My Wife Maria Callas

Giovanni Battista Meneghini

My Wife
MARIA
CALLAS

Written with the collaboration of

RENZO ALLEGRI

Translated, with an introduction, by

HENRY WISNESKI

Farrar Straus Giroux / New York

Library of Congress Cataloging in Publication Data
Meneghini, G. B. (Giovanni Battista), 1895–1981.
My wife Maria Callas.
Translation of: Maria Callas mia moglie.
Includes index.
1. Callas, Maria, 1923–1977.   2. Singers—Biography.
3. Meneghini, G. B. (Giovanni Battista), 1895–1981.
4. Husbands—Italy—Biography.   I. Allegri, Renzo.
II. Title.
ML420.C18M43   1982   782.1′092′4   [B]   82-12041

Illustrations

Illustrations

Maria in June 1947 on the ship to Italy

With Meneghini before their marriage, Verona, 1948

The Meneghinis at home in Milan, 1953

At a restaurant in Venice, 1956

Backstage at La Scala during *Fedora*, with Silvana Zanolli, May 1956

The Meneghinis at Lake Garda, probably summer 1955

Backstage at *I Puritani*, Florence, 1952

Maria in Frankfurt, 1959

Convalescing at her hotel on tour

With her chauffeur, Paris, 1976

OFFSTAGE *(following page 236)*

Maria curtsies to the Queen after the Covent Garden centenary gala, 1958

Greeted by King Umberto of Italy, Lisbon, 1958, with Maestro Ghione, Alfredo Kraus, and others in *La Traviata*

Visconti and Callas rehearsing *La Vestale*, La Scala, 1954

With Zeffirelli for his new production of *Tosca*, Covent Garden, 1958

With Marlene Dietrich and Meneghini after her Met debut in *Norma*, 1956

With David Webster after *La Traviata*, Covent Garden

With Rudolf Bing after *Tosca* at the Met, 1958

Curtain call after *La Sonnambula*, at the King's Theatre, Edinburgh, 1957

With Elsa Maxwell in doge's hat, Venice, 1957

With Lady Churchill, Tina Onassis, her husband, and others, Greece, 1959

The Meneghinis and Elsa Maxwell with Onassis aboard his yacht, 1959

During recording session of *La Gioconda*, Milan, 1959

The author at work on his book

Leaving the stage after *Anna Bolena*, La Scala

[*viii*]

Contents

Contents

Introduction

Maria Callas was approached frequently throughout her career to write her autobiography, and on several occasions during her last years, she tentatively agreed to consider the undertaking. Unlike her excursions into recording studios, however, where the late Walter Legge flattered, reassured, and cajoled her when she needed moral support, this new situation was one in which she found herself alone in her Paris apartment, unable to apply herself to the task of sifting her memories and committing her thoughts to paper. It is true that, among the more than twenty books published about her by the end of the 1970's, not one was written by a person who had known her well during her greatest years as an opera singer. (Even her mother, who published a biography emphasizing the earlier years, was in her own words completely alienated from her daughter in the triumphant years.)

After he and his wife had separated, Giovanni Battista Meneghini steadfastly refused to discuss Callas in print, and it seemed unlikely that he would be persuaded to change his mind. Fortunately, for reasons which he explains in the opening pages of this book, he decided in 1980 to write frankly about virtually every aspect of their life together—from their first words in a Verona restaurant late one evening in 1947, when (after the chef had departed) Callas offered to share her veal chop with him, to their last words at the conclusion of a telephone conversation in 1959, when they threatened each other with mortal harm.

Introduction

It is obvious in reading *My Wife Maria Callas* that Meneghini's main purpose is to convince even the most skeptical
observer that Callas had been genuinely in love with him. The
generous quotations from her letters and his accounts of her
behavior during most of their twelve years together help him
achieve this aim. In 1958 Callas told an interviewer for Italy's
Visto magazine: "Few wives, I think, can boast of a marital
happiness like mine, a husband with the heart, sensitivity, and
courtesy of mine." This declaration of love for Meneghini was a
leitmotif of her interviews during the 1950's, and she maintained
it up to their fateful voyage on the yacht *Christina*, which
Meneghini describes so graphically.

The book ends with Callas's death in 1977, his discovery of
her final note to him, and his successful search—which he says
she ordered in his dreams—for her will of 1954, in which she
named him as her sole beneficiary. After the will was probated
in France, it was contested by Callas's mother. For the next six
months Meneghini and Evangelia Callas were engaged in an
acrimonious legal dispute; in May 1978 they agreed to divide
the estate equally. A month later, the contents of Callas's apartment in Paris were auctioned off at the George V Hotel during a
two-day period. At both auctions, the biggest buyer was
Meneghini himself. His acquisitions included most of the paintings he had given Callas during their years together, her bed,
and an eighteenth-century silk carpet. Other buyers acquired
her piano and her collection of antique Chinese vases. Newspaper accounts described Meneghini's anguish on this occasion,
with his emotional outburst at one point: "This auction is a
disgrace! We are insulting the memory of a great artist. This
should never have been allowed!"

Meneghini devoted his last years to honoring his wife's memory. Shortly after Callas's death, he donated a sixteenth-century
altarpiece in her name to a small church in Sirmione, the resort
town in northern Italy where they had lived during the last

years of their marriage. In 1979, to commemorate the second anniversary of his wife's death, Meneghini arranged for a performance of Mozart's *Requiem* in the church in Sirmione, followed by a lavish reception at a hotel for his invited guests, during which Callas's recorded voice could be heard in the background. Meneghini's dream was to establish a Callas museum at Sirmione to house her memorabilia, but he died before he was able to implement his project. It is not surprising, considering what he tells us of his brothers' animosity toward him and Maria, that he did not name his family as heirs. His entire estate was left to Emma Brutti, his housekeeper, who with her husband served Meneghini faithfully for over twenty-five years.

Most of Callas's operatic triumphs were on the stage of La Scala, and she considered the theater in Milan to be her artistic home. One baffling aspect of her relationship with Antonio Ghiringhelli, the director of La Scala, was the precise basis of his aversion to her. Even after he knew she would be an invaluable asset to his company, he resisted engaging her for almost three years. No biographer of Callas has suggested a plausible reason for this antagonism. It may simply have been a manifestation of chauvinism on Ghiringhelli's part, a preference for Italian singers. (Soprano roles at La Scala during the late 1940's were regularly distributed among Renata Tebaldi, Mafalda Favero, Maria Caniglia, Margherita Carosio, Catarina Mancini, and Elisabetta Barbato.) Although Meneghini writes about Ghiringhelli's hostility at length, he, too, fails to explain it.

He mentions in passing (chapter 11) that Arturo Toscanini was anxious to have Callas sing the leading part in the Scala premiere of *The Consul,* an opera written by his protégé Gian-Carlo Menotti, which Ghiringhelli decided to present at La Scala in January 1951. (Callas had appeared at La Scala only as a guest artist in three performances of *Aida,* and Ghiringhelli had pointedly ignored her.) Meneghini states that after Callas studied the score of *The Consul*, she decided the music and the personality of the heroine were unsuited to her voice and temperament. The truth is that Callas wanted to sing in the Scala premiere of the opera, if only to secure a place on the company's regular roster. She, in fact, auditioned for the part. Menotti's version of the incident is that he went to Milan to audition various sopranos, including Callas, and after he had done so, she asked him, "Well, do I get the part?" He decided that she was indeed the best prospect for the role, and telephoned Ghiringhelli: "I've found my singer. Her name is Maria Callas."

Ghiringhelli replied: "Maria Callas, oh, my God! No, never, never, never!"

Menotti started to protest, "Well, listen, you promised me I could have . . ."

"I promised you that any singer you chose would be acceptable to me, but I will *not* have Maria Callas in this theater unless she comes only as a guest artist," the director answered.

Menotti then met with Callas and told her, "Ghiringhelli would be very happy to have you at La Scala, but only as a guest artist."

"Unless I go back to La Scala as a regular artist," Callas said, "I will not set foot in it." Menotti tried to persuade her, but she was adamant. Callas's parting words were: "Mr. Menotti, I want you to remember one thing. I *will* sing at La Scala, and Ghiringhelli will pay for this the rest of his life." The subsequent capitulation of Ghiringhelli and Callas's artistic triumphs at La Scala are well chronicled by Meneghini.

An interesting by-product of the Scala experience was her association with Luchino Visconti in a series of memorable operatic productions. Meneghini gives us a vivid portrait of Visconti. Even though it is sometimes unflattering, he allows the man's personality to emerge through extensive quotations from his letters and telegrams. It was widely maintained in print that

Callas was enamored of Visconti, but the persuasive new information presented by Meneghini suggested instead a love-hate relationship between singer and director which at base was a wholly artistic one.

There are several reasons for welcoming Meneghini's unique account of life with Maria Callas, but perhaps the most compelling is that he helps us to understand the tragic, and very human, woman behind the extraordinary artist. As for her artistry, this continued to be evident even after she was no longer singing in opera. In 1971–72, when I saw her conducting her master classes at the Juilliard School in New York, some of the most unexpected moments occurred in sessions with male singers. I have described these in *Maria Callas: The Art Behind the Legend* (1974), from which I take the liberty of quoting a paragraph:

> Possibly her most overwhelmingly powerful singing came after a discussion of the "Cortigiani" from *Rigoletto*. She told the young baritone that Rigoletto "should be fiercely savage, like a blind animal here." With her left hand, she suddenly set an extraordinarily fast tempo for the pianist and launched into the lines beginning "Cortigiani, vil razza dannata" ("Courtiers—despicable, damned breed"). As she hurled out the short, vituperative phrases—with her hands curved toward her like talons and her face reflecting the jester's terror and rage—the observers in the audience were frozen in their seats. Those who had only read of the electricity generated by Callas at her most intense were experiencing for the first time the full impact of her interpretive gifts. At the conclusion of the section, which lasted less than a minute, many in the audience were in tears.

Finally, a note about the Italian edition of this book, on which Meneghini had the collaborative help of Renzo Allegri, music critic of *Gente*, the Italian weekly. Allegri conducted lengthy interviews with Meneghini, who relied on his extensive private files to substantiate his statements and to refresh his memory. The first sixteen chapters of the book were serialized in *Gente*.

Introduction

After Meneghini's death on January 20, 1981, at the age of eighty-five, Allegri completed the remaining chapters; on these he had the help of their taped conversations and Meneghini's notes and diaries. In a few instances where Meneghini's version of important events (such as Callas's audition at La Scala) differs somewhat from other reliable printed versions, I have reported the latter in footnotes. The bracketed comments and explanations in the main text are also mine. I would like to thank Robert Giroux and George Louis Mayer for their editorial suggestions and assistance.

HENRY WISNESKI

New York
May 1982

My Wife Maria Callas

Chapter 1

Why I've Written This Book

I have decided to write a book of reminiscences about my life with Maria Callas. Everyone has been writing about Maria recently, and the most absurd things are finding their way into print. People feel qualified to set forth their conclusions, judgments, and opinions after having seen her on stage once, or having spoken with her a few minutes. Worthless books and disgraceful, inaccurate television and radio documentaries are produced, their sole purpose being to speculate about the greatest opera singer of all time.

I was Maria Callas's husband for ten years, and during all that time we lived in the most beautiful, perfect intimacy. We did not wish to be apart from each other for even a day, and chose to live in seclusion so that we would have more time to spend together. That was Maria's happiest period, as the dozens of her letters which I have saved testify. I do not believe I am guilty of presumption if I say that I am the only person in the world who truly knew her. Neither her parents nor her friends, and not even the people who socialized with her after our separation, knew the confidences that Maria shared with me. She herself was aware of this and said as much. Just a few months before her death, she replied to a journalist who asked her when she would write her memoirs :"The only person who knows everything about me, and who could write my biography, is my husband."

On October 23, 1980, I turned eighty-five. I am here, in my house in Sirmione, on Lake Garda in northern Italy, where I have spent unforgettable days with Maria. The lake is foggy, the day cold; winter is coming. A little while ago I opened the portfolio in which I keep the letters and little notes that Maria often wrote to me expressing her love. While reading them, I have the impression she is here beside me. She was a marvelous woman. The morning of each of my birthdays I would find a small gift with a note of perhaps only a few sentences, but overflowing with touching tenderness: "Battista, you are my entire life. I love and honor you like a god and, as always, I beg you to keep yourself well for me. Your Maria."—"My happiness, I adore you more than you can imagine. You are the dearest husband in the world. Without you I would have neither life nor joy."

I had previously decided to keep this moving and spiritual inheritance to myself, even though, after Maria's death, various magazines asked me to write my memoirs. One Italian publishing house dispatched two representatives with a contract ready for signing. A French publisher actually sent a blank check, with the amount to be entered. I have always refused. It seemed to me to be a betrayal of Maria to make public what we had shared together, what she had confided to me. But reading the things people continued to publish, and even suffering because of them, I was compelled to reverse my decision. I lived for Maria, I dedicated a large part of my life to her, and I never stopped loving her. Now it is my duty to defend her memory.

A book published in England and America, and translated into several languages, was the deciding factor for me. This book was signed by Arianna Stassinopoulos. I skimmed it quickly, lingering over the pages concerned with the period during which Maria and I were together. To give credence to her work, the author claims to have gathered a great amount of firsthand material about Maria Callas's life, including interviews with people who were friends of Maria and knew her well. As I have already said, I lived with Callas for twelve years,* day and night, and at least for that period no one knew her better than I. Stassinopoulos, however, never got in touch with me, nor met nor spoke with me, nor even telephoned. Yet in her book there I am, speaking, recalling facts and events as if she had had a long conversation with me. It seems to me that this is enough to justify my indignation.

On page 239 of the English edition of her book the author presents me as discussing a most serious incident—one that never took place. She quotes me as stating that one day in 1957 Maria expressed the desire to have a child, and that I was opposed to this, saying that she would lose a whole year of her career, and could easily set it back forever.†

This is an absurd fabrication. I would never have dreamed of objecting to such a human desire on the part of my wife. Maria did not wait until 1957, almost eight years after we were married, to wish for a child. From the very beginning of our marriage both of us dreamed of having a baby. We consulted doctors and did everything possible, as I will recount later in this book when I quote from Maria's letters on the subject. She, however, was not able to have children. This sad fact became a certainty when Maria underwent a long series of clinical examinations in 1957. She was passing through a very difficult time

---

* The figure previously given (page 3) was ten years. They lived together as husband and wife for two years prior to their marriage, and thus were together twelve years.

† The passage attributed to Meneghini: "One day when she was thirty-four Maria confessed to me that, above everything, she wanted a child. She went on saying that again and again. But I told her that having a child would have put her career in jeopardy for at least a year. In fact a child would have destroyed the great diva that she had become." From *Maria Callas* by Arianna Stassinopoulos (London and New York, 1981).

in her life; she was always tired, and was aware of a serious loss of strength in general. Our physician, Dr. Arnaldo Semeraro, was very much concerned. "We must discover the reason for this malaise," he said, and he advised a thorough examination by various specialists. We went to a cardiologist, a neurologist, an otorhinolaryngologist, and a gynecologist. The gynecologist found symptoms of a rather early menopause (Maria was only thirty-four), and he prescribed a series of injections. It was during one of these visits that Maria once again brought up the subject of maternity. She told the gynecologist of her longing to have a child, and this specialist, Dr. Carlo Palmieri, explained that it would not be possible because of a malformation of the uterus. Maria was distraught. The doctor suggested that perhaps an operation might offer some hope. He asked Maria if she wished to undergo one, but she refused.

My wife, therefore, did not have a child because she was physically unable to have one. For this reason, I consider what Stassinopoulos wrote concerning Maria's alleged later pregnancy to be without basis in fact. In 1966, seven years after our separation, Maria, according to the writer, became pregnant by Onassis, and was persuaded to have an abortion. I do not have documentary proof in this matter, but it seems unlikely to me that Maria, not being able to have children in her youth, could have acquired the capability at the age of forty-three. Knowing her character and her great yearning for motherhood, I am also certain that if she *had* become pregnant, she would never have agreed to an abortion, for any reason in the world.

Concerning my actions as Maria Callas's manager, Stassinopoulos's book, and other books which preceded it, contain offensive statements and gratuitous judgments. They say that I was more detrimental to my wife's career than helpful, that my presence caused negative, hostile reactions, and that I abused my position as manager, keeping theater directors and festival organizers on tenterhooks for the sole purpose of exerting my authority. There is one fact that is irrefutable: when I met Maria she was an unknown, even though she had seven years of singing behind her. With my assistance she became, in just a short while, the Number One singer in the world. When she left me, artistically she lived in the glow of her reputation for a while, and then the career faded. These are indisputable facts.

Let there be no misunderstanding: Maria sang with her voice and all of her capabilities. Her art was extraordinary, incomparable. Those who know the world of opera intimately understand the value of a good manager. Maria told everyone: "I have a husband in whom I have total confidence. He can make of me whatever he wants." The secret of her success was also that, in having a manager like me working on her behalf, she did not have to protect her financial interests. Generally speaking, a manager wants to arrange the greatest number of contracts possible because he receives a percentage of the fee. My one goal, on the contrary, was to make Maria preeminent. I thought solely of her career and prestige. The fee did not interest me as much as the quality of what was being offered. This is why I kept directors of various theaters at bay, because Maria was to sing only under circumstances where they treated her like a queen.

When I met my wife, I had behind me extensive managerial experience. I owned twelve factories and had amassed a fortune in industry. My entire family had become rich. My brothers did not want me to marry Maria, and they waged a ruthless battle against me. I had to make a choice and I renounced all that I had created, just to be with her. I put my experience and my organizational skills at the service of her art, and in a short time Maria became the reigning star of the operatic world. Every move that she made in her career was evaluated and decided by me.

Many of her controversial opinions and aggressive attitudes which earned her the appellation "the tigress"—and are still mentioned in the newspapers today—were suggested by me. She was a pacifist, a tranquil woman. I told her to make certain decisions, to assume certain attitudes, to make certain statements, and she went along with them. The famous cancellation of *Norma* in Rome after the first act, which caused such a furor because President Giovanni Gronchi was in the audience, was my doing. Maria was indeed not well, but she was almost willing to continue the performance and would have if I had urged it. I told her not to; she had to have the courage to stop because she was ill, even though the President of Italy was present, and they were urging her to risk having a musical fiasco. She acquiesced in my decision, for she knew I was acting on her behalf.

Not one knowledgeable professional in the international operatic world has ever questioned my capabilities as a manager. Giacomo Lauri-Volpi, the great tenor, who certainly knew something about these matters, wrote me after Maria's death: "Without you, La Callas would not have reached the heights that she did in the field of opera, rising above the hostility of the theater world, and leaving behind the imprint of her personality on the history of drama. It was Maria Meneghini who triumphed, before losing herself in the morass of the international social whirl. Maria Callas took over when the miracle was already completed."

But the insinuations that hurt most, appearing in various publications about my wife after her death, were those that insulted our most intimate feelings. Every page concerning our matrimonial life has a mocking, derisive tone. They want to negate the fact that we were in love, perhaps for the sole reason that I was considerably older than my wife. It was an ungracious bias that only reflected the meanness of the writers.

For the entire period of our union, Maria and I were profoundly in love. Our mutual feelings had a tenderness and a freshness that some people are incapable of comprehending. Every moment of our life together was happy, and the proof is not in my assertions but in the dozens of letters and little notes that my wife wrote me. When she was away, there were lengthy letters. When she was at home she let me discover—on my desk, by the bed, in a bunch of flowers—notes of a few sentences or just a few words, telling me of her love. If this practice had lasted a month, a year, two years, one could think that it was prompted by a general enthusiasm for married life, for the joy of finally having found happiness. But it lasted for the duration of our marriage. The final notes are dated a few weeks before the ill-fated cruise on Onassis's yacht, the *Christina*, the cruise which was Maria's downfall. For the entire twelve years we lived together, Maria's love for me was vital and unwavering.

Religiously I saved all those notes and letters, which are, to me, of inestimable worth. They are kept on my desk and I often reread them. Maria's short sentences were like outbursts of joy, almost a need to express what she felt inside. "I adore you, my soul!!!" or, "To the dearest husband in the world." Other times the notes were longer: "I adore you more than you can possibly imagine. Remember that when I am away and you find yourself annoyed and tired, think that you are living for me, just as I exist for you. Your Maria." Or else: "My dear, beloved, adored, blessed husband. I only want to tell you that I adore you and that I thank the Eternal Father for giving us so much joy. I know that you are never satisfied and would like to give me the entire world. But I am happy because I realize you have wanted to give me so much and I want you to know that there is no woman in the world as fortunate and happy as I. Wish me well and ask God that we always remain this content. Your faithful wife Maria."

On some occasions she was playful. She jokingly used to call herself, in Veronese dialect, *paiassa* ("clown"). She would end her notes: "with all my heart, all my love, all my devotion, your *paiassa*." And again: "As the years pass, dear, I adore you even more. Be sure to wish me well, otherwise I will slap your face."

My Wife Maria Callas

On one of my birthdays she wrote this note: "My dearest everything, I have nothing to give you as a gift because you already have all of me. As a souvenir of ten birthdays spent together, I am giving you a chain for your bread that they are always clearing away. Know only that you would not have been able to do more for your wife, because that woman is already the happiest wife in the world." The cryptic reference needs an explanation. When I'm eating, I have the habit of putting aside small pieces of bread, which I eat at the end of the meal. But often the waiter would sweep them up before he could be stopped, thinking I left them there for him to clear away. This would upset Maria, and it was incredible thoughtfulness on her part to give me a tiny chain with a little harpoon, with which I could spear the pieces of bread so the waiter couldn't remove them.

Considerate gestures like this emanate only from the mind of someone who is deeply in love. At this point the reader will ask himself, "But if she was so in love with her husband, why did she leave him to go away with Onassis?" It is a question that has been put to me a thousand times in the years following our separation, and one for which I have never succeeded in finding an answer.

I have never allowed myself to sit in judgment of my wife, however, not even on this question. I have refused to understand, and that is that. I will not go into the matter in detail in this book. I will tell what happened, without any elaboration, just as it is recorded in my diary for that period.

Following the advice of journalist Renzo Allegri, my collaborator in the writing of this book, I have scrupulously limited myself to the period during which I lived with Maria, leaving to others the job of discussing what happened afterwards. And for my narrative I have limited myself only to facts for which I have documentation. I have given ample space to Maria's letters, convinced of their inestimable worth. With over a dozen of

Maria's letters incorporated into the text, this book, one can say, was in part written by her.

The most important thing about the letters, some of them quite long, is that they were not written when Maria was at the apogee of her career, a period when she tended to be guarded in her comments because of concern that strangers would discover her true feelings. They are letters from the period when she was young, poor, and unknown, written at the beginning of her career, or when she was experiencing her first successes—documents, therefore, that are open and sincere. In them Maria speaks of her work, her preoccupations, her future, her convictions, her goals, and her aspirations. She speaks of her passion for singing, but especially of her love for me. I am not a literary man, but I believe they are extraordinary love letters, and it is through them that one can seek to understand this marvelous woman.

Chapter 2

First Meeting with Maria

Maria Callas arrived in Italy on June 29, 1947. I met her on that evening, and within a day our lives were already intermingled.

Almost invariably when people speak of this period, they say that I began to show interest in Maria after hearing her sing. That is not true. The emotions that triggered my interest were those of compassion and of sorrow. It was a desire to help a person desperately in need of assistance.

At that time I lived above the restaurant Pedavena, in Verona's Piazza Bra, a restaurant managed by my friend Gaetano Pomari. During the war the Germans had appropriated my apartment and I had yet to find another one. There were a few empty rooms above the restaurant and my friend rented one room to me. Since I returned from work at odd hours, I didn't eat at the restaurant; my meals were served to me upstairs. Pomari was also one of the organizers of the opera season in Verona's ancient Arena, and he used the rooms adjacent to mine as offices for the Opera Association of the Arena. The official director of the amphitheater was the Veronese tenor Giovanni Zenatello, a famous singer from the time of Caruso. Zenatello, however, usually lived in New York, and all of the actual work fell on Pomari's shoulders.

Everything that concerned the Arena was dealt with in the two rooms next to mine. While I had lunch or dinner, I would participate in the discussions, the projects, and decisions; in effect, I was one of them. I have always been a great opera lover. I went to the performances, and I knew the artists and the conductors. I was a real aficionado. I also enjoyed aiding young singers who wanted to make a career. I had tried with several unknowns, some with truly exceptional gifts, but none had gone on to success.

The evening of June 28 I was eating dinner as usual while in the other two rooms were gathered the organizers of the opera season that was to begin in about a month. Maestro Tullio Serafin, Gaetano Pomari, Giuseppe Gambato, Augusto Cardi, Ferruccio Cusinati, and others were seeing to final arrangements before the commencement of rehearsals.

The series of opera performances that year was of particular importance, for it was Verona's first complete season to be held after the war. The previous year only a token series had been offered. Three works were being mounted—*La Gioconda,* *Faust,* and *Un Ballo in Maschera.* The roster included such well-known names as baritone Carlo Tagliabue and mezzo-soprano Elena Nicolai, but the general anticipation centered on two young singers who were making their Arena debuts, American tenor Richard Tucker and a home-grown soprano, Renata Tebaldi.

That evening each member of the association summarized the plans for his own assignment. I was listening, but at a certain point, if only to join the conversation, I said: "I have heard that each one of you has a specific task. Serafin conducts, Cardi is the stage director, Cusinati is chorus master, and so on. But what am I to do? I'm one of the directors. I'm always here among you. I'm acquainted with all your problems. I'm present at all your meetings. You should give me an assignment as well."

"That's fair," said Maestro Serafin. "I agree that you also should carry out some task. Let's see, what could you do?"

"Why not appoint me supervisor of the ballerinas?"

My remark was in jest. Besides, ballerinas—so thin, and all skin and bones—are not my type. Titianesque, fleshy women appeal to me more.

"No, not the dancers," Serafin said. "You are a distinguished man. They tell me you are the major representative of Verona's industries. You should, therefore, have a prestigious job. I recommend that you accompany this season's prima donnas. This year we have two very good young women. One is Renata Tebaldi, a splendid girl. She already has a certain fame because she sang at La Scala under Toscanini, who said of her that she has 'the voice of an angel.' However, she doesn't strike me as your type. The other one, though, should be just right. She's Greek, but she grew up in America. Her name is Maria Callas. She hasn't done anything of importance yet, but Zenatello, who engaged her in New York, wrote me and spoke highly of her. He says that she has a remarkable voice and that she should be an excellent Gioconda. It's her first time in Italy, so she doesn't have any acquaintances or friends in Verona. It would certainly be useful for her to have someone as important as you acting as her guide."

"Fine, I accept," I replied.

"This Callas will arrive tomorrow," Serafin said. "In the evening we are all eating together, here at the Pedavena. You should join us so I can introduce you to her."

The conversation was only half serious. I didn't have any desire to waste time escorting singers around. At this time I was the head of a large brick-manufacturing business. Several of my factories were damaged in the war, and I was traveling constantly to make them operative again. I was working up to twenty hours a day, with scarcely any time to sleep.

The next morning, as part of my work, I went to Trento. Returning to Verona late in the evening, I went to my office and remained there until around eleven at night. I was dead tired when I left. My office was near the Piazza Bra, and walking toward the Pedavena, I saw the company of the Arena eating at tables outside. I recalled the conversation of the night before, and said to myself, "Good Lord, I have to escape before these nuts get hold of me." I ducked around the corner so that I could enter the restaurant from the back, but Serafin spotted me and called out, "There's Battista, bring him over here." Two waiters caught up to me. I said I was tired and wanted to go to bed, but Serafin came over and insisted. I couldn't refuse.

The group had almost finished eating, but Serafin said that everyone would stay and keep me company. He asked what I would like to eat. "I'm not that hungry, I'll just have a veal cutlet," I said. Sitting across from me at the table was a young girl whom I didn't know, with a plump face and sweet features. She said in perfect Italian, but with a trace of an accent: "Sir, if you don't mind I would like to offer you my cutlet. It was the last one. There aren't any more. I haven't touched it."

"Don't worry about me, signorina, have it yourself," I said.

"No, I'm not going to eat it, so please take it." And she passed the plate over to me.

"You haven't met," interjected Maestro Serafin. "This is Maria Callas, whom I told you about last evening." And then, turning to her, "This is Battista Meneghini, a special person, an industrialist who is a friend of all the singers."

I looked at the girl and made the smile required by the situation. She also managed the suggestion of a smile. Because she had a rather commanding presence, she made an impression on me. Her face, as I have mentioned, was very round, she was full-breasted, her shoulders were powerful, and she had black hair and intense eyes.

I ate the cutlet and listened to the conversation. Those who arrived from America along with Callas were the Veronese bass Nicola Rossi-Lemeni, whom I knew very well, and a woman named Louise Caselotti, wife of Richard Bagarozy, a lawyer and an opera impresario who had Callas under contract.

Mrs. Bagarozy continued to speak of the beautiful sights in the United States, of the power of the country, of its grandeur. Finally I couldn't take any more of it. "Excuse me," I said. "I don't have firsthand knowledge of the United States. It may be an enormous, powerful country, but our tiny things can be worth more than your great things. We have an ancient civilization with art treasures, churches, palaces, and marvelous monuments. Have you seen Venice? No? Well, I am convinced that one old brick, half-decomposed, from the foundation of one of the Venetian palaces is worth more than one of your skyscrapers."

Swept along by the ardor of my own defense of Italy, I added: "Tomorrow I'm taking you to Venice as my guests, and you will be able to see for yourself whether it is an incomparable city. And now, to show you something fantastic this very evening, I'm going to accompany you to the Piazza dei Signori. It's just a short distance from here. You will see a stupendous architectural jewel, the balcony by Fra Giocondo, a monument certainly superior to your Brooklyn Bridge."

We arose from the table and it was at this moment that I experienced my first genuine feelings toward Maria Callas. When she was seated she didn't seem that large, even though she was solid and well set, but when she stood up, I was moved to pity. Her lower extremities were deformed. Her ankles were swollen to the size of calves. She moved awkwardly and with effort. I was doubly embarrassed because I perceived a few little smiles and disdainful glances from some of the others. I don't know if she was aware of it, but she stood off to one side, silent, with her eyes lowered.

We proceeded on foot by way of the Via Mazzini to the Piazza dei Signori, paused to admire Fra Giocondo's Loggetta, and then returned. Before saying good night at the Hotel Accademia, where Mrs. Bagarozy, Rossi-Lemeni, and Callas were staying, we confirmed our date for the excursion to Venice. Then, alone, I continued on my way to the Pedavena.

At five the next afternoon I was waiting before the Accademia in my car. Rossi-Lemeni was also there with his car. After a few minutes, Mrs. Bagarozy appeared with Giuseppe Gambato, who was sent to fetch Callas. Unexpectedly, she informed him she would not be coming. She apologized, but said she could not accept the invitation "for personal reasons." I said to Gambato, "We're not going without her. Go, insist, talk her into it. Who knows if there will be another opportunity?" He returned and after a good half hour finally succeeded in convincing her to come, and she got into the car.

She scarcely said five words during the entire trip to Venice. As I continued to comment on the various areas through which we passed, she listened attentively and observed everything, but she remained mute. "She's certainly not a lively traveling companion," I said to myself.

It was late when we arrived in Venice. I decided to take the group directly to the Piazza San Marco. We climbed into a vaporetto, disembarking at the stop that permits one to enter the great square from the back. When we had passed along the colonnade and had come upon the piazza, illuminated, with the basilica in the background, Maria Callas could not contain her astonishment. "Oh, how beautiful!" she exclaimed. Her eyes were shining and her entire body seemed to reach out toward the sight. Her reserve vanished immediately, as if by magic. She thanked me repeatedly for having urged her to come along.

"You were right," she said. "Something like this is worth a trip from America. Who knows when I might have had another chance to see anything comparable." She walked around, observing the basilica from various vantage points. Moved, excited, emotional, she solicited running commentary from me. I saw that Venice fascinated her, and it was a joy to witness so

[*17*]

much enthusiasm for the city I adored. Venice, for me, had always been like a balm. When I had problems or things were going badly, I would get in my car and drive to Venice. I would stroll about the city for hours, visiting specific churches and art treasures, especially the famous painting of the Assumption by Titian, behind the altar of the Church of S. Maria Gloriosa dei Frari. Each occasion restored to me my faith and sense of peace. Now the joy I observed in Maria Callas touched me and won me over. At that moment I understood that the woman had to be a great artist. "Anyone who delights in beauty to that degree," I said to myself, "must have special sensibilities which sooner or later will burst forth."

Our trip to Venice was limited to the Piazza San Marco. I took them to dinner at a restaurant there, and then we drove back to Verona. Maria was now a different person. She did not stop talking about what she had seen earlier that evening. Then, little by little, the conversation turned to other subjects, her early years, her career. She told me of her difficulties in New York, and how she had been unsuccessful in finding an engagement. She had auditioned at the Metropolitan, and was even heard by Toscanini.* No one in New York had lifted a finger for her. At one point it seemed she might sing *Madama Butterfly* at the Metropolitan, but because of some quirk in her character, she had turned it down.

She spoke of her family. Her mother didn't get along with her father, and for several years had lived in Greece with her daughters, dividing the family. Callas said that she never had anyone

---

* Callas was anxious to sing for Toscanini in New York and had petitioned their mutual friend, the bass Nicola Moscona, to arrange an audition. According to Callas's cousin and biographer, Steven Linakis, Moscona told her, "Don't be ridiculous. Unknown sopranos don't ask for auditions with Toscanini." After that, Moscona ignored her completely. (Steven Linakis, *Diva*, 1980.) Callas's first and only audition with Toscanini was to take place in Milan in September 1950 (see page 138).

whom she could confide in or go to for advice, and had to fend for herself. Her career was uncertain. She said she considered the trip to Italy to be her last hope: the forthcoming *Gioconda* in the Arena meant everything to her. If it went badly, her career would very possibly be over.

When she spoke of her career and of her future, she didn't have the enthusiasm characteristic of young people. She was sad, pessimistic. Her words were cold and a little bitter. They were those of a person accustomed to disillusionment, sacrifices, humiliations. She also disclosed the real reason why she hadn't wanted to go to Venice with us: she didn't have anything to wear and was ashamed to appear wearing the same blouse from the evening before. "I would have bought something," she explained, "but I don't have any money."

When we reached Vicenza, we stopped in the Piazzale Garibaldi. It was now two in the morning, but we continued to talk. I asked her, "But didn't you ever find anyone who was interested in you, someone who gave you a helping hand?"

She looked at me with a sad smile, somewhat embarrassed by my question, and said, "But who would be interested in me, with my shape?"

"Don't underestimate yourself," I said, seeking to console her.

"I'm not in the habit of kidding myself," she replied.

We conversed at length. I had already decided. I wanted to help this girl and was searching for the proper way to tell her, so as not to be misunderstood. I began by saying, "I'm interested in opera. I have already helped other young people. I am certain that you are gifted and can make a success of it. So, if you would allow it, I would also like to help you a little. Think about it, and don't give me an answer now. I want you to have confidence in me."

She was touched. I gave her a kiss, tenderly. I started up the car and we returned to Verona.

The following day I wrote her my first letter: "Dear Miss

Callas, I hope the all too brief excursion to Venice last evening was, for you and for your most charming friend, agreeable, comfortable, and a pleasure. May I hope that we will return to Venice soon, and in less haste? I am sending you yesterday's local paper with the mention of your arrival in Verona. I will look for the book about *Gioconda.* You will have to tell me the name of the Colonel again for me to locate the information you want. Being at your service, please remember me to Louise and pass along my warmest regards. G. B. Meneghini. P.S. My telephone number is 3846." It was a formal letter but it had the dual purpose of also sounding out Maria's reaction to my kiss of the night before. Inserting my telephone number at the end of the letter worked perfectly. Maria telephoned and I sensed that she was pleased.

Two days later I picked her up at her hotel and took her to dinner on Lake Garda. I wanted to clarify our agreement. "It's six months until the first of the year," I said. "During that period I will take care of all necessities—hotel, restaurants, wardrobe, everything. You will concern yourself only with singing and studying with the *maestri* that I choose for you. At the end of this year we will evaluate the results. If we are both satisfied, we will draw up an agreement that will cover our future professional relations."

She accepted the arrangement, and that day I began to orchestrate the *modus operandi* of Maria Callas. Within a few days, however, our business agreement also became a perfect personal relationship.

Little by little I discovered what humiliations she had endured. How many people have bragged of having helped Maria Callas at the beginning of her career? They spoke of their good deeds after Callas became famous, but in reality, they exploited her. Her contract drawn up in the United States for the Verona Arena was an insult to fairness. The only one who tried to help Maria in the United States was Nicola Rossi-Lemeni.

First Meeting with Maria

In 1946 he and Maria had tried to make a success out of forming a company of young singers, which included tenor Luigi Infantino, who was married to Sarah Ferrati at the time; the conductor Georges Sébastian; and another woman singer, an Italian, whose name escapes me. After having visited various cities without success, they were forced to disband the company.*

Before leaving New York for the summer opera season in Verona, Nicola Rossi-Lemeni paid a visit to Giovanni Zenatello. While discussing the forthcoming season in the Arena, Zenatello told him that, although the casts for the various operas were set, he had not settled on a definite choice for the role of Gioconda. The part had been offered to Herva Nelli, who had been recommended by Toscanini himself, but they were unable to agree over the fee. Herva Nelli was demanding a sum way beyond the means of the Arena. It was at this point that Rossi-Lemeni mentioned Maria Callas, saying that his friend had a voice ideally suited to that role. Zenatello asked to hear her, he found her "rather interesting" (his evaluation of her in a letter to Verona), and he engaged her.

The one thing I have always held against Zenatello was his having profited by Maria's unfortunate situation. He saw that she was down-and-out, and he offered her a hangman's contract. I have saved this document and it is, I repeat, an insult to fair-

* Meneghini is undoubtedly referring to the ill-fated United States Opera Company, formed in 1946 by Callas's lawyer friend, Eddie Bagarozy, and Italian impresario Ottavio Scotto. The roster included, in addition to Callas, Rossi-Lemeni, and Infantino, Mafalda Favero (apparently the name Meneghini could not remember), Cloë Elmo, Galliano Masini, and Max Lorenz. The company's first performance was to have been a production of *Turandot*, presented in Chicago in January 1947, with Callas, Favero, and Masini in the principal roles. Shortly before opening night, the American Guild of Musical Artists insisted on a substantial deposit to protect their chorus members, and Bagarozy and Scotto, unable to cover the amount, were forced to declare bankruptcy.

ness. It stipulated a fee of 40,000 lire per performance,* with four performances guaranteed. Maria, however, was required to be in Verona a month in advance for rehearsals. He did not offer her one cent for the trip, or lodging in Verona, or incidental expenses. Maria was also bound to a contract with her agent Bagarozy, even though the Verona engagement was procured by Rossi-Lemeni. Bagarozy expected his ten percent, and he even sent his wife to Italy to collect the commission.

To be able to make the trip, Maria had to ask her godfather for a loan. She left for Italy with a cardboard suitcase, held together with twine, like some destitute emigrant. She sailed on a Russian cargo boat, which turned out to be very bad in every respect. She had scarcely disembarked in Naples when she was robbed of the little she owned. From Naples she went to Verona by train—then a trip of a day and a half. The train was overcrowded and she had to stand in the aisle.

These were the straits in which I found Maria Callas when I offered to help her. To read in books that Callas was discovered at her debut in *Gioconda* at Verona either by Zenatello or by I don't know who else, absolutely infuriates me. No one discovered Maria Callas. It is all fabrication. Even before hearing her sing, I was moved by her story. She was a young girl desperately in need of help, and I offered it, without asking for anything in return.

* Approximately $60 or about £20 at that time.

Chapter 3

Debut in Verona

My first undertaking after having decided to help Maria was to find a first-rate teacher who would prepare her properly for her Arena debut. When she told me about her life, she also talked a little about her vocal background. She had had a very good musical preparation, but she hadn't sung on stage in two years.

Her first voice teacher in Greece was not Elvira de Hidalgo, as is often stated in print, but rather Maria Trivella, who taught at the National Conservatory of Greece. Maria was not pleased with Trivella, and after a year with her she was able to transfer to the Athens Conservatory. There she studied with the Spaniard Elvira de Hidalgo, who was at one time a coloratura soprano. She was an outstanding teacher who understood Callas and helped her to place her voice. She was the one who really developed her. During her two years in the United States following the war, Callas only studied intermittently, and virtually never sang in public.

I am not a musician, but I do have a feeling for music. Shortly after we first met I had a clear impression of Maria's vocal resources, and I implemented a plan to have her voice developed to the maximum of its capabilities. I told her, "You're here for the season at the Arena, and you have a binding contract with the Verona theater, so you'll have to go along with whatever they require of you. At the same time, however, you must work with a teacher whom I will select for you."

In Verona there was a voice teacher, Ferruccio Cusinati, who was also chorus master for the operas in the Arena. I knew him very well and had enormous respect for him. He had a thorough understanding of the human voice. I had already entrusted to him other young singers in whom I was interested, and I had observed how much imagination and skill went into his teaching. Even though he did not have the renown that he deserved, he was a professional of rare accomplishment. I took Maria to him, and after listening to her, he told me that she indeed had a truly remarkable voice. "She's at your disposal," I said. "You must help her to make her voice more flexible, more supple, and, in short, eradicate any faults. From now on, she will come for a lesson every day. You must mold her into a perfect Gioconda."

From that moment on, Ferruccio Cusinati became Callas's teacher. Whenever she was not in the midst of rehearsals at the Arena, she went to his studio in Via Valverde. I still have the receipts from those lessons. I also had her study her debut role with Cusinati. Elvira de Hidalgo taught Maria the technique of singing and she opened up the world of music to her, but it was Ferruccio Cusinati who taught Maria all the operas in her repertory. It was he who helped her to create her famous interpretations. Books and magazine articles have never given credit to this teacher in Verona. His name never appeared in any of the biographies of Maria, but he was Callas's teacher. Maria herself has commented in some manuscript notes which she prepared to refute a *Time* magazine article that was full of misinformation: "It is not true that my husband asked Tullio Serafin to coach me in my roles and that it was he who taught them to me. My teacher was Ferruccio Cusinati." Tullio Serafin was Maria's favorite conductor, but not the coach with whom she first studied her roles.

She studied with enthusiasm and made exceptional progress. She was happy, content to be working. She realized my assistance was a serious matter and of great importance to her. Probably for the first time in her life, she felt secure and free of economic worries. She repaid my concern for her with fondness and touching devotion.

I continued to pursue my own vocation. We saw each other only in the evenings, when I returned to the city. Maria stayed at the Hotel Accademia but took her meals at the Pedavena. When I was not there she ate alone, on the upper level of the restaurant in the corner. No one ever spoke to her, because she was a stranger and, as I have mentioned, not that attractive. She waited for me even when I returned to Verona rather late, and we had dinner together. I still have fond memories of those evenings. Maria would tell me what she had done during the day, how the rehearsals at the Arena were going, and so on. I would offer suggestions, and we would talk about projects for the future.

I was happy. I took an active interest in her lessons and her progress because I was anxious for her to make a splendid impression at her debut, but I was not inordinately optimistic about her chances for a career. I knew that having a success in opera was in large part a matter of luck. Of the other young people I assisted, who had showed great promise, none had gone on to make a career. I did not have any illusions, even with Maria, nor did I expect repayment or consider profiting from any success she might have.

As each day passed, our conversations became more personal. A strong bond developed between us, and it became apparent that we were meant to remain together. I discovered myself to be in love to a degree I could never have imagined possible. We both wished to marry. For the first time in my life I was certain I would not regret this decision. There were, however, a thousand difficulties to surmount, and I had to convince Maria that it was necessary to wait. She did not understand, but agreed reluctantly.

What compelled me to delay our marriage? First, the hostility that my relationship with Callas engendered in town and especially within my family. When the Veronese realized there was a special rapport between me and the young American singer, one would think the world had come to an end. I was well known, respected, and considered to be a good businessman. Major industrialists throughout the Veneto region sought my advice when they found themselves in serious difficulty. My romance with Maria elicited criticism and snide remarks. I was attacked from all sides. "What are you doing?" my friends asked. "Don't you see that she's built like a potato, like a sack? Can't you see how ugly she is, how clumsy? Have you lost your head? You're not yourself," and other comments of that nature. The members of my family were even more vehement. They banded together and waged a battle that was to last ten years.

To explain this absurd, incredible phenomenon, I must say a few words about my family. I was the eldest of eleven brothers. Even as a young boy, I was enthusiastic about my studies. My father, who had a small brickmaking business, decided to send me to the university. After I finished my basic studies in Verona, he enrolled me as a business and economics major in a school in Venice that was the equivalent of a university. I enjoyed writing and traveling, and considered becoming a journalist.

World War I interrupted my studies. I became a field artillery officer, earning three military awards (two for merit and one for valor), and other honors. I resumed my studies after returning from the front. I was to graduate soon when my father summoned me. He was only sixty, but he considered himself to be old. He said to me: "Battista, I have decided to retire from the firm, and I'm turning it over to you. I am also placing your ten brothers in your care. You must watch after them and see that they finish their schooling, grow up properly, and make something of themselves."

I felt as if part of me had died. All my dreams of world travel disappeared. I considered my father's wishes to be sacred, and I accepted the responsibilities which he entrusted to me. I put my studies behind me and plunged head first into my new assignment. That was in 1920. My father's business at that time was modest and employed a few artisans. They made the bricks by hand, shaping the clay in the courtyard of the shop and baking them in kilns heated by wood.

From that point on, my only concern was for the business and the future of my brothers. I became their surrogate father. I kept after them to study and later helped them to enter the professions of their choice (one became a doctor, another a university professor of gynecology, a third a general, and a fourth a chemist). I also found employment for my sisters. The business grew from a few craftsmen in a small building to one of the most modern and important industries in Italy. In 1947, when I met Maria, I had twelve factories, each employing scores of workers.

It was a full-time job just coping with my many obligations. I sometimes worked up to twenty hours a day. While all my brothers were raising families, I had to forfeit even this. At the age of fifty I found myself rich, known in the world of industry, and respected by everyone, but also alone, as alone as a stray dog. I hardly even had a home, as I practically lived in hotels.

My meeting Maria, her tender affection, and her desire to have a family, suddenly opened my eyes. I, too, discovered a longing for domesticity, and realized the time had come to begin thinking of myself. I decided to get married.

When the members of my family realized that Maria was more than a caprice or a liaison of a couple of weeks, they flew into a rage. They feared that if I married her, their well-being would no longer be paramount in my mind, and in the event of my death, my estate would not pass into their hands in toto. If they had reflected on what I had already done for them, they could have said, "Our brother has devoted his best years to us, and it is only fair that he thinks of himself now." Instead, they joined forces against me.

With regard to Maria, they were unspeakably malicious. They judged her in the worst possible way, without giving her a chance. They even refused to meet her, and I was never able to bring her home. The only one to speak up on my behalf was my mother, who wanted to meet Maria. She could tell that Maria was a nice girl and that we would be happy together, but her siding with me only exacerbated the situation with my brothers.

Eventually our problems passed from our home to the courts. My family initiated a legal battle that lasted ten years. At one point, among the lawyers and various experts and consultants, there were about sixty professional men involved in the controversy. They were to eat up hundreds of millions of lire, a large part of our family fortune. I didn't want to give in to them, not only because it was I who built up the business and made them secure but because I believed that my brothers would be unable to continue to move forward without me.

They fought me, hoping that I would "regain my senses," but they never listened to what I had to say. Their position was clear: the Meneghini family or Callas. Finally, exasperated, I said: "Take everything. I'm staying with Maria. But remember that you will still need me." In a few years the business was in ruins. I had to intervene so the losses would not be even worse. Now the great firm of the Meneghinis no longer exists.

This is a sad chapter in my life, and one that is linked to Maria. The woman who revolutionized opera was also responsible for the rending apart and destruction of the Meneghini family. She suffered because of what had happened, and would say: "Battista, I feel I'm to blame. Look at what has happened because of me. You must leave me, and forget me."

She wanted only what was best for me, and I never regretted

having left my business and family for her. I was always convinced that she would have done the same for me, and recently I found proof of it. In one of her articles she wrote, "If Battista had asked it of me, I would even have given up my career for him." It is not true that her art was the most important thing in her life, as people have always maintained. Her singing was a profession which she pursued with enthusiasm and dedication. But what mattered more to her, at least during the years we lived together, was our love and mutual happiness.

The month of July passed in this tense atmosphere. The rehearsals at the Arena were held regularly, but scarcely any interest was shown in Maria. The singer who captured the imagination of the press and public was Renata Tebaldi, who was to sing in Gounod's *Faust*, the second opera of the season. It was during the dress rehearsal of *Gioconda* that I became aware of Maria's potential. On stage her presence dominated everything; she was mesmerizing.

But Callas was invariably pursued by misfortune. During the final rehearsal she almost lost her life. While leaving the stage, she didn't see one of the open chutes which lead to the subterranean areas beneath the ancient amphitheater, and she stumbled into it. The fall could easily have been fatal, as it was in the case of poor Mario Riva a few years later. Fortunately, she survived the accident with only a bruise and a badly sprained ankle.

The day of the *prima* arrived. I was very nervous, but Maria, despite the pain in her ankle, seemed perfectly calm. She told me: "I'm as myopic as a mole. When I walk on a stage, I don't see anything. I do what I'm expected to do, and I don't concern myself with extraneous matters."

I watched the performance from the wings. Maria would not allow me to watch from the audience, as I would have preferred. She wanted me to be near her.

My being close to her, and our spending as little time away from each other as possible, were obsessions with Maria, even from the very first days of our relationship. "We must eliminate everything that keeps us apart," she would insist. Before going out, even for half an hour, she would badger me to accompany her. It was not unusual for her to cancel a visit or even a short walk if I couldn't go along. In each of the various houses in which we later lived, my studio had to be near her bedroom. "You have to get up early for work," she would say, "while I must stay in bed a little longer. But I don't want you to be far away from me. You have to work nearby, so that I can hear you."

She always wanted me backstage during her performances so that I could accompany her to her dressing room as soon as the opera was over. My presence seemed to calm her. For me, however, each one of her performances was torture. I was always afraid that something would happen, that she would lose her voice, or that she would trip and fall. I was in a constant state of anxiety, perspiring and pacing about.

Many people still remember the famous concert of December 19, 1958, for the gala benefit of the Légion d'Honneur at the Paris Opéra, when Maria sang for an elegant public that included the President of France, René Coty; the Duke of Windsor, the Begum Ali Khan, the Marquis de Cuevas, Jean Cocteau, the Rothschilds, Charlie Chaplin, and many other celebrities.* I was, as usual, backstage watching from the wings, and enduring the tortures of hell. I must have been unusually agitated, because a man walked over to me and asked, "Are you Mr. Meneghini, Madame Callas's husband?" "Yes," I answered. "I am the theater's physician," he said, giving me his calling card. "Please allow me to tell you that it is very bad for your health to follow your wife's performance with such concern. At your age this constant tension could be fatal." At this point I had

* A kinescope was made in France of this televised concert, and excerpts from *Norma, Tosca* (in costume), and *Il Trovatore* were included in the 1978 public-television tribute to Callas.

already been suffering through her performances for eleven years.

But to return to the *Gioconda* in the Arena—her debut went well. Maria was not able to move around much with her swollen ankle, but she was in extraordinary voice. It was not a triumph, however. In all of the books and articles about Maria, the writers speak of that evening as if it were now legendary. The truth of the matter is that nothing unusual happened. She had a nice success, and that was it. No one proclaimed a miracle. If they had, offers for engagements would have arrived immediately, as always happens when a new star is heralded. After her series of four *Giocondas*, Maria did not receive a single offer of work.

Not even Maestro Serafin, the conductor for *Gioconda* and a leading expert in the world of opera, realized at the time what Maria was capable of doing. He could have signed her for other productions, recommended her to other theater managements, or at least encouraged her. He did none of these, for he considered her to be just a competent singer, like so many others. In a letter sent to me immediately after the Verona opera season, Serafin wrote that Maria had excellent vocal gifts which would allow her to essay a specific repertory, but that she didn't possess "an Italianate voice." He said that she needed to continue studying, and recommended Emma Molaioli, a teacher in Milan. In short, he told me that Maria should not expect to have a great career.

Chapter 4

La Scala Audition Fails

With the final performance of *Gioconda* on August 17, the curtain fell on the opera season in the Arena. Maria Callas collected her small fee, turned over ten percent of it to Eddie Bagarozy's wife, and joined me in celebrating her first important venture in Italy.

As I have said, nothing out of the ordinary happened in the Arena. Maria was liked and Serafin had expressed his satisfaction, albeit without enthusiasm. Even though Maria's debut in Verona did not elicit any new offers, we were satisfied and prepared to begin ascending the ladder of success.

A few days later I said to Maria: "The moment has come for you to make a definite commitment. I repeat my offer to be of assistance; you have only to decide if you want to accept it. If you stay, we must develop a plan of action and implement it. If you decide to return to the United States, we should arrange passage for you."

Maria replied, without hesitation: "I can no longer leave. Not only because I'm certain that your help will be the determining factor in my career, but because I have found in you the man of my life. I cannot live apart from you."

My plan for Maria's future was elementary. "First of all," I told her, "you must devote yourself to intense study. We already have Maestro Cusinati for this. Then we will look for engagements, and rest assured, they will be forthcoming."

Maria's life continued as before. She still lived at the Hotel Accademia. I arranged for her to have a piano so that she could study in her room, if she wished. She took long walks around the city. Nobody knew who she was, except for a couple of gossips who pointed at her as she passed, and said, "That's the American singer who turned Meneghini's head."

I told Maria to buy anything she wanted in the dress shops, because I wanted her to dress well. She showed herself to be restrained and dignified. She purchased only what was necessary and continued to dress modestly. One day she said to me, "Battista, I would like to ask a favor. I do not own one piece of jewelry—a little necklace, a bracelet, earrings, anything. But I have always wanted to have something to put on. I saw a bracelet in a window. It doesn't cost much, and I would so like to have it." I accompanied her to the shop. She was referring to a simple, inexpensive silver bracelet. I bought it for her and it made her very happy.

She had arrived in Italy with a travel visa that was valid for only three months. It expired around the end of September and she had to request an extension. We went to Venice, where she applied at the American consulate. I had assumed it was something that could be taken care of in a few hours, but the clerk told us that the request had to be forwarded to the United States, and a reply would take at least a couple of weeks.

We took advantage of this unexpected delay by exploring Venice, my favorite city of all cities. After our visit the day after we met, Maria had spoken often of Venice, and now it meant a great deal to her also. Maria had a remarkable capacity to assimilate beautiful things. Although it was only our second visit, I discovered that she knew Venice well. She had read about it and was very knowledgeable. She wanted to visit specific churches and palaces which were even new to me. I often visited the Friars' Church, which contains my favorite painting, Titian's *The Assumption.* I was convinced that this painting brought me luck and I had reproductions of it in my office. Maria was also drawn to Titian's masterpiece. It became "our painting" and "our Madonna." Our trips to Venice at that time were wonderful diversions. The climate was ideal, the evenings delightful. With the excuse of following the progress of the visa extension, we went there often.

The reply finally arrived from the United States. "It turns out to be a rather involved matter," the clerk in the embassy informed us. He showed us a dossier full of various documents which indicated that Maria had a rather considerable outstanding debt with the United States government. It concerned expenses the government had underwritten so that she could return to the United States from Greece after the war. Maria was aware of debts with certain people whose generosity allowed her to come to Italy, but she knew nothing of a financial obligation to her government. It was about a thousand dollars, a not inconsiderable sum. "If it is not paid," the clerk explained, "we will not be permitted to issue her a regular passport." "That's not a problem," I said, and I paid the amount. Thus Maria had her passport and was now able to remain in Italy as long as she wished.

Her papers were in order, and Cusinati was increasingly enthusiastic about the progress she was making with her studies. The only thing lacking was employment. I thought about having Maria audition for La Scala. I said to myself, "If they engage her there, everything is set." Remembering the positive response to her *Giocondas* and Cusinati's encouraging remarks, I was optimistic.

I was a friend of the splendid conductor Antonio Guarnieri. We first met at the Fenice Theater in Venice, where I often went in the company of a friend who was an ardent Wagnerite.

This acquaintance, Amleto Faccioli, had been a professor of literature, but he gave it up to become a building contractor. He had such an intimate knowledge of Wagner's operas that he amazed even Maestro Guarnieri, who was himself thoroughly versed in these works. We always went to hear Guarnieri when he conducted Wagner at the Fenice. My friend Faccioli followed the performances with such intense emotional participation that I feared for his health. He would become so involved that his face was damp with perspiration. I said to his secretary, "Someday he'll waste away and we won't find him in his seat."

When I decided to take Maria to La Scala, I asked Guarnieri to put in a word for me. He wrote a letter of introduction to the artistic director, who at that time was Mario Labroca, a composer of some repute. The absolute director of the theater was Antonio Ghiringhelli, who was unapproachable. Ensconced in his office, as if in a fortress, he directed the theater through a network of assistants in mysterious offices. Of Ghiringhelli and his court, I will have opportunity to speak later, and at length.

One day I said to Maria, "Let's go to Milan tomorrow."

"Fine, what time are we leaving?" she asked. She didn't even wonder what we were going to do. She was totally content. She had complete confidence in me and did not worry about anything. The fact that she was without engagements was for her of secondary importance. She thought of me before her singing.

When we were on the train I told her, "We have an audition at La Scala at five this afternoon."

"Then this is an important trip," she replied.

At the appointed hour we went to the desk inside the theater and told the receptionist that Maestro Labroca was expecting us. "Please sit down, he'll be here in a moment," he said. We waited with a young tenor who also had an audition with him.

Labroca arrived shortly, and we followed him into the auditorium. On the stage, off to the side, was a piano at which was seated an accompanist. Labroca said to the young tenor, "Let's hear you first, please." The tenor went up to the stage and sang "Che gelida manina" from *La Bohème*. He had a modest voice and a technique which I judged to be disastrous. Labroca, however, liked him. "The schedule is set for this year," he told him, "but we can use you the following season. Please make yourself available to us. I will send you a letter in the next few days indicating the period when we will be able to use you." With that, he dismissed him.

I thought to myself: "They don't seem to have very high standards at La Scala. If Labroca was enthusiastic about him, God only knows what will happen when he hears Maria."

"If you would be so kind, signorina," Labroca said, turning to Maria. She walked across the stage to the piano. "What would you like to sing for me?" Labroca asked.

"What would you like?" Maria replied.

"No, no, just select the aria in which you feel yourself best prepared."

"Would you like to hear 'Casta diva' from *Norma?*" she inquired.

Labroca looked at her somewhat skeptically. "Casta diva" is among the most demanding of all arias. Only presumptuous or foolhardy novices offer it at an audition. Upon hearing what she suggested, I believe that Labroca assumed he was face to face with another pretentious, dumb soprano. "Do the 'Casta diva' if you wish," he said, with an irritated tone to his voice.

Maria waited calmly while the accompanist played the opening measures, and then she began to sing. "Casta diva" is the aria for which Maria Callas was most famous, even among those who were not opera fans. She sang it like no one else in the world. The timbre of her voice, the breath control, and the haunting melancholy she managed to bring to music were unforgettable. And on this occasion she sang it in the most marvelous way. I was very moved. Labroca, however, seemed

restless and was evidentally not too pleased. When she was finished, he didn't make any comment but asked her if she could
also sing "O patria mia" from *Aïda.*

"Yes," she replied, and sang it.

"That's fine," he said, breaking in. "We don't have an opening
now, so there's nothing I can do, but I'll keep you in mind."

While Maria was coming down from the stage, I approached
Labroca and asked him what he thought of her. He knew that I
was interested in Maria's career, because Maestro Guarnieri had
written to him. He knew that I wanted an honest opinion. He
said without hesitation: "There is nothing for her here. You
should send her back to America, whenever you want. She'll do
fine there. On the other hand, if she waits around here, she's
wasting her time, for there's nothing for her, absolutely nothing."

This was the evaluation of Maria Callas by the artistic director of La Scala in September 1947. I was dismayed, and also
profoundly disheartened. I tried to hide my feelings from Maria,
because I didn't want her to be sad.*

Since we were in Milan, I took advantage of it by making a
few business telephone calls. We went into a café, where Maria
waited for me at a table, and read. We then had dinner at
Savini. The elegant shops, the cathedral, the illuminated streets,
and the famous arcade all made Maria enormously happy. I

---

* Toward the end of 1956, Callas wrote a lengthy autobiographical series
for the weekly magazine *Oggi.* Her more immediate recollection of the
Scala audition with Labroca is somewhat at variance with Meneghini's
account, and is worth quoting. Callas wrote: "Maestro Labroca, at that
time artistic director of the theater, had me sing arias from *Norma* and
Un Ballo in Maschera. I nervously awaited his evaluation and I heard him
say that my voice had too many defects. 'Try to correct them,' he added,
'and within a month you will be hearing from me. But don't go home
upset. I promise that you will have the part of Amelia in *Ballo in Maschera.'*
I waited a month, two months in vain." It is possible that Labroca did
consider her for *Ballo;* Verdi's opera was given five times during the
1947–48 season, but with Elisabetta Barbato in the role of Amelia.

enjoyed seeing her so carefree, but I was unable to block La-broca's words from my mind.

At one point during dinner Maria asked point-blank, "The audition didn't go very well, did it?"

"On the contrary, it went very well," I replied. Maria had been more perceptive than I thought. She looked me straight in the eye and said: "That's not true. That Broca person"—that's how she referred to him— "didn't like me. But neither he nor La Scala mean a thing to me. I have you, and I am very happy, do you understand? I will continue studying, and when the right moment comes, I'll succeed on my own merits. I'll come out on top in this world without having to depend on anyone. With you at my side, I'm not afraid of any obstacles. And I am certain that I will succeed."

I had never heard her speak so decisively, and with such determination. Her confidence reassured me. After the disappointment at La Scala, her words were encouraging. We finished our dinner contentedly, and then took the train back to Verona.

Chapter 5

No Parts for Maria—
and Then Isolde

Maria had misled me with her remarks at Savini's restaurant. She managed to convince me that she had limitless confidence in herself. In fact, she was as concerned as I. Not so much because of her career, but for the complications she was bringing to my life. She was a woman of great dignity. She was accustomed to fending for herself in difficult situations and not asking favors of anyone. It made her suffer when she saw that she was the cause of my problems.

She knew of my family's hostility. She often asked me about my mother and my brothers, because she wanted to meet them. For a while I told her that it was best to wait, but when she finally understood the degree of my brothers' aversion to her, it grieved her. Only one of my brothers, Nicola, showed a little understanding, but he was circumspect about it because he didn't want to antagonize the others. They, too, were the object of snide remarks from friends and acquaintances in town. We found ourselves alone. Outside of work, where my personal contacts were dictated by financial interests, I no longer saw anyone.

All this preyed on her mind and filled her with remorse. To this was added the fiasco of the Scala audition. Seeing me tired and taciturn, she began to think that I had wearied of her but was hesitant to tell her. While all this was going through her mind, she had no one in whom she could confide.

Around September 20, a few days after the unsuccessful trip to Milan, she decided to return to the United States. She wrote me a letter of farewell and packed her bags. Then her love for me won out. She tore up the letter, and wrote another in which she expressed what was in her heart. I found her letter when I returned to my office the evening of September 22. I read it with tears in my eyes.

"My dear Battista," she wrote. "Yesterday I tore up a letter that I had written to you. Now I am writing you another. I feel the need to tell you that my love for you is so strong that it causes me to suffer. The other evening and all of yesterday were a nightmare. I had decided to leave because it seemed to me that you were tired of me. Yes, I had made up my mind, but I had found so many excuses for not going through with it. I finally began preparing my bags, and then I stopped. Leaving you would have been too great a punishment for me. Life could not hold such a great sorrow in store and I do not believe that I deserve it. I need you and your love.

"Yesterday I understood that my insecurity was wrong. You gave me a great proof of your love. I needed to hear and see that I do not bother and annoy you. I had been so miserable, and you made me so happy staying with me yesterday the way you did. I would have been in a terrible state if you had left last night. I needed to be in your arms, and feel you near me, as I did. You are everything to me and I am grateful. I ask only for your love and your affection.

"My Battista, I am all yours, even my tiniest feeling and slightest thought. I live for you. Your wish is also mine, I will do whatever you want, but don't take my love and relegate it to one corner of your life. I need to be part of your house. Every home needs to be cared for. Do not forget that a woman thinks of and lives for her husband; she depends on him. For me, you are my husband. Battista, it is not possible for a woman to have greater love for you than I have.

"You have an obligation in your life now, and that is to be well for me. You have me and will continue to have me forever; always remember that. I am your friend in love, your confidant, your support when you are tired; and everything that I am, I would like to be even more. Your Maria."

Our relationship emerged strengthened from her emotional crisis. I now realized that Maria loved me more than I had ever imagined. I ordered construction to begin on an apartment above my office in Verona. This was to be our home. Maria, meanwhile, continued to study relentlessly.

Everything in our lives proceeded smoothly, with the single exception of the fact that I could not find an engagement for her. At that time I was totally unknown in theatrical circles, and I didn't know the ropes. But I asked questions and gathered information, and every now and then I would try a different approach. I was told there was a theatrical agency in Milan, the Alci, headed by a certain Liduino Bonardi. He was a strange person, almost devoid of culture, but one with a genius for organization. Sitting alone in his bare office, with a telephone, sheets of paper, and a pencil, he controlled the lives of theaters in half the world. He deployed singers, replaced those who didn't work out, and made dramatic rescues in crisis situations. If he received word from New York that the person scheduled for the title role in an opera was sick, and that it was imperative they find a substitute immediately, he resolved the problem with one or two telephone calls. He was, in short, a magician.* I also decided to place myself in his hands.

The way this happened, the choice of the day, the details of the meeting that were decisive in Maria's career, are unlikely to the point of being improbable.

* Rudolf Bing, in his autobiography, described Bonardi as "an amiable old bandit."

Early in October of that year, Maestro Nino Cattozzo, director of the Fenice in Venice, began to block out the schedule for the forthcoming season. Born in Adria, a composer of talent, he was for several years the artistic secretary of La Scala. Now he was the new head of the Fenice. I had first met him in 1928, when he was director of Verona's music conservatory.

Cattozzo wanted his inaugural season at the Fenice to be impressive, and he hoped to open with Wagner's *Tristan and Isolde* [to be sung in Italian, as was customary in Italy at that time]. This complicated and difficult opera demands interpreters intimately familiar with their roles, and Cattozzo was searching desperately for an Isolde.

He had attended a performance of *Gioconda* in the Arena and heard Maria sing. He had admired her voice, and when he decided to mount *Tristan*, she was one of the sopranos who came to mind. Before engaging her, however, he wanted to know if she knew the music. It would have been pointless to offer Isolde to her otherwise, for opening night was less than three months away and no one would have been able to learn the role that quickly.

Cattozzo telephoned Angelina Pomari, sister of the manager of the restaurant Pedavena, where Maria and I ate dinner every evening. He asked her to find out if Maria Callas knew the role of Isolde. "I have to have an answer as soon as possible. I'll wait to hear from you until tomorrow morning. If you don't call, that means that Callas doesn't know the part. Then I'll have to look elsewhere."

Angelina Pomari, who was also a singer, pretended to be Maria's friend, but in reality she was jealous of her. Because of her envy she played a vicious trick. She neither mentioned the plans for *Tristan* to us that evening nor telephoned Cattozzo. Who knows by what arcane intuition I sensed this petty act against Maria. Cattozzo had telephoned Verona Tuesday evening and was waiting for an answer by Wednesday morning.

The following day he planned to go to Milan to look for a soprano who knew Isolde. Wednesday afternoon, without knowing
why, I felt I should go to Milan. I said to Maria, "Tomorrow I
want to try another approach for finding work for you. Let's look
up Liduino in Milan."

Around ten the next morning we were in the office of the Alci
agency. Liduino was seated on something that resembled a
throne. I introduced myself and presented Maria to him. He was
a man of few words—curt, straightforward—and he made one
feel a little uncomfortable. Since he had never heard anyone
speak of Callas, I showed him a list of her operatic repertory. I
told him that she had made her debut at the Verona Arena and
had received good notices. He listened to what I had to say and
then pointed out that the theaters were all closed at the moment. He added that the various schedules for that year were
set. In other words, there was nothing.

I insisted. "Listen," I said, "Callas has done *Gioconda* in the
Arena. Maybe there's another theater that's staging this opera."

"I don't believe so," he said. "It's rarely performed, so there is
little demand for a Gioconda."

Trying flattery, I said, "But is it possible that you, who know
everything that's going on, the Napoleon of theatrical agents,
cannot find even some little engagement for this young singer?"

Seeing that I was going to be persistent, Liduino said: "See
that woman over there," and he nodded toward a lady at the
back of his office, a corpulent woman of coarse mien. "She's the
director of the opera house in Pavia," he continued, "and they're
doing *Gioconda*. Give her a try."

"There we are," I thought. I walked over to her and introduced myself and Maria. She had heard of the young American
singer. I explained to her that Maria didn't have any more contracts, despite her success and good reviews. "Illustrious maestri
have predicted a great future for her," I said. "Let her sing in
Pavia, and you will not regret it."

"It's too late," she replied. "I'm only doing two performances and I've already promised the part to another soprano."

"At least give one of the performances to this young girl," I begged.

"Okay," she said, "if you insist, I'll do you this favor. She can sing the second performance. However, bear in mind, I don't pay more than 20,000 lire [about $30]."

I was a businessman who was accustomed to paying a fair price for a product. To have charity offered in that despicable manner made my blood boil. I had been in that office for almost an hour, begging like a man dying of hunger. Her offering this pittance to a singer I considered the best humiliated and offended me. Flushed with rage, I took Maria's hand and said, "Let's get out of this stinking office!" Liduino had a door that opened out, and I gave it a forceful shove. At that moment someone was approaching from the other side, and the door hit him in the face. I heard an inhuman moan and, in the dialect of the Veneto region, "*Maria Santissima*, my nose is broken!" A man stood in the doorway, doubled over, cupping his bloody nose.

Liduino rose from his throne and rushed over. "Oh, God," he exclaimed, "you've broken Maestro Cattozzo's nose!" I apologized while Liduino looked for alcohol. We examined the wound. His nose was bloody, but it was nothing serious, only an abrasion. Unable to find a bandage, Liduino wanted to put a stamp on it.

While we were talking, I observed the man. It seemed to me that I knew him. He also had a puzzled expression. Then suddenly he said, "But aren't you Titta Meneghini?" "Yes," I replied. Cattozzo was a likable person. He only spoke in dialect. He was so thin his friends nicknamed him "the sole." He told me he wanted to open his season at the Fenice with *Tristan*, and that he had come to Milan to look for an Isolde.

"Why don't you give the part to Callas," I suggested.

"What do you mean?" he asked, surprised. "She knows the part?"

"Certainly," I assured him. Maria started to interrupt, since she hadn't studied a note of the opera, but I stopped her with a glance. "I tried to get in touch with you two days ago," Cattozzo informed me. He told us of the telephone call to Angelina Pomari and their arrangement. When she didn't return the call, he assumed that Callas didn't know the part.

"I'm satisfied," he said. "I wound up with a broken nose, but I also have an Isolde." Cattozzo said that before we signed the contract, however, he had to have the approval of Serafin, who was conducting the opera. As Serafin happened to be in Milan, he telephoned him that moment. Serafin made an appointment with us at three that afternoon. We had time to kill, and we went to get something to eat. Maestro Serafin was happy to see Maria again. He asked me if I had taken his advice and sent Maria to study with Emma Molaioli, the teacher in Milan whom he had recommended. "No," I replied.

"You made a big mistake," he said.

"I sent her to another maestro who lives closer to us," I told him.

"Let's see the results," he replied tersely. He took the score of *Tristan* and asked Callas what portion she would like to sing. Since she wasn't acquainted with any of it, she replied, "You choose, maestro." He opened the score at random. "Let's start here," he said, indicating a certain measure, and he began to play. Maria, sight-reading the score, sang with confidence and extraordinary accuracy. "Fine, fine," Serafin told her. "I see you do know the opera."

They continued on for several pages. Then he jumped to Act II and had her sing the great "Liebesnacht" duet. Maria sang her part magnificently. "I am very pleased," Serafin said. "The voice has improved. The lessons were beneficial. I think we have an interesting Isolde here. However," he added, turning to me, "since I want to do a truly beautiful performance, you must promise to send Maria to my home in Chianciano for at least a week, so I can coach her in the role and indicate to her what I expect from those who sing Isolde under my baton."

"Maria is available whenever you wish," I assured him.

That evening we returned to Verona happier than we had ever been. Serafin had voiced some reservations about Maria at the end of the season in the Arena, but now he was enthusiastic about her. He was one of the most venerated operatic conductors, and his opinion was extremely important.

Maria continued to study with Cusinati with the greatest enthusiasm, working exclusively on *Tristan.* She was certain she could do it. Shortly before I was to accompany Maria to Serafin's home in the village of Chianciano, the maestro had a change of plans and asked that I send her to work with him in Rome instead.

Maria left Verona October 28. She was away for a week. It was the first time that we were apart since we had met, and it was that separation that revealed to us just how much in love we were. I was sad and depressed in Verona, and she, in Rome, felt even worse. I briefly considered saying to hell with my business obligations. In six days she wrote ten letters to me. On two of the days she sent me three letters. I also wrote or, more often, sent telegrams.

The morning of October 30, before she was scarcely settled in her hotel, she wrote me: "Dear Battista, first of all, I would like to know how you are, and if everything is going all right. Then I want to tell you that I miss you very much . . . too much.

"Last evening was the first time that I have eaten alone since we met. I cannot tell you how unhappy I was. I would not even have gone to eat if it were not necessary. Since I left you I've only managed to eat green salads and eggs. I just don't have an appetite. We've only been apart a couple of days and I'm miser-able; what will happen tomorrow and the next day?

"You're very busy with your work, but I do ask you to send me your news. Yesterday I had my first lesson with Serafin and it went very well. His wife paid me many compliments. She says that the part suits me very well, both from a physical and a vocal standpoint.

"The trip was comfortable. It is pointless, however, to tell you how I was. By morning my eyes were puffy, with dark circles. It's good that you didn't see me. I was so ugly! It was pouring rain. I had to go looking for a hotel, because the one that Serafin recommended was full. I went to six or eight hotels until I found this one. I have a small, rather nice room, although it's a little damp. I hope I don't catch a cold. Unfortunately, it's without bath. I am paying nine hundred lire plus tax, in all about a thousand lire. The *pensioni* charge about four thousand lire a day. I think it's better that I remain here. The hotel is also a short distance from the bus that takes me to Serafin's.

"I don't want to tell you to join me, my love, because you know I hate to pressure you, but it would be so nice if you could come to Rome. Don't leave me here. I'm very alone, you know, so alone. I'll let you go, but please write me. Think of me when you have a chance. *Ciao, amore*, take care of yourself and be sure to eat well. I wouldn't want to see you any thinner than you are. Always, your Maria."

That evening she wrote me another long letter. I had been writing a lot about my work, and she replied: "I'm very tired at the moment. We worked for more than two and a half hours. Serafin went over the role with me word by word. If I do just what he says, it can only result in something marvelous. I'll have to work very hard, but I would do it gladly, to please you. There is also Serafin, whom I must please. But who is thinking about my happiness? I do what I can to please everyone, and I wind up with glory, while my personal feelings go by the wayside. Let's not become philosophical, because it makes me sad and unhappy. Sometimes you too are in love with Callas the artist, and lose sight of the person. Your letter was very beautiful, so sweet, but I wanted to find more 'Battista and Maria' in it, and less 'Meneghini and Callas.' Let's see if I find my Battista in your other letters.

"Today, my love, I had a lot of trouble with my leg. At one point tears came to my eyes. It happened as I was climbing into a bus with a very high step. The pain was terrible. I also have one of those dreadful headaches that come now and then to plague me. I don't know what to tell you; when I am far from you I am not well. Battista, I miss you, you can't imagine how much. I can't wait for the hour when I will see you again and am in your arms.

"I have been in good voice, and the more I sing *Tristan*, the better it goes. Isolde is an impetuous role, but I like it. Write to me, I only have you and your letters. I just received your wonderful telegram. You know so well how to make me happy. I didn't say a word to you, but I wanted so much to receive a few words from you from Padua. I am so touched, my dear, and I am not ashamed to tell you that I cried. You alone know the depth of my love for you . . . I am, I have been, and I always will be yours."

On the first of November, Maria wrote three letters to me. Here are a few excerpts. "My dear Battista, My joy in life is to receive letters from you, and words of approval from Maestro Serafin . . . Cattozzo telephoned Serafin yesterday and Maestro spoke so glowingly of me that I almost wept. Are you pleased, my love?

"You know, they're all against Serafin because he's using a foreigner. That means that they are also against me. In the United States they wrote a negative article about me. I don't know how much longer I will remain in Rome, but I don't believe it will be more than two weeks. Even at the end of two weeks I won't know the part well. I'll know what Serafin expects with the score in front of me, but then I have to memorize it. That's the hard part, and for this I have to be at a piano . . .

"Rome is a grand, beautiful city, at least the little I've seen. I like it, although nothing is really beautiful if you're not there with me. . . . Here in Rome I'm alone. How I would like to have you near me right now! I would like to hear you say, 'You know, you speak Italian very well!' Then I would like for you to look at me in that special way, and hear that name that you call me."

And here is the third letter she wrote on November 1. "Dear, this is the third letter I'm writing to you today. I must be crazy, you're saying. But this time I have an important reason for writing: we will be together in a few days. Serafin says it is pointless for me to wear myself out, and he's allowing me to return to Verona. I'll rejoin him in Venice at the beginning of December, when we begin the regular rehearsals.

"Now, my love, how shall I make the return trip? Will you arrange it for me? I would prefer that. Write me what I should do. I hope you're not displeased to see me so soon. I am so very happy. When Serafin told me I could leave, I almost kissed him. I can't wait to see you again."

The following day she wrote: "Battista my love, I'm touched. While I was studying feverishly your telegram arrived. Battista, you are so thoughtful and bursting with tender thoughts. I was so moved that I cried, because today I felt particularly alone. Your letters hadn't arrived. The coaching session was in the morning, and we finished at 12:30. I have spent the afternoon alone, studying. I'm enormously depressed . . .

"If I put everything that I feel for you into Isolde, I will be marvelous. I will do my best . . . Once again, think of me, be sure to eat well, and again, think of me. Maria."

November 3, I received a very long letter in which Maria complained of the delays in receiving my letters. "I hate the mails," she wrote, "because they always play nasty tricks." Then in conclusion: "Your Isolde greets you; stay well, but also work hard. Today is a marvelous day, sunny, a clear sky, not the least bit chilly. How happy I would be if Verona were like this, but one cannot have everything in life. You will be my warmth in Verona . . . and not the way you're thinking . . . and then again, maybe yes . . . !"

Chapter 6

Triumph in Venice

Maria returned from Rome around November 10. She was very happy to be home again. The separation had only been for twelve days, but it seemed an eternity to both of us. By now we were so accustomed to living close to each other that the hours we passed apart seemed empty, heavy, devoid of significance.

The trip to Rome was certainly not without its artistic fulfillment. Serafin, coaching her two and a half hours a day, had had the opportunity to gain an in-depth understanding of Maria, and also more accurately evaluate her capabilities. *Tristan* demands not only musical preparation but experience, style, intelligence: attributes which are almost never combined in a singer who is still a novice. Serafin discovered that Maria—only twenty-four and at the beginning of her career—possessed extraordinary maturity. The maestro's enthusiasm was such that, in contrast to his customary behavior, he was not at all niggardly in his compliments.

Even more enthusiastic about Maria during her Roman sojourn was Serafin's wife, Elena Rakowska, a former Polish soprano who had married the conductor in 1915. Born in Krakow, Rakowska had studied singing in Vienna and had begun her career in Genoa at the age of seventeen. Engagements followed in Warsaw, at the Vienna Opera, and then again in Italy. Her La Scala debut was in 1918 in Boito's *Mefistofele*, conducted by

Toscanini. Later she appeared at the Metropolitan in New York and at other important American theaters.*

A superb interpreter of the Wagnerian repertory herself, Elena Rakowska was in a position to evaluate competently the suitability of the young Maria Callas for the difficult role of Isolde. After sitting in on a lesson, she was not able to contain her enthusiasm: she said that in both voice and physical attributes Maria was the ideal Isolde. Rakowska had only one reservation. "I and all my other colleagues who have sung Isolde spent at least two years learning the part," she told Maria. "I don't know how you will manage to do it in less than two months." After a few days, however, she no longer had any doubts.

Observing how quickly Maria mastered and retained the part, Rakowska added new admiration to her enthusiasm. She offered Maria the wig she had used in her performances as Isolde. It was still lovely, and valuable because it was made of real hair.

Upon returning to Verona, Maria resumed her regular schedule. In the morning she went for her lesson with Cusinati, and in the afternoon she studied alone in her hotel. Around evening she often came to my office and stayed there, sitting off to the side, just to keep me company. She knew all our employees, and they all loved her.

At the beginning of December, when Tullio Serafin went to Venice to begin rehearsing the orchestra of the Fenice, I went there with Maria for a couple of days. She and Serafin went through the entire opera again, which Maria now knew by heart. Opening night was announced for December 30. We returned to Venice around the twentieth and took rooms at the Hotel Fenice, which was adjacent to the theater. I stayed with

* Rakowska made her debut at the Metropolitan on December 23, 1927, as Rachel in *La Juive*. She was on the roster for three seasons, singing mainly in *La Juive* and *Cavalleria Rusticana*. She also appeared as Brünnhilde in a single performance of *Siegfried*.

Maria for a day, but had to return to Verona because of business obligations.

Her debut at the Fenice was important, certainly more than the one in Verona. The Fenice is very prestigious, even outside Italy. The careers of many famous singers have taken flight from the stage of that theater. Maria was also singing a very difficult work. If everything went well, that performance could be the true springboard for her career.

Thinking about her debut, the general anticipation, and the attention which Serafin had lavished on the preparation of the opera, I knew this would be a memorable evening for Maria. Every performer wishes to live these special moments surrounded by the people most dear to them. Maria's colleagues had invited intimates, family, friends, acquaintances. They scurried about reserving hotel rooms and finding extra tickets, happy and in a state of excitement. Maria, however, did not have anyone other than me and a few of my own friends. I thought she would like having her mother know about the event. I took the initiative to send her a long telegram in New York, and then I told Maria.

It was the nicest present I could give her. She replied with a letter: "My love, I do not have words to tell you how much pleasure and happiness you have given me with this gesture of sending the telegram to my mother. You see, this says so much to me because it is another example of your kindness, your thoughtfulness and especially your interest in the people who are most dear to me. You have made me so very, very happy. I thank you and I love you even more, if that is possible."

The first *Tristan* took place on December 30, 1947. Maria's colleagues included Fiorenzo Tasso (Tristan), Boris Christoff (King Mark), Fedora Barbieri (Brangäne), and Raimondo Torres (Kurwenal). It was a triumph. The general public, the aficionados, the critics, all understood that they had found a great artist in Maria Callas. I knew the opera fairly well from having heard it on other occasions with my Wagnerite friend Amleto Faccioli, but *Tristan* seemed to me to be completely new when I heard Maria sing it. Faccioli told me he had never heard an Isolde of that caliber.

Even Serafin was pleased. Probably because of his normal reticence and reserve he didn't express in words all that he felt, but his eyes sparkled. The enthusiasm of his wife, however, was boundless. Rakowska kept repeating loudly to her husband, without caring if everyone heard her: "I told you it would be a triumph. You weren't convinced, but I knew. You are the only idiot who doesn't understand anything." Serafin, accustomed to his wife's exuberance, smiled and remained silent.

After the *prima*, Maria and I went to dinner with some friends. She was not at all dissatisfied, but she was also not triumphant. She really seemed to derive greater pleasure from my being with her than from the applause she received in the theater. The first thing in the morning I ran to buy the newspapers, but Maria scarcely looked at them. She had her own standards by which she judged her performances, and she relied on her own opinion.

After Maria's success at the Fenice, my thoughts returned to La Scala, and the negative evaluation of the artistic director of the theater, Mario Labroca. Her triumph was a great vindication for me. I said to myself, "Let's see if La Scala wants to talk now," and in my mind I composed the high-handed answers I would give. But I was rather naïve, and did not understand the lugubrious, mysterious machinery that ran La Scala. I had to wait four years before its directors stirred.

There were four performances of *Tristan* at the Fenice—December 30, 1947, and January 3, 8, and 11, 1948—all conducted by Serafin. Maria then began to prepare for Puccini's *Turandot*, which she sang at the same theater on January 29 and 31 and February 3, 8, and 10. *Turandot* was under the baton of Nino Sanzogno. The other principal singers were José Soler,

Elena Rizzieri, and Bruno Carmassi. Maria also had a great success in this opera. In fact, the reception was even more glowing. *Tristan* was a success among connoisseurs who could fully understand the enormity of the challenge, while *Turandot* was a popular success. After the *prima* Maria found herself a favorite of the Venetian public.

The year 1948 began well. The two months spent in Venice were marvelous. Then, since none of the important theaters approached us despite the successes at the Fenice, we decided to accept whatever offers came our way. In March, Maria sang in two performances of *Turandot* in Udine. Oliviero de Fabritiis conducted; with Maria sang José Soler, Silvio Maionica, and Dolores Ottani, in the part of Liù.

In April she was invited to Trieste for four performances of Verdi's *La Forza del Destino*. Mario Parenti conducted, and the other singers included Cesare Siepi (Padre Guardiano), Benvenuto Franci (Don Carlo), Anna Maria Canali (Preziosilla), Giuseppe Vertechi (Don Alvaro), and Ottavio Serpo (Fra Melitone). The reception was enthusiastic. On the eve of her debut, the *Corriere di Trieste* published a lengthy interview. The reviews were mainly favorable. "Maria Callas has a penetrating voice, not always of the loveliest timbre, but noteworthy for its security and power," wrote the reviewer for *La Voce Libera.* "Maria Callas proved herself to be a first-rate actress, thoroughly prepared and secure in her top register," observed *Il Lavoratore.*

Maria then went from Trieste to Genoa, where she sang in three performances of *Tristan* at the Grattacielo Theater under the direction of Tullio Serafin. The other interpreters included Max Lorenz (Tristan), Elena Nicolai (Brangäne), Raimondo Torres (Kurwenal), and Nicola Rossi-Lemeni (King Mark).*

---

* The Grattacielo was, and still is, a movie theater. Genoa's historic Carlo Felice opera house was totally destroyed during the war. One of Callas's

The reviews from Genoa were particularly important. Beppe Broselli wrote of Maria in the *Corriere del Popolo*: "Noble, almost solemn, superb queen and passionate lover, her Isolde was one of the great interpretations. Her magnificent figure brought to the part an added appeal and irresistible grandeur. But the greatest fascination, the most moving quality was that projected by her voice, a majestic, splendid instrument, vibrant and warm, smooth and equalized in every register—the ideal voice for an Isolde."

July found Maria in Rome for two performances of *Turandot* at the Baths of Caracalla, led by conductor Oliviero de Fabritiis. With Maria sang Galliano Masini (Calaf), Vera Montanari (Liù), and Giuseppe Flamini (Timur). The reviewer for *Il Messaggero* wrote: "[Maria Callas] has a large, penetrating voice, well schooled and expressive, at least as far as one can judge in the inhuman part of Turandot. She has excellent diction and a most remarkable dramatic sense. She embodied the cruel Chinese princess with a sensibility, art and intelligence truly out of the ordinary."

During July and August she returned to Verona's Arena for four *Turandots* led by Antonino Votto. Appearing with her were Antonio Salvarezza, Elena Rizzieri, Era Tognoli, Disma de Cecco, and Nicola Rossi-Lemeni. The middle of August she was back in Genoa for two *Turandots* with Mario Del Monaco, Vera Montanari, Silvio Maionica, and conductor Angelo Questa. In September she was in Turin for four *Aïdas* with Serafin. Her colleagues were Roberto Turrini as Radames, Elena Nicolai and Irma Colasanti alternating in the role of Amneris, and Marco

---

favorite anecdotes was describing how she and her less than sylph-like colleagues had to navigate around each other on the Grattacielo's postage-stamp-size stage. At one point Wagner had allotted Brangäne a certain number of measures to cross the stage. Because of cramped conditions, Elena Nicolai began pirouetting in one spot, much to the enjoyment of the other singers.

Stefanoni as Ramfis. The following month she went to the Teatro Sociale in Rovigo for two additional *Aïdas*, this time conducted by Umberto Berrettoni. The other principal singers were Roberto Turrini, Miriam Pirazzini, and Andrea Mongelli, as Ramfis. At the end of November she made her debut in Florence, singing *Norma* for the first time. She had a great triumph, to which we will return later.

As is obvious from this panorama, Maria sang often in 1948 and the critics in the various cities recognized in her an extraordinary voice and exceptional artistry. The references to the "strange quality" of Maria's voice, which is still a topic of discussion among certain critics, began to appear at a later date, when Maria first went to La Scala. In my opinion they were not unbiased observations, but were prompted by specific comparisons with the pure, smooth voice of Tebaldi, who at that time ruled La Scala.

This apprenticeship was very valuable for someone who knew how to mine even the smallest experience. She accepted these engagements with enthusiasm, but each time she had to leave Verona she was distressed when I was unable to go with her, and it usually was impossible for me to accompany her. I had my work, and there was no one else who could step in for me. As it was, the criticism from my family for the time I had already devoted to Maria was becoming increasingly acrimonious.

Each one of our separations was painful. The long letters which Maria wrote to me when she was away, reread now, offer a valuable insight into her personality. They illuminate aspects of her character, sensibility, her thought processes, and the way in which she lived the adventure that was carrying her to the summit of her art.

When I went to Udine for the two performances of *Turandot*, I was struck by the warmth with which she greeted the public, by the enthusiasm of her colleagues for her voice, the interest of the journalists, and even by the amount of her bill in the restaurant, which was much lower than anyone would have expected. They are simple, genuine impressions which indicate that Maria's head was not turned by her successes in Venice and elsewhere. She almost always made a report of her expenses in her letters to me. She had grown up in economic straits and now, even though she had begun to earn money, she refused to allow herself any luxuries.

She wrote me a letter from Udine, March 10, 1948. After apologizing for not having spoken affectionately with me on the telephone—she had called from a café and there were people around her listening to her conversation—she continued: "I was very tired. We arrived at five in the evening. The rehearsal began thirty minutes later and lasted until eight. When they heard me sing they were all enthusiastic, and I wasn't even singing out because I felt it was unwise to push my voice, but they were especially surprised at my *marvelous pronunciation*. Then later, after dinner, the reporters came and asked about my life and my career. I was on my feet until midnight. They also complimented me on my beautiful appearance. In short, I have had a most encouraging welcome.

"Yesterday, paying my bill for lunch, I almost fainted from surprise. Imagine: I had buttered rice, two eggs, fennel, fruit salad, bread, coffee; 505 lire [eighty cents] for everything! I have never paid such a small check. Tomorrow I will be very busy. A general rehearsal at 12:30, then the dress rehearsal in the evening. The *prima* is the following day. And you, what did you do yesterday and today? Did you eat, sleep, and work well? Did you also think a little about me and us? I lied to you on the telephone. I am not well. On the contrary, while I was talking to you I felt as if my heart were breaking. You know how I am when we're apart. It's not realistic for you to come here. It's a long trip and we could only spend little time together. I would like you to come, but it's not fair. Since you probably can't come, perhaps for the trip home you could have Rodolfo pick me up. That would be nice. It's a matinee performance, so I could return to Verona that evening. I would like to write more, but I cannot express myself well. I'm leaving it up to you to guess what I have in my heart, what I feel and think . . . Your Maria."

Her letters from Trieste also reflect her unhappiness over our temporary separation, as well as her appreciation for the compliments paid her by her colleagues and the reporters. I had accompanied her to Trieste, but was unable to stay. She wrote on April 14: "Everyone was pleased at rehearsal today. The conductor Benvenuto Franci and the others paid me many, many compliments. Franci says that there is no one in Italy singing Verdi the way I do. I would like to believe him, but you know how pessimistic I am about doing *Forza*. I can't wait for Saturday to arrive. How happy I would be if you were here. You were never missed as much as now!

"A reporter came in the evening for an interview. When I returned to the hotel I found they had given me a nicer room, and that pleased me enormously. The new one is large and very lovely, with a beautiful, spacious bath. I just took a very hot bath, which I thoroughly enjoyed.

"My dear, when will I see you? My Battista, I am so unhappy when you are not with me. Do you think of me a little? Now, Battista, I'm reminding you to rest and also to eat. With all your work you have to eat properly . . . I love you so very much, I am all yours, Maria."

Two days later she wrote me again from Trieste: "My dear love, I am writing you these lines because it is my way of feeling a little nearer to you. You see, despite yesterday's telephone call, I feel very, very sad and lonely . . . You are extremely busy at work and therefore don't notice my absence as much, but for me it's much more difficult. When I think that I must sing my first

Forza alone, without you here, I cry, not only in my heart but with my whole being . . . When I feel alone, I take out your letters and in that way feel you are near me.

"The dress rehearsal is this evening, but I don't know what the outcome will be. We have never rehearsed my scene in the second act, so I don't know what the staging is. I also feel a little run down and enervated because of my indisposition.

"And now I must tell you—please excuse me if I mention something distasteful—that the costumes have such a smell of sweat (not disinfectant) that they make me nauseous. God only knows how I'm going to manage to put them on. The smell is so acrid that this evening when some colleagues stopped by to see me, they commented on the pungent odor in the dressing room. How awful!

"After the *prima* I will write you at length. I hope to have some news."

All of Maria's letters during that period were full of tenderness and concern for me, but one in particular was unlike the others. I consider it to be the most beautiful and perhaps the most interesting of the group. She sent it November 18, 1948, from Rome, where she was studying Bellini's *Norma*, which she was scheduled to sing at Florence's Teatro Comunale. Maria again speaks of her love for me, but in a different way. She analyzes her feelings, as if to help me understand them more fully. Then she speaks of her art, revealing her thoughts, ideals, uncertainties, preoccupations, her fears. It is a beautiful and touching sharing of her feelings. It is also a remarkable document for the insight it contains into how she worked to become the great interpreter that everyone was to acclaim. Here are Maria's thoughts on the eve of her first *Norma*, the opera in which her histrionic gifts reached supreme heights:

"Dear, I am studying *Norma* after having returned from the first rehearsal with the mezzo-soprano. You would not believe how depressed I am right now. So much so that I must write to you, if only to feel a little closer to you and to unburden myself.

"You see, dear, I am such a pessimist that everything upsets me. I am convinced that everything I do I will do badly. Then I undermine my confidence even more, and become increasingly disheartened. At times I reach the point where I wish that death would release me from the torment, the anguish that is always with me. You see, I would like to give so much more in everything I do: be it in music or in my love for you.

"In singing I would like my voice to always *obey* me, and do what *I want*. But it seems that I demand too much from it. The vocal organ is ungrateful, and doesn't do as I wish. You could even say that it's rebellious and doesn't wish to be commanded or, more precisely, dominated. I always want to run away, and I suffer. If I continue in this way, you'll have a nervous wreck on your hands.

"It is the same with my love for you. I suffer because I cannot give you more. I would like to always be able to offer you more and more, but I don't know how. I know that I cannot give more, because I am only a human being, but I would like to be able to. I am sad when we are apart because I can't share your life with you—your thoughts, sorrows, joys—or give you a smile when you are tired, laugh along with you when you're enjoying yourself, guess what you're thinking (that's easy for me to do), and so many other things. I'm lonely without you. I don't have or want friendships. You know that I am a misanthrope, and I'm right in being that way. I live only for you and for my mother: I'm shared by both of you!

"Art should be my whole life, in the opinion of others. As far as I'm concerned, it's only the smallest part of it. The public applauds me, but I know inside myself that I could have done more. Serafin says that he is very pleased with my Norma, but I am not at all. I am convinced I can do it a hundred times better, but I'm unhappy with my voice. It will not do what I want.

"My love, why am I like this? I believe I'm the only person

with such a dissatisfied nature. The only time I don't long for something other than what I have is when I'm where I belong— at your side. I realize that we must be apart sometimes because of day-to-day demands on our time, but I am not the kind of person who takes things as they come. I want the best in every- thing. I want the man in my life to be the best of all. I want my art to be the most perfect. I want, in short, to have the best of everything. I also want what I wear to be the nicest that exists. I know that all this is not possible, and it torments me. Why? Help me, Battista. I'm not exaggerating. That's the way I am.

"Dear, just as I want everything to be perfect, I also want to be yours, and I am totally that. Love me in return and don't give me any reason to have regrets. Even an unintentional cross re- mark wounds me deeply, more than you can imagine. I am probably too sensible and understanding in all matters, but I would also like for you to be a little more that way with me, if possible.

"I must end now, my love. Please don't laugh at me, but rather try to understand and help me. And I ask that if you love me just a third as much as I love you, I will be happy. I am more with you than I am here, especially now. Your Maria."

In whatever city she was singing, Maria wanted to go home as soon as the performance was over, even during the period when she was at La Scala. Then it would be quite late, because she remained in her dressing room for as much as two hours signing autographs. But even if she finished at two or three in the morn- ing, she would say, "Battista, let's go home." When she said this she wasn't only referring to her apartment, but to Verona, which she considered to be her city. Maria was in love with Verona, the Veronese, the churches and palaces, the surrounding coun- tryside, the air, and even the dialect. She understood and could speak six languages correctly, and no one, only by listening to her, could determine which was her maternal tongue. When speaking Italian, one heard very clearly the inflection of the

Veronese dialect. During her audience with Pius XII, the Pope said to her, "You are Greek, and grew up in America. Yet the way you speak Italian, one would say that you are from Verona."

Her career began in Verona with *La Gioconda* in 1947. During the following season she sang *Turandot* at the Arena. In 1952 she appeared there in two works: *La Gioconda* and *La Traviata*; in 1953, two others—*Aïda* and *Il Trovatore*. In 1954 she sang in Boito's *Mefistofele*. She was also to have sung in Verona in 1955, but then declined the invitation so that she could be near me while I underwent a serious operation. The Arena was without an artistic director that season, and it was organized by a special commissioner, Piero Gonella. Finding himself in difficulty at the last moment, he turned to Maria. He sent this telegram on July 9: "I am confident that you will not deny the Arena and your friends in Verona the prestige and pleasure of your collaboration, which would elevate the opening of the season to an exceptional artistic level. The arrangements, although somewhat rushed, are nothing that would trouble an artist such as you. I therefore await your affirmative reply." Maria, not wishing to leave me, wrote Gonella: "My husband's illness keeps me in Siena. I would have accepted in a spirit of understanding, but I do not feel I can leave Battista." Maria, who always scrupulously insisted on long, meticulous rehearsals, was willing to appear in the Arena at the last minute because of her love for the people of Verona. However, her affection was not reciprocated. As I write these memoirs, three years have passed since her death: there were various tributes to her memory in most parts of the world; in Verona, they have done nothing.

Chapter 7

A Spectacular Year; Marriage

After Maria Callas's success in *Tristan and Isolde* in Venice at the end of 1947, Maestro Tullio Serafin realized that he had come across a great singer. Although he only worked with her on two other occasions in 1948—*Tristan* in Genoa and *Aïda* in Turin—he kept her in mind and continued to look for a new, important showcase.

It was after the *Aïda*s at the Teatro Lirico (formerly the Vittorio Emanuele) in Turin, October 19, 21, and 24, that Serafin decided to present Maria to Francesco Siciliani, the artistic director of Florence's Teatro Comunale.

Siciliani was a talented musician. He had recently been appointed artistic director of the Comunale (which included the Musical May Festival), after having served in the same capacity for eight years at Naples's Teatro San Carlo. Shy and reserved, he was rather uncommunicative, even though his musical and cultural background was of a level far superior to that of most other theater directors. Siciliani, who was unfamiliar with Maria, may only have listened to her because she had been recommended by Serafin, but he recognized her exceptional artistic gifts immediately. Perceiving what she was capable of doing, he offered her *Norma* for her debut opera, to be staged at the Comunale at the end of November 1948.

If Serafin was the first conductor to realize Maria Callas's potential, Siciliani was the first artistic director to utilize her gifts intelligently, even searching for operas which would challenge her. It was Siciliani who suggested to Maria—after the success of her *Norma, La Traviata,* and *Lucia di Lammermoor*—Rossini's *Armida,* which was virtually never performed because of a lack of singers capable of singing it, and Cherubini's *Medea,* which later constituted one of her most memorable triumphs at La Scala.

In 1948 the Comunale was run by Pariso Votto, a former baritone and brother of the conductor Antonino Votto. Pariso Votto was not particularly interested in Maria. Siciliani was a tranquil person who was never given to polemics, and he was careful not to antagonize his superior. Even though his enthusiasm for Maria was boundless and sincere, he was always restrained in his remarks because of Votto. For her initial appearances in Florence in 1948, he gave Maria only two performances of *Norma.* He considered this engagement to be crucial, and he didn't want to take any risks. Siciliani was always apprehensive, even years later, after Maria had become famous. He would be afraid that Maria would not have the strength to sing a particular role, that her voice would give out; he was in a state of constant tension on the eve of each of her opening nights.

Maria also realized that her first *Norma* was a major step in her career, and she prepared herself with fastidiousness and a nervous tension to which I referred earlier, when I quoted the letter which she wrote to me while she was studying Bellini's opera with Serafin.*

* During a 1968 BBC interview with Lord Harewood, Callas referred to one of her first *Norma* rehearsals with Serafin and his advice for the proper delivery of the words. After the first run-through he told her: "Fine, you know the music perfectly well. Now go home, signorina, and speak the words to yourself. Keep on speaking them. Let's see with what proportions and rhythm you come back to me tomorrow . . . Forget that you're singing and that there are note values. Respect the values, yes, but also be free."

She mentioned *Norma* in every single letter written during that period. She wrote on November 11, 1948: "I have never seen Serafin so happy. I am not, however, because I always ask too much of myself. If I had more time I believe it would be so much better, because one can never study *Norma* enough."

She was very concerned about her costume and particularly the wig, which she never liked to wear. She wrote: "The unpleasant, annoying news is that I must wear a wig in *Norma*. I must be a reddish blonde: what nonsense! So now I also have to provide for a wig. I am to have a kind of breast-band or halter, and my waist will be exposed. In addition to that, the robe is very sheer and I will have to wear stockings that are flesh-colored, not like the dark ones I wore in *Aïda*. Poor me and poor you, who will have to see all this to believe it."

A week later she wrote telling me that she felt much better, and then returned to her discussion of the wig: "I have done a great deal of running around for this wig, but I have finally found one. It was difficult selecting precisely the right wig. One has to be careful with red: it can be an eyesore. I chose one somewhere between chestnut and Titian red. I found a really beautiful one, even though it was a lot of effort. My wig for *Norma* must also be very long and reach almost to my waist. Since I'm so tall, and taking into account that it will seem shorter when it's shaped, I need one that's at least ninety centimeters [three feet] in length. Frankly, I was lucky to find one this long. Do you remember all the work that went into lengthening my wig for *Tristan?* I'm pleased because now I can concentrate on my singing."

Norma was a triumph. The other singers were Mirto Picchi, who was singing his first Pollione, Fedora Barbieri (Adalgisa), Cesare Siepi (Oroveso), Lucia Danieli (Clotilde), and Massimo Bison (Flavio). This time Maria received unqualified praise from the critics. Virgilio Doplicher wrote in *Il Nuovo Corriere*: "Maria Callas found in the title role the fulfillment of her significant dramatic-musical gifts. She persuaded one with her considerable intelligence and impressive display of her vocal ability, which is especially evident in the gracefulness and harmonious balance of the melodic phrases. This young artist is already versed in the most demanding traditions of Italian bel canto."

Gualtiero Frangini reported in *La Nazione*: "Maria Callas was new to us, but after her entrance in the first act, we were immediately aware of finding ourselves in the presence of a soprano of truly significant ability. She has a powerful voice, one that is steady and attractive in timbre, penetrating in loud passages, and sweet in the more delicate moments. Her technique is secure and perfectly controlled. Her voice has an unusual color, and her schooling—although rather different from what we are accustomed to hearing—has its undeniable merits. Callas has created an interpretation rich in subtle and touching accents of femininity. She offers in *Norma*, besides the implacable priestess of the last act, the woman in love and then betrayed, the mother, and the friend."

Siciliani was very pleased with the way Maria negotiated the role, and he signed her for a project that was to take place in September 1949 in Perugia.

After singing her second and last performance of *Norma* on December 5, Maria returned to Verona. For the next two days she didn't feel well. We attributed it to fatigue, but the evening of the seventh Maria experienced sharp abdominal pains. I telephoned my brother-in-law, Gianni Cazzarolli, who was a doctor. He diagnosed an attack of appendicitis and said that it was necessary to operate. To be absolutely certain, I also called in Salvatore Donati, who was at that time Verona's leading surgeon. Donati corroborated my brother-in-law's diagnosis.

Maria was taken to Verona's Borgo Trento Hospital, where she remained from December 8 until the eighteenth. The operation was a success, but the period in the hospital afterwards was difficult for her. Maria especially suffered from loneliness.

She didn't want strangers around her, not even the nurses. She only wanted that I keep her company. Naturally, this was not possible during the day, because I had a thousand obligations, but every evening I went to the hospital and stayed with her until the following morning. When she dozed off I also tried to rest, sleeping in my suit on a small folding bed. I spent nine nights that way, and Maria was very grateful for my attention. She often recalled those nights in the hospital and said it was in a situation like that that one came to know the true extent of a person's love.

We were in Verona for Christmas of 1948. It was our first one together in the city which Maria had adopted as "hers." The previous Christmas we were in Venice, where Maria was appearing in *Tristan*. In Verona we went to hear Mass in a poor little church, and then the two of us dined alone. Maria enjoyed spending holidays in the closest intimacy.

A few days later I accompanied Maria to Venice, where she was to sing her first Brünnhilde in *Die Walküre*, at the Fenice, under the direction of Serafin—a most demanding role. Everyone in Venice remembered her *Turandot* and *Tristan and Isolde* from the previous year, and there was considerable anticipation. Maria did not disappoint them. *Die Walküre* went very well. The cast included, in addition to Maria, Giovanni Voyer, Ernesto Dominici, Raimondo Torres, Jolanda Magnoni, and Amalia Pini. Enrico Frigerio was the stage director.

Critic Giuseppe Pugliese wrote in *Il Gazzettino*, January 9, 1949: "Maria Callas was a Brünnhilde of genuine Wagnerian spirit, forceful and touching, simple and incisive, with a splendid voice and power in the high passages and in the declamation. Visually she was superb." Vardanega commented in the *Gazzettino-Sera*, "Callas was perfect: it is unlikely that one will soon hear a comparable Brünnhilde."

Serafin, Cattozzo, and the others threw a large party for the cast. Putting aside my responsibilities, I decided to spend a few days in Venice. The night of January 10, around midnight, when we were already asleep, the telephone rang. It was Maestro Serafin. He apologized for calling at that hour but said that he had to speak with Maria: "It's an urgent, important matter. Wake her up and have her come downstairs," he said. "I'm here in the restaurant below the hotel."

"Can't it wait until tomorrow?" I protested. "Maria has to rest." He insisted, so I woke her up. We went downstairs and found Serafin, his wife Elena Rakowska, and Maestro Cattozzo, with long, sad faces. "What happened?" I asked.

"We're in trouble," Cattozzo said in dialect. "Only Maria can get us out of it."

Immediately after *Walküre*, the Fenice's schedule listed Bellini's *I Puritani*, a remarkable opera that in recent times had been rarely produced because of a shortage of suitable interpreters. One of the important singers who was able to sing this opera was Margherita Carosio, who was about forty at the time, but still in her prime. This production of *I Puritani*, to be conducted by Serafin, had been mounted at the Fenice specifically for Carosio, but she came down with the flu and was unable to sing. Serafin and Cattozzo had just learned of Carosio's indisposition. They had spent the evening searching for a replacement, but they were unable to find a soprano willing to undertake the part, especially with only nine days to opening night.

In the midst of the crisis, Elena Rakowska said to Cattozzo and her husband: "Listen, it's pointless to continue searching. You are not going to find anyone. The only person who can sing *Puritani* is Maria Callas."

"That's absurd," Serafin told Rakowska. "Maria is involved in *Walküre*, a strenuous opera with an entirely different tessitura from that of *I Puritani*. It's impossible for her to sing these operas alternately."

"Oh, be quiet, you don't know anything, as usual," she interjected with her usual exuberance. "Shall we wager on whether or not Maria does *I Puritani*?"

The idea to wake us up in the middle of the night and to have us come down was the result of Rakowska's challenge, and the joint hope of Serafin and Cattozzo that this miracle would somehow be possible. After explaining the situation in detail to her, Serafin and Cattozzo nervously awaited her answer. Their eyes were fixed on Maria, who was obviously upset by their proposition. Removing her glasses and passing her hand across her face, she asked, "Isn't it possible to find another singer?"

"We've tried everyone. There's nobody left to approach," Serafin told her.

Maria was silent for a few moments, and then said: "All right, give me a score to look over. Let's meet here tomorrow afternoon, and I'll give you my answer then."

Serafin already had an extra copy at hand and he gave it to her. We went back to bed. Maria propped herself up with a couple of pillows and began to page through the score.

"What do you think?" I asked after a while.

"Yes," she replied quietly, "I can do it."

"But do you realize that there are only eight days left and in that period you have three performances of *Walküre*? When will you find time to learn *I Puritani*?"

"Don't worry," she said. "You'll see what I can do."

I fell asleep. She continued to study the score for I don't know how long. The following day she told them her decision and began to learn the music with Serafin. Maria sang her three scheduled performances of *Die Walküre* on January 12, 14, and 16. The nineteenth was the first night of *I Puritani*. The theater was packed. Most of the people in the audience were fans of Margherita Carosio, and had purchased their tickets weeks in advance. Maria was superb. She had a triumphant success which has now passed into operatic history.

Only those who know how different are the technical difficulties of the two operas, that of Wagner and that of Bellini, can fully understand Maria Callas's achievement. The news had scarcely begun to circulate that Serafin had given *I Puritani* in Venice with Maria Callas, when a Milan newspaper contemptuously commented: "We hear that Serafin has decided to conduct *I Puritani* at the Fenice with a dramatic soprano as Elvira—specifically with La Callas. Three cheers for these old-timers without artistic conscience who amuse themselves by mangling Opera and sending it to the dogs. When can we expect a new version of *La Traviata* with [baritone] Gino Bechi as Violetta?"

Maria not only managed to memorize *I Puritani* in eight days, but she also learned it during a period when she was singing *Die Walküre*. In the space of twelve days, from January 12 to 23, she appeared at the Fenice six times, singing in three performances of *Die Walküre* and three of *I Puritani*. It was a terrifying tour de force which vividly called attention to the strength and range of her voice, her willpower, and her extraordinary technical preparation.

I Puritani premiered January 19 under the direction of Serafin. The cast included, in addition to Callas in the role of Elvira, Boris Christoff (Giorgio), Antonio Perino (Arturo), Ugo Savarese (Riccardo), Mafalda Masini (Enrichetta), Silvio Maionica (Gualtiero), and Guglielmo Torcoli (Bruno). The following day Vardanega reported in the *Gazzettino-Sera*: "But the most surprising triumph was that of Callas, who offered an unforgettable Elvira. From the heavy roles of Turandot and Brünnhilde burst forth an agile creature, sensitive, vital in every note, who breathes melody filtered through a superior intelligence."

Critic Mario Nordio wrote: "A few days ago many were startled to read that our magnificent Brünnhilde, Isolde and Turandot would interpret Elvira. Last evening everyone had an opportunity to hear her Elvira. Even the most skeptical—aware from the first notes that she was not the standard light soprano of tradition—had to acknowledge the miracle that Maria Callas accomplished, in large part due to the rigors of her early vocal studies with de Hidalgo (perhaps the greatest Rosina and Elvira of her time), the flexibility of her limpid, beautifully poised voice, and her splendid high notes. Her interpretation also has a humanity, warmth, and expressiveness that one would search for in vain in the fragile, pellucid coldness of other Elviras."

Maria had been signed—several months before her undertaking of *I Puritani* at the Fenice—for two performances of *Walküre*, to be given at the end of January at Palermo's Teatro Massimo. Even if she had been at the point of exhaustion from her engagement in Venice, she would not have been able to extricate herself from her Palermo contract, and she had to go to Sicily. She was not at all happy at the Teatro Massimo. The ambience was not that of Venice and the performances were thrown together. This annoyed Maria. She wrote on January 28, 1949:

"My dear, I'm writing you a few words from this Palermo that I find so irritating. Firstly because it is so far away; secondly because I don't know how I will manage down here to study *Parsifal*, which I must sing in Rome a month from now; thirdly because their method of rehearsing down here is a disaster.

"Yesterday was the dress rehearsal. I can't tell you what a fiasco it was. Nothing was ready. There were at least thirty workers on stage, but I have no idea what they were working on. All they did was stand around and watch. I didn't have my headpiece, and neither the spear nor the shield was ready. The orchestra made hash of the score. All the conductor [Francesco Molinari-Pradelli] managed to do was talk. I have a feeling that tonight's performance will be one that I'll remember forever! I am accustomed to perfect, orderly rehearsals, so you can imagine how I feel here, in the midst of this debacle.

[72]

"The one positive thing is that they treat me well—as if I were a goddess! Everything is going well that I have to do.

"Dear Battista, I could have done without Palermo; it's a waste of time and very boring. At least I have the consolation of knowing that I will be finished Tuesday and can leave. It would be better if you didn't come down; it's pointless. And who said that I would find spring here. *Nuts to them!* It is *so bitter cold* and windy that I could curse, if I were so inclined.

"I don't have any other news. Only a terrible headache from this morning. I can't do anything. Let's hope that it passes by this evening—I interrupted this letter because my pen ran out of ink. I used it as an excuse to go out and have a large coffee. Who knows when this headache is going to stop. —The theater telephoned to remind me that the performance begins at 8:45 this evening. I laughed so hard! It would appear that here singers forget some of their performances, and they need someone to remind them. What crazy people . . ."

On January 30 she wrote me a rather testy letter from Palermo. The first performance of *Walküre* did nothing to reconcile her to Palermo, for she did not have the success with the public that she had expected: "Dear, I just wrote to you the other day telling you about my arrival, and of the horrendous surprises here, but the worst was yet to come. Can you imagine, the newspapers here act as if Jolanda Magnoni [the Sieglinde in *Die Walküre*] had the title role. They only devoted a couple of lines to me. One paper wrote: 'Maria Callas as Brünnhilde— even though she sang with intensity and her voice was beautiful and the timbre attractive—did not succeed in being a barbaric Walküre.' What an imbecile! The same writer said that Giulio Neri, the Wotan, was always extremely musical. I will never forget the mistakes Neri made and the wrong notes that he sang. If they knew the opera better, they would have whistled. I swear, and I swear again, I will never again set foot in lower

Italy. It seems that I am too musical and too ladylike on stage to be appreciated here. They want to see the people on stage pulling their hair out. I am incensed and most annoyed."

Walküre was given twice at the Teatro Massimo, on January 24 and February 10, 1949. The other singers were Giovanni Voyer, Bruno Carmassi, Giulio Neri, and Jolanda Magnoni; Francesco Molinari-Pradelli conducted.

Maria went directly to Naples, where she sang at the Teatro San Carlo for the first time, appearing in four performances of *Turandot*. Jonel Perlea conducted and the other singers included Renato Gigli (Calaf), Vera Montanari (Liù), Mario Petri (Timur), Mario Borriello (Ping), Luciano della Pergola (Pang), and Gianni Assante (Pong). Mario Baccaro wrote in *Roma* of February 14, 1949: "Maria Callas is a most unusual singer. In softer passages her voice is beautiful and insinuating, yet her high notes are metallic and piercing. She has a nightmarish upper extension—awesome, sinister, and inexorable."

Maria was in Rome at the end of February for Wagner's *Parsifal*, conducted by Serafin. Her colleagues included Hans Beirer [who sang the title role in German, while the others sang in Italian], Cesare Siepi, Marcello Cortis, Armando Dadò, and Carlo Plataria. Renzo Rossellini commented in *Il Messaggero*: "Maria Callas is a highly gifted singer who is well versed in the exigencies of the stage." Ettore Montanoro wrote in *Il Popolo*: "Maria Callas was an excellent Kundry, both dramatically and in vocal prodigiousness." In the opinion of Adriano Bellin in *Il Quotidiano*: "Maria Callas was a magnificent Kundry. She seemed to us today a more polished singer [he was, perhaps, referring to her previous performances in Rome in *Turandot*]. This soprano, who has security of vocal production, marvelous equalization of registers, and a fine upper extension, victoriously overcame every difficulty. She also knows how to personify most effectively the fascinating and tormented figure of Kundry, the sinner longing for redemption."

A Spectacular Year; Marriage

Her last *Parsifal* was March 8. Maria's next contract was for a long season in Argentina with Tullio Serafin and a troupe of Italian singers. The departure of the company was scheduled for April 21, 1949, from Genoa. We had, therefore, more than a month together to relax.

As I have mentioned earlier, Maria and I knew from the first that we were meant to remain together. After the *Tristans* in Venice at the beginning of 1948, we decided to get married. Our parish church in Verona was the Chiesa dei Filippini, the poorest in the city. We spoke with the priest, who I believe was called Don Ottorino, and he told us what documents we needed. It was a rather complicated matter, for Maria had to obtain papers from both Greece and the United States. Since she was Greek Orthodox and I was Catholic, it was also necessary to obtain a special dispensation from the Vatican.

By the end of 1948, all the papers were in order, at least as far as I was concerned. We decided to take advantage of this month-long break in Maria's work to become husband and wife. I telephoned the church authorities to verify that all the requirements had been met. I was told that some signatures were still lacking. I explained the situation and summarized my nuptial plans. I urged them to finalize the papers as quickly as possible, because I intended to have the ceremony take place at the beginning of April. I noticed, however, that the cleric was reticent. "Something's up," I thought.

I continued to harass the people in the office of the Curia by telephone. Every time I called there was something missing—a signature, a stamp, or some other trifle. It became obvious that they did not intend to give me the documents. Only later did I learn that the papers, which had been ready for quite a while, were being withheld at the request of one of my brothers. He was the most antagonistic of all toward me because of Callas, and he succeeded in convincing the Curia of Verona that they should not cooperate because this marriage would be deleterious to the Meneghini family. I don't know what he promised— perhaps to donate the tiles for the repair of the roofs of the old churches of Verona—but the fact was that they were not going to give me the documents.

Maria continued to ask for news, and I would inform her of everything I was doing. It was soon the eve of her departure for Argentina, and nothing had been resolved. The evening of April 20 I said to Maria: "So, tomorrow you're sailing for Argentina. As you know, I cannot join you there, but I'll accompany you to Genoa. I promise you, though, that when you return, the papers for our marriage will be ready. We'll get married and go to live in our new home, which is just about finished."

"All right," she replied. "You know that I'm always at your disposal." She said exactly that—"at your disposal." Maria was rather taciturn and pensive that evening. Knowing how depressed she became each time she had to leave, I attributed her sadness to the departure the next day. I tried to distract her, but without success.

The next morning I awoke early, but Maria was already up. "What's this?" I asked.

"You see, Battista, I didn't sleep last night," she said. "You know how agonizing these departures are for me, taking me away from you. Imagine how I feel about this trip, which will last more than three months. When I sang in Venice, Rome, Florence, Genoa, you could visit me, but Buenos Aires is very far. We will not see each other for months. It's terrible. Last night I cried so much thinking that I would have to leave you here alone for such a long time. You see, I have made a decision. I will go, but only on one condition. Perhaps what I am going to say will displease you or create some difficulties for you, but I will not change my mind: I will sail only if I am your wife."

I was disoriented for a moment: I thought I had misunderstood her. "But it's not possible today," I replied. "The departure is set for tonight, and you know that the papers are not ready."

"Battista, I am not leaving if I cannot call myself Maria Meneghini Callas."

She spoke with a measured calmness I had come to recognize by now. When her voice had that even, sober tone, it meant that she had made a decision from which nobody could make her deviate. I had no other choice but to throw myself headlong into the desperate undertaking of trying to obtain the documents from the Curia. "I'm going directly to their office," I told her. "I will do everything possible to please you. In the meantime, begin packing your bags."

"I'll get them ready," she replied. "But I will close them only after we're married."

I had at the time an exceptional secretary, Elvira Sponda, a very beautiful girl, svelte, intelligent. When I gave her an assignment, she understood it immediately and dispatched it with alacrity. I explained the situation to her and sent her to the Episcopate to fetch the documents.

She telephoned at ten that morning. "Commendatore, they absolutely do not want to give me the papers. Although they say that there are details which have not yet been resolved, I was talking to one of the secretaries and I learned that everything has been completed for a while. The obstacles are all your family's doing. I also spoke with the chancellor, Monsignor Amedeo Zancanella, upon whom everything depends: he told me there is nothing that can be done."

"Where can I find this chancellor?" I asked.

"He went home. He lives in Via Garibaldi."

"Let's go to Via Garibaldi. I'm driving over there. I want to talk to this monsignor."

Monsignor Zancanella's home was bordered on one side by a savings bank and on the other by a small church. Elvira Sponda rang the bell and after a few moments the monsignor appeared. Recognizing the girl, he said rather dryly: "It is useless to continue to bother me. Those papers are not ready."

"Commendatore Meneghini is here and he wants to speak with you," Elvira said.

"I cannot receive him," the priest replied, and he shut the door. I was at a loss as to what I could, or should, do. I began to lose my temper but forced myself to remain calm. The little church next to the monsignor's home was lovely. "I'm going to take my problems to the Lord," I thought. I pushed open the door and found myself in a church rather different from mine: it was, if fact, an evangelical church. On the cornice was sculpted an inscription which I still remember very well: "God is spirit and those who worship Him must worship in spirit and truth." I entered the little church, where I reflected on my dilemma. When I left, I said to Elvira, "Let's try again."

My secretary attached herself to the bell and rang it long enough to awaken the dead. The priest finally rushed to the door and this time I spoke with him. At first I tried to explain my situation, and then I exploded. I said whatever came into my head. Some of the expressions are probably still reverberating in his ears. The priest was speechless. Still unyielding, he refused to give up the documents.

It was now 11 a.m. What could I do? I had a friend, Mario Orlandi, with whom I was very close. He was a very intelligent person. In addition to being a manufacturer of electric stoves, he spent much of his time visiting vestries, archbishoprics, and convents, serving on committees of charitable organizations, and being of assistance everywhere. I thought, "Let's try Orlandi."

I managed to locate him by noon, and explained my difficulties. He knew and respected Maria and was in favor of our marriage. He pondered the situation, and then mentally reviewed all his ecclesiastical friends. Eventually he said, "Let's go to the vicar of San Tommaso." I drove him to San Tommaso's.

He went off with his friend while I waited in the car with my secretary. He returned in about an hour and said, "Battista, here are your papers."

"How did you do it?" I asked incredulously.

"Don't concern yourself with that. You're to get married now."

I drove my secretary back to the office, where I telephoned Maria and told her that everything was proceeding quite nicely. Then I raced to my parish church of the Filippini and handed the papers to Don Ottorino.

"Fine," said the priest. "However, there is still one slight problem. Because Maria is not Catholic, we cannot celebrate the rite in the main church. We will have to find a consecrated place which is not, however, in the church proper."

"Select whatever spot you wish, as long as we can be married," I told him.

"There is the sacristy, where we house old statues, candlesticks, and objects for funerals. It serves, in fact, as a storage area, but it is a consecrated place. There is also a small altar. I will clear it out a bit, and we will perform the ceremony there."

"Fine. At what time?"

"At five o'clock."

"I'll be on time." I returned to the hotel.

"I was thinking . . ." Maria said.

"Everything is ready," I announced. "We will be married at five."

Maria became pale and sat down on the bed. Starting to cry, she thanked God and the Madonna. I had never seen her so happy. We had lunch together, but neither of us managed to eat very much, we were in such an emotional state. I then helped her close her bags. Shortly before four, we headed toward the church.

The witnesses at our wedding were my friend Mario Orlandi and my brother-in-law Gianni Cazzarolli. A little clearing had been made near the altar in the sacristy storeroom. Two large

candles were lit, but there were no flowers or any other adorn-
ment. The priest was assisted by Beppo, the old sexton. There
among broken chairs, headless statues, funeral palls covered
with dust, and century-old canopies and banners, we became
husband and wife. Rarely could there have been a marriage
ceremony in a setting more superficially squalid than ours, but
it didn't matter a bit to us. Maria and I, as long as we were
together, always remembered that afternoon as the most beautiful of our lives.

As soon as the ceremony was over, we returned to the hotel to
fetch the luggage. We left immediately for Genoa, where
Maestro Serafin was waiting for Maria. The steamer *Argentina*
was scheduled to depart for South America at midnight.

Onstage

Callas as Maddalena in *Andrea Chénier*,
La Scala, 1955, with Aldo Protti

An early role, Leonore in *Fidelio*, Athens, 1944

Her first *Norma*,
Florence, 1948, with
Maestro Tullio Serafin
and tenor Mirto Picchi

Norma, Epidaurus, 1960

La Gioconda, Verona, 1952,
with Maestro Antonino Votto

Rehearsing
I Vespri Siciliani,
La Scala, 1951, with
Eugene Conley

Il Pirata, La Scala, 1958

Il Barbiere di Siviglia, La Scala, 1956, with Luigi Alva

Iphigenia in Tauris
(Visconti production),
La Scala, 1957

Fedora, La Scala, 1956

Medea, Dallas, 1958

La Traviata, La Scala, 1955, with Ettore Bastianini

Tosca, the Met, 1965

Backstage after *Lucia di Lammermoor*, the Met, 1957

Anna Bolena, La Scala, 1957

Chapter 8

Debut in Buenos Aires

My farewell to Maria on the pier in Genoa, the night of April 21, 1949, was one of the most heartrending of my life. She was sailing for Argentina and would be away for three months. It was not an eternity, but we had only been married eight hours, and this made the separation especially difficult.

Maria considered not making the voyage, even up to the last minute. Shortly before she was to board the ship, she said, "Let's ask Serafin if he can substitute another soprano." I went to discuss it with him, but he replied that it was impossible. Serafin pointed out that the *tournée* included the guarantee of Maria Callas. The ship sounded its whistle at midnight and began to leave its berth. I stood in the darkness, waving goodbye. I then returned to my car and drove back to Verona.

Besides Maria and Maestro Serafin, the company for the South American tour included Mario Del Monaco, Fedora Barbieri, Nicola Rossi-Lemeni, and Mario Filippeschi. Almost everyone traveled with someone they loved. Serafin was surrounded by his entire family—his wife, his daughter Vittoria, and his granddaughter Donatella. Maria, however, was totally alone.

It was the first lengthy journey she was making since we met two years earlier. That period we had spent together had been most affectionate. We had always lived in close proximity and our separations because of her work were never more than six or seven days in duration. For that reason, this trip turned out to be particularly trying. In order to have the strength to face it, Maria wanted to become my wife before she left.

The marriage gave her a certain euphoria, which lasted, however, but a short while. As each day passed, her feeling of melancholy became increasingly more oppressive, and Maria suffered greatly. Her only solace was in our correspondence. She wrote to me almost every day. Her letters were overflowing with love and tenderness, but they also reflected her sadness, pain, and concerns. It was enlightening when I recently relived that Argentinian season through Maria's letters, which constitute a kind of diary of her thoughts and feelings. They reveal that, although music and her art were extremely important to her, they did not represent her ultimate goals in life. In fact, she dwells more on our temporary separation than on her operatic activities. By 1949 she was rather famous, and had many reasons for being preoccupied with her career and reputation. However, that was not the case. If it had been up to her, she would have abandoned the tour and returned home.

These letters are a reply to those who have always said and written that Maria was a cold, egotistical creature who lived solely and exclusively for her career, that her love for me was just a pretext for my economic protection, and that, in fact, she never loved me. Anyone reading these letters can ascertain that nothing is more false and defamatory than such statements.

April 22, 1949

My dear Battista, I am sending you a "hello" from Barcelona. I remember you more than ever in these days, days which should be *ours!* As I told you a couple of days ago, I am leaving with my soul so much lighter. Hopefully this trip will be less oppressive than those in the past. The joy of totally belonging to you comforts me to an unimaginable degree.

And you, dear? How was your return trip back to Verona, and how was our room? I urge you not to become angry; eat well and get lots of sleep. In the past you didn't have anyone to worry about. Now you have *your wife*, who lives only for you. Just imagine if something happened to either of us! If you want me to be happy, take care of yourself. We belong to each other and share the greatest happiness. I will be well for you (with the help of God), and I will sing and be a success for you. But you must stay well for me.

We've had an opportunity to see a little of Barcelona and I like it immensely. It's Sunday and all the shops were closed, but I did notice that handbags and shoes are inexpensive. We're sailing in a couple of hours. I don't have anything else to tell you. I hung *our* Madonna above my bed. I send you a kiss and a warm thought every minute of the day. Fortunately, I am in the company of Maestro Serafin and his wife. They never allow me to become too despondent. The weather has been good and I'm trying to exercise and lose a little weight. Think of me as I think of you.

April 24, 1949

My love, I am writing you because in this way I feel nearer to you. Your telegram today made me so happy. You know that I'm always uneasy when I'm traveling. You see, Battista, when a person is as in love and as happy as I am, he always fears losing that happiness. What I have seems too beautiful to comprehend. I adore you so much, so very much: remember that. How I would like to have you near me! How aware I am of your absence, the absence of your thoughtful gestures, your caresses, the tiny bell with which you awake me in the morning, and finally the *jujubes* that you give me! I miss our coffee together, the telephone calls I make to your office, to which you always respond so warmly, saying that you were fatigued and my voice was a balm.

My Battista, why did you allow me to go? I hope that you will never again permit me to go so far from you, and that we will remain together forever. Remember that I am alive only when I am with you, my husband. Please write to me often, dear. I only have your letters to comfort me on this voyage. They are playing through *La Traviata* right now and the music makes my longing for you even more acute.

There is no one special on board. Ordinary people, couples or families. The children show great respect toward me, and this pleases me. The sea is rough today. The ship is rolling, but it doesn't seem to bother me. They're having a film later; it helps to pass the time.

April 26, 1949

Caro, caro, caro, we have been sailing for only four days and I already miss you terribly. I don't have words to describe how bored I am. I pray to God that this trip ends soon so that I can return to you. I am only happy and relaxed when I'm near you. And you, what are you doing? How is everything at home? What have they said to you there? What has your mother said? I'm a little concerned because I haven't received your telegrams yet.

Everyone is having fun on board the ship and we eat very well. One evening they have a horse race (I won six pesos!), another evening a dance or a movie. Serafin had a liver attack, so we haven't begun to study. I must tell you something strange: each morning at 6:30 or 7:00 I suddenly open my eyes with the impression that someone had passed by to awaken me. I think that it's you, and I'm happy.

It seems that they want to play a nasty trick on me at Buenos

Aires's Teatro Colón, but they will have to pay me! They want to open the season with *Aïda*, but not sung by me. It seems that a certain Minkus will sing.* I believe it will be fifteen days more before we arrive.

May 2, 1949

My love, how are you? What do you think of our situation? I don't know if you're happy about our marriage. You say you are in your telegrams, and I hope that's true. I'm enormously happy. Perhaps this separation will even serve to show me just what I have. I'm always alone when I'm on tour, but here, because of circumstances, I have to be with others. I swear to you, I see and hear so much that is vulgar and banal that it makes me appreciate even more the treasure that I have. I thank God for His having given me a companion in life such as you.

I don't have anything else to tell you, dear, except that I adore you, I honor you and I respect you, and that I am so proud of my Battista! No woman is as happy as I am. Even though I'm well known for my singing, most of all I have the man of my dreams! I challenge any woman to say that she has as much as I do.

Serafin had me go through *La Forza del Destino* with him yesterday. He said that I was marvelous. Rakowska was also enthusiastic. Maestro told me that my contract in Trieste for *Forza* was made with the sole purpose of embarrassing me. They wanted to say that, yes, I had had a success in Venice with *Tristan* but that in Verdi I was a disgrace. They wanted indi-

---

* Sara Menkes was a dramatic soprano who appeared regularly at the Teatro Colón between 1934 and 1953. Her repertory included the soprano leads in *Tosca, Suor Angelica, Aïda, La Forza del Destino, Il Trovatore,* and *Mefistofele.* She did not sing at all during the 1949 season in Buenos Aires. Their careers converged in the spring of 1953 when Callas was obliged to withdraw from a performance of the Verdi *Requiem* in London and was replaced by Menkes.

rectly to give Serafin a box on the ears. What disgusting creatures they are. I'm sure they were in agreement with Ghiringhelli and Labroca.

May 6, 1949

Dear, I'm continuing with the letter I interrupted the other day. I wasn't in a condition to write one word. I thought of you and the tears welled up. Let's not even mention yesterday. If it is true that souls can commune over great distances, then you were awakened by my sobs. I was inconsolable. At the movies they showed a war film, with torture and destruction, that was horrible. You know how much those films upset me. I began to cry and I couldn't regain control of myself. I tried thinking of you, recalling all the things you say to calm and reassure me, but that only made things worse. Thinking of you only intensified my sorrow . . .

The other evening they had a masked ball on board ship, and I was so beautiful that you would have fallen in love with me all over again. Everyone tried to come up with some disguise. I was at a loss for what to do, not having anything suitable for a costume. Then Maestro Serafin said, "Why don't you go as the Empress Messalina?" This in turn prompted Rakowska to dress me as a woman from ancient Greece. I adapted a plain bed sheet and arranged my hair on top of my head in the style of the Greek women of the past, and you know, I won the prize for the most original costume. They took a photograph of me which I'm sending to you.

The Teatro Colón informed us that when we arrive in Rio we can continue on to Buenos Aires by air, but Serafin is against it. After the disaster in Turin, he's afraid. It seems that they want to open the season with *Aïda* conducted by Serafin, but they didn't specify if I'm to sing. Serafin cabled saying that without La Callas he wouldn't be available for *Aïda*.

Debut in Buenos Aires

May 10, 1949

My love, today I'm very unhappy because I've caught—I don't know how—a terrible cold. I was so well, in such good health! But don't worry: I'll be fine again by the time you receive this note.

May 13, 1949

The other day I was not able to continue with my letter because I was truly ill—so ill that I went immediately to bed and have remained there until today. Three days in bed! You can imagine how annoyed and unhappy I've been. I curse the hour I left Italy. I'm furious that you allowed me to go. I don't know how to manage without you, and I want you to realize that!

We have arrived at Rio. The directors of the theater here came on board to take us to dinner in the city. They told me they would like to do *Norma* with me, but I declined their offer, explaining that it was necessary for me to return to Italy. Now, if you truly want me to return, you must help me. Write immediately to Serafin saying that you want me back in Verona without fail, as soon as possible, otherwise you will not permit me to accept engagements for next winter, or make up something else along those lines. Also write a similar letter to me, so that I can show it to Serafin. You must do this quickly, though, because they also want me to go to Montevideo. You should say that you allowed me to go to Argentina only with the understanding that I would return directly home and would not accept any other offers.

May 14, 1949

My great, eternal love, I cannot find the appropriate words to convey what I felt while reading your letters. You have made me the happiest, proudest, most loved woman in the world. I had to wait twenty days for news from you. You can imagine the immense joy, and love, and ineffable tenderness I felt for you as I read them . . . Thank you again for having married me before I left. In that gesture you have heightened my love for you. I will live for the sole purpose of making you the happiest and proudest husband in the world. Fortunately there are no rehearsals tomorrow, because I continue to cry like a baby from the joy your letters have brought me. I also received one from your mother, and that also made me weep. I am happy.

I forgot to tell you that I purposely left behind in the wardrobe my beautiful pink nightgown. I left it behind because of you. It is exclusively for you—I'll only put it on when you are there. I will wear it the first night that I return. Do you think about that night?!!! We will be bursting with love and tenderness.

I have not been well the past few days. I have had that type of influenza that I came down with at the hospital that time, do you remember? I was in bed for three days, coughing, with a temperature constantly over 100°. Thank the good Lord I'm better today, but I have absolutely no appetite. I forced myself to at least eat the second course, but I hardly managed to swallow a thing. Don't worry, though, I'm now on the road to recovery . . .

Now to tell you the news. The opera season will open May 20 with *Turandot*, and I will sing. They were going to begin with *Aïda*, sung by Rigal, Del Monaco, Rossi-Lemeni, etc., but the good Lord is always with me, so I will have the first performance. Everything is very expensive here. Serafin found an apartment for me, but it was too tiny, and I moved to a hotel. I have a small room with bath and pay thirty-eight pesos a day, without meals. This afternoon I tried the restaurant in the hotel. Can you imagine, I paid sixteen pesos for soup, a steak, vegetable, fruit salad, and coffee. That's too much. This evening I ate in another restaurant, less grand, but the food was good, and I spent only seven pesos. That's a big difference, the louses!!! If the directors of the Colón insisted I stay here three months I'd murder them.

I can't wait until I return. I'll take a plane, because I don't want to lose twenty days in transit: I would go crazy. If you are considering coming here, do not travel by air. It doesn't matter if something happens to me, but it would destroy me if something happened to you. If we must die, it's better that we die together.

May 15, 1949

Fortunately the Serafins have left their small apartment to me, which, besides the bedroom and sitting room, has a small kitchen, where I can warm milk and fix a little something. This way, when I'm not up to going out, I can prepare something for myself. I do think I'll like it here. Buenos Aires is a beautiful city, big, full of enormous cars, the kind that you call "houses." Despite the elegant stores and spacious avenues, my heart is always with you, and I don't see or derive pleasure from any of the lovely things. You are the reason for my existence. I adore you so much that I would like to die in your embrace.

Evening of May 16, 1949

I contacted Mrs. Covies, the lady who wrote me from Buenos Aires, do you remember? I worked out an arrangement whereby she will help me a little. I'll give her something each month, and she will take care of my wardrobe. Her daughter will be my secretary. They said they don't want anything in return, but they don't have much money and I can help them.

The coffee is dreadful here. From what I see when I stroll about, the elegance is a façade. It's better in Italy where the people are more courteous and the way of life is more gracious. My love, what are you doing? Do you feel our separation the way I do? Write to me often, dear, because your letters are the only things that keep me alive here. I reread all of them every morning when I wake up, and also before I go to bed at night. I also reread your letters when I'm sad, and they give me courage.

May 17, 1949

My dear, beloved Titta, I receive one of your letters almost every day. You cannot imagine the joy, the exultation, and the strength they give me. They put me in such a wonderful mood. Dear, I see and read between the lines that as the days pass, the more you miss me. Now, apparently, you are beginning to understand what I must endure when I go on tour, leaving you alone . . .

I'm very at home in this small apartment. I have my little kitchen which I take full advantage of. Just this moment I went to turn off the gas because I had milk on the stove. Now I'm drinking a wonderful glass of hot milk, with a lot of sugar and a lot of cognac to try to chase away this persistent cold. Today I'm slightly better, but only a little.

I awoke this morning around seven with the strangest headache. I swear, it felt as if I had a tumor. My head was even painful to the touch. I had to get up and take two aspirin. The truth is that I am not well at all. I am only writing you this because by the time you receive my letter this will all be in the past, and you won't have cause for concern.

I hope to do *Norma* soon, and then they will allow me to leave. Please write to Serafin telling him to send me home right away. Remind him that we're newly married and that you have the right to expect me to be with you. Please write him immediately. You must prod him because he's old and, after so many years of matrimony, perhaps he no longer remembers the joy of newlyweds as much in love as we are.

May 19, 1949

My dear Titta, my treasure. It is a little past midnight. I drank three glasses of cognac and honey, took two aspirin, and went to bed, trying to make myself a little drunk so I could sleep and perspire. You see, I have a terrible case of influenza. I'm positive that no one as sick as I could even open their mouth, let alone sing, and tomorrow night is the *prima* of *Turandot*. I am so unlucky. I was right in dreading the voyage by sea. Do you remember when I would say to you, "Don't let me go"? You must admit that I am *supersensitive,* and have premonitions about certain things. I sensed that I would suffer greatly on that ship . . .

May 23, 1949

My dear Battista, I am writing to you from bed, where I've been since the day before yesterday, following the performance, and where I always am when I'm not rehearsing. I don't know what this influenza is that refuses to go away. Every morning I'm fine. I don't have a fever. Then, in the afternoon, my temperature climbs to 100°. I have that strange, unremitting headache, as well as blemishes all over my skin.

Dear, I have to be near you to be well, because you mean everything to me. No one can take your place or give me the comfort and sense of well-being that you do. You cannot leave me alone again. You're asking, "But how did you manage in the past, before you knew me?" My answer is: when one falls in love, one exists only for that other person. Neither singing nor fame—nothing—can be a satisfactory substitute. Deprived of your love, I am lost. God, if only you were here with me, I am certain that I would regain my health immediately.

The performance went very well. The press, fortunately, was very favorable. Only one paper wrote that I have a small voice that is incapable of opening up, but that newspaper doesn't count for anything. All the others were positive, even Evita Perón's paper. I don't know how I managed to sing, I was so sick. The Serafins were very apprehensive, but God always helps me.

They've written from San Sebastiano, Spain, offering me two performances of *Norma* in September. They all want me down here—Montevideo, Rio, São Paulo—but I've turned everyone down. I want to return to you! Today I so looked forward to receiving your letters, but none arrived. If you only knew how much happiness and reassurance your words give me.

May 24, 1949

Dear Battista, I received your letter of the eighteenth today. I see that you have yet to receive the long one I wrote upon my arrival here. This underscores all the more how great the distance is which divides us. It takes at least six days for one of your letters to arrive. I sensed a certain melancholy in your latest one, is it not so? You have every right to be sad if you haven't received my letters. Dear, I have written to you often, and I continue to do so, feeling an ever increasing need to communicate with you. I no longer know how to express the extent of my love for you and also how much I suffer, being so far from you.

I still have a fever, but tomorrow I'd like to get up and go out for a while. I have a performance Sunday, and I don't want to be too weak. It seems that the first *Norma* will be given on June 10. In that case I would be able to be back in Verona by the end of the month. I would like that so much because it would coincide with the anniversary of our first meeting. Just imagine if I could be back by June 29!

It is now one in the morning and I cannot fall asleep. I continue to write to you and I feel as if I'm there, with you, in our bedroom. I don't know if you're sleeping, or if my soul—which is part of you—has awakened you. Hold me tightly, tell me lots of lovely things, squeeze me until I become as one with you, and let me die under your kisses. You see, Battista, we should consider ourselves God's favorites, because He has given to each of us the other. He has also given us understanding, devotion, and a melding of souls. If I were asked to offer my life itself for you, I would do it without hesitation, just to prove how much I love you.

May 26, 1949

This morning I was awakened by the chambermaid who delivered one of your letters. It was the most beautiful "good morning" I have ever had! Dear, it is not necessary to ask me to come back. I *wish* to return, I *must*, and I *will*. Only if I were to die would I not come back.

Tomorrow is the first *Aïda*, and I'm very displeased. Rigal will sing, and she is also to do *La Forza del Destino*. *Forza* doesn't matter to me in the least, but *Aïda*, yes. Serafin says that perhaps he can persuade Grassi-Diaz to give two of the performances to me, if only so the public can compare us.*

May 27, 1949

Dear Battista, I waited all day for one of your letters. Nothing . . . They do things so stupidly here. They allow ten days to elapse between one performance and the next. They want to have a varied season, and I, who sing in only two operas, must wait my turn, which never seems to come. It's really getting on my nerves.

I've lost weight because of this flu. My face is very gaunt. If you saw me you would be furious. I'm thin and, as you say, "washed out and run down at the heels!" Rossi also told me that I'm wasting away. And you, what are you doing? How do you

---

* Delia Rigal, a native of Buenos Aires and a protegée of conductor Ettore Panizza, was a great favorite at the Teatro Colón. In addition to guest appearances at La Scala and the Paris Opéra, she was on the roster of the Metropolitan Opera for seven seasons. In November 1951, at the time of her Met debut, she informed an interviewer of *Opera News*, "I have always found artists with American experience so generous to fellow artists, so completely devoid of jealousy."

spend your time? I'm not jealous, because no woman would ever be able to love you as I know how to love you, nor would she ever be able to give you the understanding I have given you, and continue to offer. And you are not jealous because you know me well. Then, I never go out. I hate Buenos Aires . . .

This evening they're giving *Aïda* with Rigal; you can imagine how I feel. I swear that I haven't been as ill for a long time, perhaps not since Venice, when I was doing *Tristan.* I suffer tremendously. It seems as if there is something wrong throughout my entire body, and I have such pain in my heart.

Everyone here is only interested in himself, and that's about it. When I was sick, only Maestro Serafin came to visit, running the risk of catching the flu himself. The Serafins aren't staying here because there was no room. They only come to eat.

It's lovely outside, almost like spring, but the air is full of coal dust that gets into your eyes and on your clothes. Going out is more of a bother than a pleasure. The climate changes from one hour to the next: it's hot, and then it's cold. The high humidity affects my legs. This whole affair is a disaster!

May 30, 1949

Dear Battista, I'm so annoyed today, first of all because of the Teatro Colón, which only gives me one performance every ten days! God only knows when they'll do *Norma.* I curse the hours I left Italy . . . I'm wide awake every night until four or five. If it continues this way, I'm going to have a relapse. I have this constant fear that everything is going to end badly.

June 1, 1949

My dear, I am so pleased. I went to Grassi-Diaz and he told me I could leave July 10. They have already promised to reserve a seat on the plane. I don't have words to express how happy I am. I'm so excited I can't write.

Debut in Buenos Aires

June 8, 1949

Oh my! I have finally received your letters. Six at once!

Norma is to be given June 17, eight days from tomorrow. I hope, with the help of God, to be good!! You see, in *Turandot* the public doesn't have the opportunity to evaluate my art. My colleagues have had the good luck not to sing with me, but rather with that horrible Rigal. They've had a triumph and now they've become very grand. Especially [Del Monaco], who has been very unpleasant to me. I will tell you why when I return home. If I ever have the opportunity to block him when something important comes along, I'll do it gladly, even though I'm not the type who derives pleasure from that sort of thing. For now, let's wait for *Norma*. If I'm in good health, we'll see which of us has the triumph.

Not one of my colleagues came to see me when I was sick. They were all overjoyed because I wasn't singing. They're afraid, the poor things. They know they're overshadowed when they're on stage with me. I have never treated any of my colleagues that way. Poor Nicolai, that woman! And Siepi too.

I can't wait for the hour when I return to your arms and to living and flourishing again. You know how to give me the attention that I need, and can help me to forget all this.

June 12, 1949

My dear beloved Battista, I haven't written to you for a couple of days because I was so busy with rehearsals for *Norma*. I've had to really work to get back in voice. Singing only every ten days is not good for me.

I'm almost ready now, but I feel sorry for Maestro Serafin. He's depressed, and that saddens me enormously. The weather down here has taken its toll on him. I also am not well, and I'm always tired. I would sleep all the time if I could, even though I never sleep well. This stinking weather.

[95]

I am so annoyed by the deviousness of my colleagues. I anxiously await the hour when I find refuge again in our pure, clean, and honorable love. Of all the things I love about you, the most important to me is the Old World graciousness that I find in you. A wife, especially one like me, must be *proud* of her husband. And that I am.

Yesterday was the first orchestra rehearsal with Barbieri—the second and third acts.* Everyone was amazed. The members of the orchestra applauded after our duets. All the others were terrified. A hostile wind is blowing! They're all spreading the word that I'm sick and that the opera should be changed. It always happens when I have a good rehearsal! They know I'll give them a run for their money. Well, they can say what they want. The important thing is for me to be in good health: then they will see. I enjoy making them uneasy.

Tomorrow I'll try to go to the little Greek Orthodox church for a benediction. God has been so good to me. He has given me health, success, a rather nice appearance, intelligence, integrity and, most of all, you, who are the *reason* for my life and my *faith* in life. My love for you is limitless, and I want you so much. This evening it seemed as if you were here beside me, and I am certain that you had the same thought in your mind. So many times I have felt that you were next to me. It must be your soul

---

* Callas was to sing with mezzo-soprano Fedora Barbieri about forty times between 1947 and 1956. Both were feted divas, neither of whom ever underestimated her artistic worth. Callas's professional difficulties with Barbieri did not receive the publicity of her altercations with such luminaries as Boris Christoff and Mario Del Monaco. As one of the contributors to a book generally eulogistic to Callas (*Per Maria Callas*, published in Bologna in 1980), Barbieri took the opportunity to mention that shortly before Callas's debut at the Met in *Norma*, the soprano told Rudolf Bing that she did not want to sing with Barbieri. Bing, after informing the latter's husband of Callas's dictum, cast the two women together for the run of *Norma*. It was the last time they appeared on the same stage together.

coming to visit me. Battista, my love, I fear that I will suffocate from emotion when I see you again. Joy, so often, can transform itself into suffering, is it not so? I'll leave you now. Pray that I sing well.

June 17, 1949

My dear Battista, I am writing to you today, the day of the big test, of the great lesson in singing I wish to give everyone. Yesterday was the dress rehearsal. You can well imagine how much interest there was on the part of everyone in my Norma, after my having sung in *Turandot*. So much so that the critics of one newspaper telephoned advising me to sing full voice because they had to base their review on the rehearsal. The morons!! Fine. The rehearsal amazed everyone. After the "Casta diva," everyone was in tears. I'm extremely pleased. I hope, God willing, the actual performance is as good as the rehearsal; then I will be satisfied.

The other evening I went with a Greek journalist and a lady to the Greek Orthodox church to light a candle for us and my *Norma*. You see, I feel our Church more than yours. It's strange, but it's so. Perhaps because I'm more accustomed to it, or perhaps because the Orthodox Church is warmer and more festive. It's not that I don't like yours, which is also mine now, but I have a strong partiality for the Orthodox Church. I'm sorry, dear. You understand me, don't you?

So I prayed and it seems that God did hear me because, truly, those who were at yesterday's rehearsal were beside themselves with enthusiasm. There was Scatto, the poor old man "whose fires have gone out," to use Rakowska's expression. He kept repeating: "This is singing. This is how they used to sing." At the end of the performance, while I was still on stage, director Grassi-Diaz came up and embraced and kissed me, saying, "I was so overcome I had to tell you: today I wept." I know the members of the chorus wanted to offer me some token of their admiration, they were so pleased with my singing. My poor colleagues! God, who is good and great, has allowed me to have my revenge. And this is certainly because I have never tried to harm anyone, and because I have worked so hard.

And you, my love, how are you? Do you want to hear something silly that will make you laugh? But then again, maybe you won't—perhaps you too are doing the same. Every so often I look at your photographs and talk to them as if they were you, uttering all kinds of tender, affectionate phrases. You're laughing, isn't it so?

My love, in just a month, God permitting, we will see each other again, and then we will always remain together, taking care of each other, cherishing each other. This is the most beautiful aspect of our love—each offers to the other. And the more one gives, the more the other offers in return. This is the love of which I have always dreamed. Now I have it, and it means more to me than sight itself.

June 20, 1949

My dear, please forgive me for not having written much the past few days. I've been totally involved in my work, which has demanded all of my energy so I could win my battle. I wasn't welcome here, as you know by now. I found a hostile atmosphere when I arrived, and it wasn't only Grassi-Diaz, but the others as well. I therefore had to give them a little demonstration of my superiority and worth by singing well. And I sang well! I brought down the house. They hadn't seen such a success even with Claudia Muzio. Now my enemies can't talk any more. They have to eat their words, the louses!

And now, with God's help, I will give them another lesson with *Aïda*. And then I will return to find comfort, peace, and love in your arms, you who are my only true aspiration. Dear, I missed you the other evening. You would have wept from the emotion of such a triumph. I wept because you were not there, *amore*.

I don't know how to stand this test without you. I'm coming back, dear, because we need each other. We must be proud of having a love so pure, so extraordinary, and rare . . . If I lost you, or were deceived by you, I would lose all my faith in life. It would destroy the most beautiful things that are within me. Please remember this always. I am so proud of being called Meneghini. When I return we will live all of our hopes and dreams. Buenos Aires is just hateful. The weather is horrible. There's coal dust everywhere. It's humid. And then, it's totally fascist. I don't mind now having refused to carry those photographs . . . Every fascist in the world is down here. And Evita totally controls the theater!"*

June 22, 1949

My beloved, I'm sending you the reviews from here. They're writing marvelous things about me. I cannot describe the enthusiasm of the public for my *Norma*. They're ecstatic. Next I'm to do *Aïda*.

June 24, 1949

My sublime love, today, the feast of Saint Giovanni Battista, is your name day. I received two of your beautiful letters. They are even the most beautiful of all. Please forgive me for having accused you of writing infrequently, but it wasn't entirely my

---

* Callas's displeasure with her season in Buenos Aires was not limited to her poor health, loneliness, and difficulties with other singers. Her mother wrote in her book *My Daughter Maria Callas* that, under Argentine law, Callas was not allowed to take the money she received for her performances out of the country. She used her fees, therefore, to buy furs, which she *could* take out of the country, and she sent them back to Italy with her theatrical wardrobe.

fault. The letters I received today are dated May 30 and 31. After your last letter dated June 18, I see these arrive! Who knows where they wound up. It's enough to drive you mad. Yes, my love, the letters are so lovely. I've already read them three times: I received them at one o'clock after lunch, and now it's only two. The Serafins send their regards. They often speak warmly of you, and I can feel myself swelling with pride and happiness. During the *Normas* they kept saying, "Ah, if Battista were only here." Dear, the Serafins adore you in the most marvelous way.

Rakowska, during the dress rehearsal, came into my room after the "Casta diva." She was weeping from happiness and satisfaction. During the *prima* I went to see Maestro Serafin in his room after the first act, and he too had tears in his eyes from emotion. Just imagine how much these two people love me. Serafin created me. You know how he worked with me, of course. You heard how he was in his home in Rome when we studied *Parsifal!* He opens his soul to me, because musically I respond so sympathetically to him. He suffered when he saw that some of the people here were against me.

Yesterday Rigal gave her last performance of *Aïda*, and she had the bad luck to have a tremendous mishap. She came to grief on her high note at the end of "O patria mia." It happened during her final performance, just as I was to take over her role. God is understanding. It's sufficient that one knows how to wait, rather than do something evil in the name of revenge. Pray that I sing *Aïda* well, so in that way I'll leave behind another of my calling cards. I would like to make a clean break with everything here.

July 3, 1949

My dear Battista, it's been a few days since I've written, but I've been so obsessed with the thought of returning that letters seem pointless. Perhaps this one will even arrive with me. God permitting, I will be home the morning of the fourteenth or fifteenth. My seat is already reserved on the flight of five in the afternoon from Rome to Venice. How glad I will be to see my— *our* Venice . . .

Yesterday I sang *Aïda*, finally. It was a triumph. I made a clean sweep of everything down here. The public adores me. Grassi-Diaz is already talking about next season. They would like *I Puritani* and one other opera. Poor Rigal!

I've also had the good luck to please the minister of state. For the Independence Day concert on July 9 I'm singing part of *Norma*—practically alone. The minister has cut the Adalgisa– Pollione duet, because the tenor [Antonio Vela] was so awful. The excerpt will begin with Norma's entrance in Act I, and will end after the "Casta diva." Then they'll do the "Jewel Song" from *Faust*, with some Argentine soprano [Helena Arizmendi] who isn't bad, and then Act III of *Turandot*. Rigal won't be singing because Evita doesn't want her. I've been fortunate, haven't I? God is always fair.

Chapter 9

Weight Problems; First Nabucco

Maria Callas returned from her first visit to Buenos Aires on July 14, 1949. I hurried to Rome to pick her up at the airport, and later that afternoon we flew to Venice, where we enjoyed a short vacation which will always remain among my most wonderful memories. We then returned to Verona.

While Maria was in Argentina, the masons had finished our apartment which I had constructed above my offices in Via San Fermo. It was a beautiful apartment, spacious and airy. Maria and I had designed it together, and now she looked forward to furnishing it. I knew how possessive she was about "her" house. From the beginning of our relationship, the subject we talked about most frequently was our home. Maria described how she wanted it to be a thousand times.

She threw herself with relish into her assignment. For weeks Maria no longer thought about singing. She didn't even go to her coaching sessions with Maestro Cusinati. She was totally preoccupied with her home. An interior decorator from Verona, Leonardelli, and a builder, Casali, were put at her disposal. At first they offered advice and made suggestions. "Trust me, signora, this is my profession; I've had experience in these matters." And they would try to impose their opinions upon her. Very quickly, however, they realized they were dealing with a headstrong and unusual person who had specific ideas of her own.

Weight Problems; First Nabucco

Maria had "her" house fixed in her mind for some time, as she would have had some operatic score committed to memory. She scarcely listened to the advice of the two consultants. She had decided upon everything: the colors, carpeting, drapes, the furniture, and precisely where it was all to go. The two men had become resigned to saying, "That's fine, signora." For Maria the apartment was the place where the two of us were going to spend a great part of our lives, and she furnished and arranged it according to practical exigencies, rather than any abstract aesthetic criteria. As soon as the apartment was furnished, we left the Hotel Accademia, where we had lived for almost two years. Maria didn't even go out for several days; she was intoxicated with her new home. She had hired a housekeeper, Matilde, and the two of them continued to push the furniture around and rehang paintings to improve the appearance of the various rooms.

Maria bought a metal box of the kind that plumbers and mechanics use to hold their tools. She glued a sticker to it which stated that the toolbox was always to be kept in order. Inside was everything needed for minor repairs; a hammer, pliers, nails, wrench, screwdriver, as well as a variety of the most impractical tools imaginable. She carried it around the apartment constantly, holding it as if it were an overnight bag. That box is still in my kitchen where she left it.

From the very beginning she enjoyed fine art, and I owned many paintings by important masters. Maria hung several of them on the walls herself, but she was never satisfied with the arrangement. She would sit in the middle of the room looking around, and then would say to Matilde, "Don't you agree that if we shifted that picture it would improve the look of this wall?" Often, returning to the apartment, I had the impression of entering new rooms, because Maria kept regrouping the paintings. If she moved one into another room, she destroyed the balance of the other canvases, and she was obliged to rearrange all of them. I personally could never have undertaken such a tedious chore, even if the aesthetics of the entire apartment were compromised. Maria, however, did not give it a second thought; she wanted her house to be perfect. She roamed from one room to another with her metal box, climbing up and down the ladder, pounding nails and, with the assistance of Matilde, shifting even the heaviest paintings. No interior decorator could have done a better job, but I was always worried about accidents and would object to much of this. Both Maria and Matilde were rather stout, and I feared that one or another would fall off the ladder and break a leg.

Maria spent a large part of her day either in the kitchen or in the bathroom. She had difficulty losing weight and tried a variety of ways to overcome her problem, including lengthy electric massages and baths of every kind. She had wanted a spacious, comfortable, inviting bathroom. When she was resting there undergoing her massages, she either attended to her correspondence or read. For the most part the books were biographies of composers or works dealing with the theater. She purchased publications in Italian, but even more in English. With her passion for painting, she read numerous volumes devoted to the history of art, various trends, and specific painters. She never bothered with romantic novels, simply because the plots bored her.

And the kitchen? Maria was quite overweight until the end of 1953. Various publications relate how she consumed enormous plates of pastasciutta, and how she gorged herself on cheese and desserts. Some people even ascribed a psychological interpretation to her "ravenous" appetite, postulating that she ate in compensation for a lack of affection. These suppositions are fantasy.

I will return later to the subject of Maria's unsuccessful diets, which were followed by her sudden loss of weight. For the moment, however, I will simply state that Maria was heavy not because she overindulged at the table but rather because she had a glandular disorder. She herself outlined the saga of her weight problems in some autobiographical notes she had written to refute certain statements published in *Time* magazine. She was still thin when she left the United States in 1937 to go to Greece with her mother. She began to gain weight in Athens after a medical treatment based on whipped eggs, and also because of a glandular disorder that was never cured. She continued to get bigger even when she hardly ate. "I remember one of my relatives would chase after me to the top of the stairs in the morning because I often went out without having had anything but a cup of tea," Maria wrote.

When she returned to the United States in 1945, she went on a strict diet. She wrote in her autobiographical sketch: "I dropped from 218 pounds to 170, or from about 100 kilos to 80. Later, when I arrived in Italy, I was down to 155 pounds. That was my weight when I was singing *Turandot* and *Tristan* in Venice, and *Norma* in Florence. After my operation for appendicitis, I gained twenty-two pounds. Then, around 1950 and 1951, I continued to get heavier, without any apparent reason."

Maria's cumbersome body frustrated her, and her determination to stay on her diet was extraordinary. I have always been a gourmand, although hardly a glutton. I enjoy having tasty meals served at home. Maria, however, was always a slave to the most severe diets. She never ate any kind of pasta, subsisting on grilled meat and raw vegetables, eaten without any seasoning or oil, like a goat. She didn't drink liquor, and only took the smallest amount of wine. She never ate desserts.

She was crazy about rare meat—filets and steaks *alla fiorentina*. When she was nearly finished, she would attack the bones like a cat. Only with her steaks did she sometimes eat voraciously. When she was singing at La Scala, we would dine at Biffi Scala around seven in the evening. Maria would consume a twenty-eight-ounce steak; everyone who saw her must have wondered how she could possibly sing with all that food sitting on her stomach.

Her dietary requirements were quite basic, and no one should have expected anything bordering on culinary art from Maria, but she always thought of me. She had a passion for working in the kitchen with pots going on all the burners. Cooking was for her a fascinating hobby. She would buy a bewildering array of knives, spoons, casseroles, whisks of every type, and so on. Every time she went into a housewares store and found something new, she bought it. She called these gadgets her "mousetraps," and the kitchen was full of them.

Another of her obsessions was cutting recipes from periodicals. Almost every morning, she bought a pile of magazines for women, and would systematically clip the recipes and paste them in scrapbooks. She had a mountain of them. She would devote entire days to her culinary experiments, especially trying to make desserts. She also concocted some absurd dishes, perhaps because she misjudged the proportions of the ingredients, or perhaps because the recipes were incorrect in the magazines. Some of her creations were inedible. I would try to grin and bear it, but often I just couldn't manage it. She was never offended; she'd laugh and the next day she would start again from the beginning.

On Sundays we went to my mother's house in Zevio. She also loved fine food. They would both go off to the kitchen, and it was a pleasure to see the two of them preparing dinner. My mother, who was a truly good person, taught Maria certain Veronese dishes, such as *lesso con la pearà* (boiled beef with a sauce of bone-marrow broth and bread crumbs), *anara fredda con polènta calda* (cold duck with hot corn-meal pudding), *baccalà* (dried, salted codfish), etc. The strange thing is that after having spent so much time in the kitchen preparing a particular dish or dessert, Maria would not even taste it if her diet did not permit it, and she was adamant about it.

We stayed in our apartment in Via San Fermo for about a year. Our marriage had exacerbated the rupture with my brothers, who now looked at Maria with open contempt. As the apartment was above the offices of the family business, my brothers occasionally ran into Maria on the stairs or at the entrance to the building. They would stare at her with disdain, never greeting her. One day one of my brothers was with our chauffeur Rodolfo in the courtyard by the entrance. Maria was coming down the stairs at that moment to go out, but, upon reaching the landing, she lost her footing and fell to the ground. My brother did absolutely nothing to help her. He merely said, in a loud voice, "So good for nothing that she doesn't even know how to walk downstairs."

In light of the situation, we decided to leave Via San Fermo so we would no longer have to encounter them. We moved into the top floor of a very high *palazzo*. Our apartment was surrounded by a beautiful balcony, from which we saw only bell towers and tiled roofs. On the front of the building was a plaque honoring Renato Simoni (I don't know if he was born or died there). Maria decorated the new apartment according to her tastes, and we remained there until 1953, when we moved to Milan.

Maria was not interested in accepting engagements for July and August. The first half of 1949 had been grueling, including, as it did, the season in Argentina, and now Maria simply wanted to enjoy being a housewife. We spent a week by the sea, at Venice's Lido, and then we went to Lake Garda, just doing whatever came into our heads. In September, though, Maria began working again. Her first contract was for Perugia, for which she had been engaged by Francesco Siciliani to sing in Alessandro Stradella's oratorio *San Giovanni Battista*. The work was to be conducted by Gabriele Santini in the Church of San Pietro. The soloists, in addition to Callas, were Cesare Siepi, Miriam Pirazzini, Rina Corsi, and Amedeo Berdini. This was a prestigious engagement at the time when Stradella was being rediscovered as one of the most original and seminal Italian composers of the seventeenth century. The first rehearsals took place in Rome, where Maria remained for a couple of days. In her letters, besides lamenting, as usual, our separation, she was also preoccupied with her home. "We're rehearsing regularly," She wrote from Rome. "A lot of it is exhausting, because the oratorio is extremely difficult. I'm exceedingly restless. I long for you and my apartment. I love you so much, my dear. I'm happy to be your wife, and if I could remarry you I'd do it with even greater enthusiasm, if that were possible."

Maria then went to Perugia, from where she wrote me on September 15: "My love, I wasn't able to hear your voice on the telephone. I'm writing you just a few lines now to tell you what I'm doing. Yesterday, unexpectedly, we went to Perugia. We left at 3:00 and arrived at 6:30. I found a room in the Hotel Brufani Palace. It's not elegant, but my room has a bath. Meals are included, so I don't have to go out to eat. Maestro Santini seems to be satisfied with the way things are going with the oratorio, but I'm not. Well, never mind.

"Yesterday I saw Siciliani and we spoke at length about you. We were right in thinking he might be the future head of La Scala. He didn't say anything to that effect, but I believe it will happen. He'll at least give them a run for their money, but don't say anything to anyone about it.*

"I spoke with Vitale, who wants me to promise not to accept any engagements immediately after January 20. They would like me to sing *Norma* and *Turandot* at the Rome Opera. I declined *Turandot* but suggested *Tristan*. That would be nice, wouldn't it? They would also like something new from me, perhaps

* Callas's reference to her friend Siciliani was probably, in part, wishful thinking. Antonio Ghiringhelli was not to relinquish his position as Superintendent of La Scala until 1972.

Refice's *Cecilia*, the work in which Claudia Muzio had such a great success. I said that it was fine with me as long as Serafin conducted, but I would not like modern operas!"

She wrote again two days later, on September 17: "My dear, you can't imagine how much I miss you, especially today, because the weather is so bad. It's raining, and that depresses me. We continue to work on *San Giovanni Battista*—three rehearsals a day. I must spend a lot of time with my colleagues, and that can be exasperating, as you know. Oh, well. The truth is that I can't stand being away from you for even a day. Everyone and everything seems unimportant. Nevertheless, every so often I must live without you.

"How are you? What are you doing? Do you miss me? I'm pleased that you're coming Sunday with your mother and Pia. I hope you've found my black dress, the long velvet one with red taffeta. Also the jacket that goes with it, otherwise I won't be able to sing in San Pietro. I hope you receive this in time. Please also bring a fur coat. It's cold here and at night I don't know what to wear. Please also bring my diamond and the necklace with matching earrings. I'm sorry if I'm a nuisance, but these things are necessary even if one is as unassuming as I am. Come join me, my love, I don't want to be . . . I *can't* be without you.

"Ildebrando Pizzetti and Maestro Vittorio Gui are here. Pizzetti has been very nice to me. Gui has gone out of his way to meet me and pay me a lot of compliments. He says that he would like for me to sing under his baton."

Vittorio Gui's desire to work with Maria resulted in a production of Verdi's *Nabucco* at Naples's San Carlo in December of the same year. She did not, however, find her collaboration with Gui to be particularly rewarding. As Maria's career gained momentum, she became increasingly demanding of herself and others. She wanted perfection in everything. In the theaters in which she appeared, though, the operas were often thrown together with little concern for detail, and with even less enthusiasm.

There was also the undeniable fact that Maria was nervous and irritable when we were apart, and that in turn affected her rapport with her colleagues. As soon as she arrived in Naples in December 1949, Maria determined when we would be able to see each other again. That this was an important production, that the conductor was famous, that the public—remembering her excellent *Turandot* from the previous year—adored her, was all of secondary importance to Maria. She wrote on December 16: "My dear, I have just received your letter, which has filled me with confidence and happiness. Dear, I can sense that you miss me, but we will be together sooner than we had expected. Opening night is December 20, a Tuesday. The second performance is the twenty-second, and the third and last one the twenty-seventh. You see, there are five days to rest between the second and third performances, but I certainly don't want to be here. I was thinking I could fly to Verona the twenty-third and return to Naples the morning of the twenty-seventh. What do you think? I'll do whatever you suggest."

She went on to discuss her misgivings about the new production. "Gui enjoys working with me. I'm not enthusiastic about him, though. He's always talking about himself. The stage director [Brissoni] doesn't have any idea what *Nabucco* is about. Dramatically I will have to rely on my own invention. Let's hope it goes well. Do you believe how they produce opera these days; it's just *awful*! Where is Serafin, who taught and supervised everything, including the staging! The San Carlo is already sold out. May God be with me. Say a prayer, because there is enormous expectancy here."

In the same letter she spoke of a season in Mexico projected for the summer of 1950. She commented that she was pleased they had asked her to sing *La Traviata,* but she was concerned that it would not be Serafin who was conducting. She hoped that he would coach her in the opera before she left for Mexico. It was now obvious that Serafin had become "her" maestro, and that she had confidence only in him.

On the afternoon of December 20, the day of her first *Nabucco*, Maria wrote me another letter, which I quote at length because it reflects what went through her mind shortly before she was to go on stage. As one can see from the tone of the letter, Maria was quite detached and almost indifferent to everything that was happening around her. High-strung and demanding in rehearsal, she was calm and at one with herself the day of the actual performance. I never saw in her the nervousness, anxiety, and fear which generally grip most singers before they walk on stage.

Especially noteworthy in this letter is the portion in which Maria informed me, with regret, that once again she found she was not pregnant. Maria wanted more than anything to be a mother. The statements that Maria lived only for her art and did not wish to have children are all false. So was the assertion in one biography that Meneghini was opposed to children. These are stupid observations which totally misrepresent Maria's and my personalities. The truth is—as witnessed by this letter of 1949—that we both ardently desired to have children.

"My dear, I'm here at a table in a restaurant where I'm trying to put down something before the performance this evening. I've received telegrams from everyone in the world—you, your mother, Pia, Gianni. Of course I would have preferred to have you here in person, but that's all right. In the meantime, I'm in fine health, thank the Lord. Let's hope everything goes the way I want it to. They wanted to have additional rehearsals, but so much for that.

"I don't know what to do in Naples. I have no interest in going to the movies alone, for I'm afraid of lice and mashers. The weather is like spring—it's truly enchanting. I'm unhappy we

[*111*]

were unable to speak by telephone. The line was out—what a pity! I feel very isolated and alone here, but otherwise I'm in good spirits.

"I have to report again—still no baby! I had my period the eighteenth, right on schedule, along with a headache fit for our worst enemies. We must be patient . . ."

The opening night of *Nabucco* went splendidly. The other singers included Gino Bechi in the title role, Gino Sinimberghi (Ismaele), Amalia Pini (Fenena), Luciano Neroni (Zaccaria), Igino Ricco (High Priest), and Silvana Tenti (Anna). Alfredo Parente wrote in *Il Risorgimento*: "Maria Callas, considered to be one of the most highly gifted dramatic sopranos today, interpreted the difficult role of Abigaille with impressive nobility of accent. The dramatic situation, besides affording a display of vocal fireworks, was also revealed through the force and incisiveness of her temperament. Her splendid voice, smoothly produced throughout its wide range, was equal to all of the requirements of the part, including the most difficult florid passages."

A. Procida reported in *Il Giornale*: "Maria Callas once again impressed us with her vocal gifts, developed through rigorous training, and displayed in Act III and in Abigaille's death scene an uncommon dramatic flair. She astonished with both the size and the range of her voice, which combines the power of a dramatic soprano and the high notes of a light soprano." In the opinion of *Roma's* Mario Baccaro: "The fiendish part of Abigaille was assumed by Maria Callas, a most musical and intelligent artist, who brought vigor to her characterization and a sense of evil, driving power."

Maria telephoned me the day after her first *Nabucco*, but instead of describing her triumph, she dwelt on how lonely she was. Seeing how she suffered, I decided to forget my business obligations for a few days and go to Naples to spend Christmas with her. When I told her this over the telephone, she was very pleased. Shortly after our telephone conversation she wrote me an enthusiastic letter, full of little projects, and various things we could do together. It is obvious from this letter, too, that singing was only of secondary importance to her. In fact, she digresses to chat about incidental purchases, shops we can visit together, and things of that nature. Only at the end does she take time to comment on her work.

"My one and only!! After having waited two hours at the communications center to place my call to you, I finally was able to hear your . . . *my* dear voice, which gave me so much comfort, as always. Now I'm back in my hotel room and I'm writing a few words to tell you that I was depressed, sad, alone, *so very alone*. But now, after our phone call, I'm better. I'm so happy that you are coming here. We can even play the true married couple a little. We can go for a walk, and see all the beautiful sights—Pompeii, the shops, the street, etc. December 26 we can go to the first *Wozzeck* [with Tito Gobbi and Suzanne Danco]. We can dress elegantly for that, but you will have to bring my long dress, whichever one you prefer, the black or the violet one. Maybe the violet one is better, if only for a change. Please also bring a dress for late afternoon, a bra that Matilde forgot to pack, and a short corset. Please also bring my long cloak.

"Titta, I've made some purchases. I bought a mirror for my dressing case, a small Christmas gift for you, and some beautiful 'mousetraps' for my kitchen. Also a small lamp for the small table with the telephone. I'm pleased because it's exactly the kind of lamp I wanted. But how will we manage to carry all this stuff? Why don't you bring a large suitcase and the black hatbox. That way we can divide up some of these things. I'm sorry if I'm a nuisance, dear, but I do need these things. Now come quickly, quickly. I've had enough of it here. It's disagreeable being alone, without anyone to talk to.

"The performance went very well, at least until Act II. They set fire to paper [for the burning of the temple at the end of the first act] instead of making steam, and the fumes parched my throat. I don't know how I managed to go on, but the third and fourth acts went very well. I had a marvelous duet, but the public and the critics didn't notice, so what's the point? Maestro Gui only thinks of himself. The stage director should drown himself—he doesn't know anything. Gino Bechi is old and full of phlegm. Amalia Pini is a nice girl, but her voice is nothing special. And then, the opera itself has beautiful music, but it's also a *big bore*!!

"Come, I live only for you. And you, do you miss me? Who knows!"

Chapter 10

Maria and Her Mother; Mexico

By the end of 1949, Maria was famous. She had enjoyed clamorous successes in Italy's most important theaters, with the sole exception of La Scala, where she was yet to sing. She was acclaimed a star of the first magnitude in the newspapers. Because her name was now a box-office draw, the possibility of a concert in Verona's Teatro Nuovo was broached.

The idea for this concert originated with a friend of mine, Ghiro, who was going through a difficult period with his business and needed to make some money. "With a celebrity like Maria Callas, we'll pack the theater," he told me. To help him out, we agreed. Ghiro was responsible for organizing the event, and Maria offered to sing without a fee. After deducting the various expenses, we would divide the balance of the receipts.

To avoid following the usual recital format of one aria after another, Ghiro decided to engage an actor also. He chose the most famous of that time, Memo Benassi, who, alternating with Maria, would recite monologues, poems, and excerpts from tragedies. Benassi was enthusiastic about the proposition. "I'm an admirer of Maria's," he said, "and just to have the honor of working with her, I will participate gratuitously."

The concert was announced for the beginning of November 1949. Flyers were printed and advertisements were placed in the papers. Everything seemed to be proceeding smoothly, and we expected an unprecedented success.

But when I accompanied Maria into the theater an hour before the start of the performance, I began to have some doubts. I noticed with surprise there was no activity in the theater. "It's probably still too early," I thought.

While Maria was getting ready in her dressing room, I peered through a little hole in the curtain. The auditorium was still more than half empty. There were a few people here and there. There were also those who entered, found the theater almost empty, and drifted away. My friend Ghiro was desperate; Benassi, amazed. It did not daunt Maria at all, however. "There aren't many people out there," I said, testing her mood. "I sing without glasses, so it doesn't matter to me whether the theater is full or empty; I can't see a thing." We were to have started at exactly ten. Hoping some other people might show up, I persuaded her to wait, but it was to no avail.

The recital started at 10:30. Maria sang as if it were a capacity house. It was an extraordinary concert from an artistic point of view, but a fiasco *sans pareil* as far as public interest was concerned. This episode underscored that, despite Maria's triumphs elsewhere, the people of Verona still did not know who she was.

My friend Ghiro, who had expected to realize a nice profit from the event, found himself burdened with more debts. He wrote to me in despair, emploring my assistance. I paid out almost 700,000 lire.

1950 was a very important year for Maria. Her art was fully appreciated, and engagements were always more prestigious. She began the new year with a production of *Norma* which was presented in Venice during the month of January. The other singers were Gino Penno, Elena Nicolai, Tancredi Pasero, Nerina Ferrari, and Cesare Masini Sperti; the orchestra was under the direction of Antonino Votto. Giuseppe Pugliese wrote in *Il Gazzettino*: "Callas knew how to project the complex, intimate drama of the protagonist with passion and an extraordinary musical abandon. Norma's lofty pride, fiery indignation, and pangs of love were captured by her in moments of the greatest musical beauty. She lavished her voice upon that wealth of trills, phrases, and melodies with a prodigiousness that is extraordinarily rare, and she achieved excellent results at the same time."

In February she appeared in a production of *Aïda* in Brescia. Alberto Erede conducted, and the other soloists were Mario Del Monaco, Amalia Pini, Aldo Protti, Enzo Felicitati, Duilio Baronoti, and Piero de Palma. In the same month she was heard alternately in *Tristan and Isolde* at the Rome Opera, with August Seider, Giulio Neri, Benvenuto Franci, and Elena Nicolai, and in *Norma* with Galliano Masini, Ebe Stignani, and Giulio Neri. Both operas were under the baton of Tullio Serafin. Her appearances in the two contrasting operas caused a sensation, and there was also considerable interest on the part of the press, and not only in Rome. The *Osservatore Romano* published a feature article about Maria. In March she participated in a broadcast concert from the RAI auditorium in Turin, and then traveled to Catania for *Norma*. Her colleagues there included Mirto Picchi, Marco Stefanoni, and Jolanda Gardino, under the direction of Umberto Berrettoni.

In April, Maria sang at La Scala for the first time, as a guest artist. Several pages will be devoted later to the discussion of Maria Callas vis-à-vis La Scala, for it is one of the most mysterious, bizarre, and comical chapters in the history of opera after the war. At that time La Scala was headed by Antonio Ghiringhelli, a person who hated and despised Maria and wished to obstruct her career. Today the name of Maria Callas is revered at La Scala, but during that period they made her suffer unjustly.

As I have already mentioned, in 1948 and 1949 Maria recorded successes in Italy's most important theaters—the Fenice in Venice, the Comunale in Florence, the Rome Opera, Naples's San Carlo, the Teatro Regio of Turin, the Verona Arena, and the principal theaters of Catania, Palermo, Genoa, Udine, Trieste, and so on. Outside Italy, she had sung at the Teatro Colón in Buenos Aires, earning triumphs which received extensive coverage in local and foreign newspapers. The reverberations of her successes certainly reached as far as La Scala, but they still chose to ignore her. After each of these engagements I expected Ghiringhelli to telephone, inviting her to his theater; however, nothing. It seemed that, as far as he was concerned, Maria simply did not exist. I was certain he was personally informed as to what Maria was doing in the various theaters, but he still snubbed her.

Given that situation, I understood full well that La Scala would not be making the first move. I needed an occasion to storm the citadel. This opportunity presented itself in April 1950. Renata Tebaldi, then the reigning queen of La Scala, was indisposed and unable to continue in a series of performances of *Aïda*. There was the possibility that my wife could substitute for her, and I discussed it with Maria. It was a fine cast: Mario Del Monaco, Fedora Barbieri, Cesare Siepi, and Silvio Maionica. Franco Capuano was conducting. It was an excellent opportunity for Ghiringhelli to evaluate Maria, and she agreed to step in.

She sang there for the first time on April 12, in what was an official gala performance. Those present included Luigi Einaudi, President of the Republic, the ambassadors of China, England, Ecuador, Greece, India, Turkey, and the United States, the consul generals of various nations, the chief magistrate and the mayor of Milan, Minister Togni, and many other dignitaries. The public's reception was warm. Maria sang very well, even though we perceived immediately that there was something suspicious in the attitude of some of the people, suggesting a prearranged hostility.* Not one director of the theater came backstage to congratulate Maria. Ghiringhelli even took advantage of the situation to be malicious. I was in Maria's dressing room after her debut, waiting for Ghiringhelli. I commented, "He must come now, and we'll see what he has to say." Every now and then, I went to the doorway to peer out. Finally I saw him coming, but he did not stop at Maria's room. He passed by the doorway without even deigning to look her way. He did stop at the nearby dressing room of the baritone, however, and told him in a loud voice, so that Maria could hear, "Fine, fine, you've managed to do it again." It was obvious from his remark that he was implying the performance went well despite the absence of Tebaldi.† As for Maria showing her mettle, not a word.

The second surprise came the following day when I read the reviews. It was the first time the Milan papers discussed my wife. *Il Tempo di Milano* was the only one to single her out for praise. Their reviewer wrote: "On stage the title role was sung by Maria Meneghini Callas, whom we were hearing for the first time, and whom we admired very much for the dark timbre and intensity of her voice, her most uncommon musicality, her always alert stage presence, and the nobility of her phrasing."

* Callas wrote in 1956 that when she arrived in her dressing room for her debut, she found that her Aïda costume consisted of a long piece of brick-red silk, stitched down the sides, with an opening for her head. (She had requested her regular set of costumes from a specific theatrical agency in Florence.) The wig could only have fit a child. Fortunately, she remembered that the Amneris, Fedora Barbieri, had two sets of costumes, her own and those of the theater. She was able to borrow the latter, which fit her very well; she then arranged her hair in a style appropriate to the opera. At the end of her aria "O patria mia," just as the audience began to applaud, someone shouted from a box, "Quiet! The piece isn't over yet." The admonition startled the members of the audience long enough to spoil any possible ovation.

† The baritone for that performance was Rafaelle de Falchi. Ghiringhelli may have been referring to an *Aïda* in 1948 when de Falchi was the Amonasro and Elisabetta Barbato took over the title role for Maria Caniglia.

The *Corriere della Sera* merely mentioned her, referring to her success with the phrase "Maria Meneghini Callas, a new singer who was applauded in the title role." The *Corriere Lombardo*, in a review signed "T.C.," fired off an unfair and totally undeserved broadside which one could spot as prejudice a mile away: "I did not care for Maria Callas, who, although she has been singing for a while, is new to La Scala. She obviously possesses temperament and a fine musicality, but her scale is uneven. She seems to improvise differently, from note to note, the method and technique of her vocal production. She does not have clear diction and she also forces her high notes, thereby jeopardizing the security of her intonation." It is a judgment completely contrary to those expressed by other more authoritative critics during that period.

Maria also sang *Aïda* at La Scala on April 15 and 18. She then went to Naples for additional performances of *Aïda* at the San Carlo. The conductor was Tullio Serafin and the other singers included Mirto Picchi, Ebe Stignani, Cesare Siepi, and Ugo Savarese.

At the beginning of May, Maria left for a season in Mexico, where she remained for almost two months. It was necessary to change planes at New York, and Maria took advantage of the opportunity to visit her parents. Maria's comportment in her relations with her family was always a mystery to me. I never really succeeded in fathoming her true feelings. Much has been written on this subject, especially in the United States. Newspapers have accused her of being a monstrous daughter, of having left her mother and father in poverty, of having refused to respond to their piteous requests for aid. Maria never said a word in her defense or chose to refute the accusations. At times her icy responses even aggravated the situation. Once, when a reporter asked her why she did not send money to her mother, she snapped: "If she doesn't have any, she can go to work. If she doesn't want to work, she can jump out the window!" These retorts also upset me, but I am certain they did not emanate from the heart. She was exasperated by the relentless publicity and by the shameful and widespread speculations about her private life and family. Her family even tried to launch her sister Jackie on a career as a singer, altering the date on her passport and telling the newspapers that she was younger than Maria. Jackie was actually six years older than Maria. This nonsense infuriated Callas and had a direct correlation to her angry responses.

Maria definitely harbored feelings of resentment toward her mother, but it was not hate. It was rather anger and antipathy or, perhaps, frustrated love. If I referred to her mother, she would say, "I don't want to hear you mention that woman's name." On certain occasions she allowed herself to speak openly to me about it, and then she would say that her mother had robbed her of her childhood. Even when she was only three, her mother forced her to practice the piano hour upon hour, forbidding her to play. She had her perform in public, like a trained dog.

Her father was of a different temperament. He was a good man, of even disposition, and passive. Maria adored him, but her mother considered him to be an injurious influence on his daughters. In 1937 she decided to sail for Greece with her two children and educate them in her own fashion. According to Maria, in Greece, all the attention of her mother Evangelia was lavished on her older sister. Jackie was beautiful, intelligent, and extroverted. Maria, however, was shy, myopic, and clumsy. Evangelia was proud of Jackie, but considered Maria to be an ugly duckling. The latter was required to do the most humble chores, and was viewed at home as something of a servant. Jackie was allowed whatever she wanted, while Maria was always poorly dressed, simply because her mother never bought her anything. When a glandular disorder made Maria swell up before her very eyes, her mother did not bother to arrange for a cure. During the terrible war years, while her mother and sister remained safely at home in Athens, Maria was constantly exposed to danger and humiliating work in order to procure food.

This is the picture that Maria painted of her mother, and I suffered on hearing her accounts. I am a "mama's boy" in that I believe a mother is the highest expression of mankind. I always adored my mother. She is constantly in my thoughts and in my heart even now. I visit her tomb every Sunday, regardless of the weather. I tried to convince Maria that her attitude in her relationship with her mother was unfair, and I wanted to effect a reconciliation, especially since I detected certain feelings which indicated that Maria's heart was full of concern and love for her mother. I have explained that when Maria sang her first *Tristan* in Venice, I sent a telegram to Evangelia. Maria had tears in her eyes and thanked me repeatedly; this surely reflected love for her mother. After our marriage, Maria was influenced by my matriarchal attitude, and gradually she stopped recalling her mother with rancor. When I suggested she spend a little time in New York visiting her parents before continuing on to Mexico, she agreed readily. She even told me she wanted to take her mother with her to Mexico, so Evangelia could keep her company during the two-month season.

However, things did not go the way Maria had planned. When she arrived in New York City, she learned that her mother was in the hospital and that her father was suffering from a heart condition. It was a difficult situation, aggravated even more by the incessant bickering of her parents. Her mother had decided to divorce George Callas and come live with us in Verona. Maria, at first grieved by the poor health of her parents, was livid at the prospect of their divorce. The fact that her mother intended to move in with us also upset her, for it prompted memories of the ugly days in Greece, and she feared a recurrence of the discord, the dissension, the hateful scenes with her mother. These thoughts plagued her for the entire period of her stay in Mexico, disrupting her sleep, and bringing her to the brink of a nervous breakdown.

Her letters from Mexico reflect these concerns, which, in turn, adversely affected her singing. This is what she wrote as soon as she arrived in Mexico City:

May 14, 1950

My beloved, I have finally reached my destination after a flight that was comfortable but also distressing. I arrived with my calves swollen badly enough to give one cause for alarm.

In New York I had the shock of finding my mother in the hospital for the past ten days with an infection in her right eye.

I was at my father's apartment and Giulietta Simionato was with me. She was thirsty and Father gave her a cold drink. Simionato became sick immediately—she was vomiting and had stomach pains, a headache, and then diarrhea. Everyone was upset all day and very frightened. Simionato thought my father had given her gasoline to drink by accident, but it was even worse. He had given her insecticide. Thank God she doesn't know the truth. Fortunately, nothing really serious happened, except that I spent the day—when I should have been resting— going between the hospital to see my mother and back home to take care of Simionato, who was dying of fright. Such goings-on!*

We arrived in Mexico City at nine this morning. The director general of the Opera, Señor Pani, was at the airport to greet me, along with the Greek consul and some women who gave me two boxes of orchids. Then, in the consul's car, they accompanied us to the hotel. I feel okay. I took a bath and then slept until 1:30,

---

* Callas's mother kept her insecticide in a Seven-Up soda bottle in the refrigerator. It was not until 1956, when Callas and Simionato were sitting in Biffi Scala in Milan, that Callas had the courage to tell her friend exactly what the liquid was that she drank.

when I was awakened by a delivery of flowers from Pani on behalf of the theater. They seem to be full of thoughtful gestures here, and I hope it continues that way.

It's terribly hot. I'm finding it difficult to breathe at this altitude, and it taxes my heart. I hope it'll pass. Everything passes eventually, isn't that so? I'm very concerned about my mother. I wanted to take her along with me because I needed a calming influence and some assistance, and here I am alone and worried. What's even worse, my father is also sick. He has a heart condition and has not been able to work for four weeks. They did take him back [at the pharmacy], but he lost a month's pay. And now my mother is in the hospital. Why does sickness always come to poor people who aren't in a position to sustain the expense?

I hope that my mother will be able to leave the hospital in a few days and that she'll be able to join me in a couple of weeks. But will that be good for me? Will she be a help to me? Who knows!!

I'm making a great effort to stay calm. I must because of the demanding schedule ahead of me, and also because I want to return to you quickly and in good health, my love. And please, enough of these long trips, with their interminable periods of separation! My treasure, how are you? Leaving you Thursday was so hateful. I didn't even have an opportunity to embrace you.

They're beginning performances here the twenty-third, at a time when I know I won't be at my best. It's fate, isn't it? I hope to God that everything goes well, and that my mother is well soon. . . . I implore you to take care of yourself. I forgot to mention that I hated New York. The city is too noisy, and has too much traffic.

Maria was not an expansive person. She dispensed details of her preoccupations with an eyedropper. Only in her next letter, dated May 19, did she tell me that her mother wanted to come to live with us in Verona: "My dear, today I received your second, sweet, wonderful letter. I imagine you have received my first letter in which I told you about the trip. I don't know anything about what's happening with my mother. I wrote, but I've yet to receive an answer. I'm going to send a telegram now requesting news. The one thing that's certain is that she is not well, and the infection in her eye does not help her peace of mind. She continues to fret and is always worrying about my sister and me. As with all good mothers, she thinks of her children rather than herself. But she does not get along with my father. He also is not well. He still has diabetes and now a heart condition. My mother wants to leave him, but I said to her, 'How can you abandon him now, when he's old and sick?'

"Battista, she wants to come and live with us. May God forgive me, Battista, but right now I want to be alone with you in our home. Under no circumstances am I willing to compromise my happiness and my right to be alone with you a little. We deserve that, don't we? But how can I explain all this to my mother? How can I tell her that I do love her, but that it is a different kind of love from that which I have for my husband? I will give her money so she can go somewhere to rest, in the mountains or the country, but I do not believe it is fair that she leave my father now. What do you think? Please do not speak about these matters with anyone.

"I've already seen to my mother's ticket, but I don't think she'll come. Perhaps my indirect refusal to allow her to come live with me will set her off.

"Everything concerning the opera is up in the air. I no longer know what's going on. We're supposed to perform Tuesday, but the tenor, Kurt Baum, hasn't arrived yet. We have not had even one rehearsal with the orchestra and chorus. It's enough to drive you crazy, but I'm not getting involved in it. I just want to be in good health and sing my performances well. Fortunately, I feel better today. When I'm healthy as an ox, then I'm in fine spirits. I realize that I have to be here for two months, so there is nothing to be gained from working myself into a state. The climate here is so debilitating one doesn't have the energy to be excitable.

"Please send immediately the letter in which the director of the theater states that I'm engaged for a period of six weeks. This does not appear in my contract, and I would not want them to insist on my staying longer. As I predicted, the *Traviata* business was a disaster. Do you remember when they protested when we told them I didn't want to do it? Well, our agent, Liduino, sent a telegram assuring them I had agreed. We'll see what happens. I struck it from my contract simply because I wanted to; I would rather lose two performances. I said I would be happy to do *I Puritani,* but they are not interested.

"In the meantime, do not go about getting a passport to come here. I'll murder you if you do. I don't want you flying here, please. I have this fear that something will happen to you. For my return trip I'll be flying directly to Italy, via Madrid. I don't want to go by way of New York. I hate the city and do not want to spend even one day there. I hope my mother joins me here. I will also send money to my godfather, repaying what he loaned me so I could go to Italy.

"The schedule here calls for *Norma, Aïda, Tosca, Trovatore.* I don't know if it will also be *Traviata* or *I Puritani.* Please take care of yourself. I will do the same, because I want to return healthy and beautiful in order to enjoy our happiness. Just think how much God has given us! He will watch over us always. He does with us as He wishes, and I have total faith and confidence in Him. I send my greetings, my love. Remember me to our little home."

Every letter Maria wrote from Mexico contains passages concerning her mother. This preoccupation was an *idée fixe* and she was unable to rid herself of it. In her heart she was struggling with two conflicting emotions: the desire to help her mother, and the fear of once again being the victim of her will. Maria's depression, her difficulties, the nervousness and the insomnia that she attributes in her letters to the weather, the lack of organization, the maliciousness of her colleagues, her separation from me, all stemmed, in reality, from her familial problems, which she never did succeed in resolving.

May 25, 1950

My dear, my adored one, I'm writing at a horrendous hour—7:30 in the morning. I did not sleep the entire night, so you can imagine how well I am.

I'm existing in this strange state of apathy. My resistance is low because of this damned climate and also the altitude, which saps you of your strength. The performances go their way in a pitiful manner, so much so that if I were in full form I would rebel and scare the daylights out of even these fools. But I don't even have the strength to do that. I move about like a cretin, in the true sense of the word, hoping just to be able to survive another month of this tiring and badly done work. I have also physical problems which have taken their toll. The past few days we've all had diarrhea without knowing why.

My mother doesn't write, I don't know how she is, and I don't see her arriving. Papa says she is better, but how can I believe him? Battista, the distance between us weighs on me enormously, not only for the simple reason of a physical need for my husband, but for a combination of things I miss. I cannot get along without you. Whatever happens—a minor indisposition, some stupid annoyance—makes me feel even more the absence of our affection, and the mutual interests which unite us and have become something belonging only to us. This oneness cannot be broken or divided. A separation causes the greatest suffering, and if it is not remedied, all could end badly. We have been apart too much. Before we were married we longed for this union. I sensed that you were my ideal. Now I know firsthand the pride, the joy in being your companion, and I suffer even more from this estrangement, from being deprived of your beloved person.

I was just interrupted by the arrival of one of your letters. I live only in anticipation of your letters. I'm pleased about the prie-dieu and also your having decided to have that damaged painting restored . . . I've begun electric massage treatments. It seems futile, but I would love to lose a little from my hips and legs. We'll see or, more precisely, you'll see when I return.

May 29, 12:30 at night

Dear Battista, once again I am unable to sleep, so I'm writing letters. Tomorrow is the first *Aïda*. I swear to you I do not know how these damned performances are going to turn out, it's so impossible to sing here. Everything gets worse instead of improving. My resistance is good but you can imagine how debilitating this has been for poor Simionato. She's flat on her back.

Today I had a long discussion with Antonio Caraza-Campos about *La Traviata*. He says he's going ahead with the costumes, and I remain adamant. I don't want to sing it. I do not want to learn two new operas—*Il Trovatore* is enough. I don't want to kill myself here. The climate is terrible enough. I can't wait to return.

My mother has not written. What could have happened? Her plane ticket has been in New York for ten days now. I hope she's not sick. There always has to be a problem.

I've estimated what I should clear after this engagement. I should return with a little more than three thousand dollars, after having repaid my godfather and having given some money to my mother. It's not much, but the important thing is that I return to where I belong. I do not enjoy being so far away from you for such long periods of time. Believe me, these separations could eventually be injurious to our wonderful relationship. This way of life is not good, at least in my opinion. Our best years are being wasted. Enough. Life has so many beautiful things to offer, and I'm enjoying none of them.

I'm not doing anything of interest here. My diamonds are sparkling only in the hotel safe. My furs are of no use because it's brutally hot. Without you near me, I don't derive pleasure from what I do have. I've lost more than seven pounds. If I continue at this rate, I'll become a skeleton. Write to me, and wish me well. I would die without you, who represent love, fidelity, courtliness, elegance, in short, all of the ideal attributes!

June 1, 1950

My dear, if you saw me at this moment you would be terrified. I'm fit to be tied. They want to do *Tosca*, then *Cavalleria*, then *Trovatore*. I'm furious with that tenor Kurt Baum. He's worse than a jealous woman. He continues to insult me and was angry because at the end of the ensemble in *Aïda* I took a high E flat. The public went crazy, and Baum split with envy.

I'm displeased with the way the company does things here. It is now 1:30 and they have just informed me that the rehearsal for *Tosca* is at 2:30. Can you imagine, and I haven't even had lunch yet! I'm fed up and thoroughly annoyed. Damn this Mexico, and woe to you if you ever allow me to go away again. I warned you, you know.

My mother sent me a note. She says I'm egotistical, I only think of myself, and I'm leaving her to die in economic straits. I'm so disgusted I'm considering severing all relations with her. Here I am, alone as a dog. At least Simionato is here, and she keeps me company a bit. One cannot work on one's roles, because there is no rehearsal hall. I'm telling you, I'm ready to murder everyone.

Aïda went marvelously well the other night. The audience was ecstatic, at least over Simionato and myself. The others had a stroke when they saw who were the favorites of the public.

My Wife Maria Callas

June 5, 1950

My dear, beloved treasure, I received two of your letters today. I'm pleased that you've decided to go through with that dental work, but my poor Titta, what discomfort you're going to have. I wish I could be near you to try to help you forget your suffering. And you, have you longed to be near me? You know I'm very jealous and don't like to leave you alone. Are you never jealous of me? That's not good, and I'm displeased. I want to see and hear that you're jealous of your wife, even if you have total confidence in me!

I'm in bed today with one of those famous inflamed throats. It's this weather that dries out one's throat. So they've had to postpone *Tosca* for two days—I'm voiceless. It will be *Tosca* that does me in!

They went berserk over the *Aïda*. Baum almost killed me. He came to apologize before the second *Aïda*, though. It's obvious he's afraid of being too brazen in his confrontations with me. He heard I wouldn't sing with him again if he didn't apologize, so the "prima donna" came to ask me to forget about what has happened. The skunk! The public was clamoring, "Aïda, *sola!*" After another ten curtain calls, I had to go out alone. My colleagues almost spit blood.

I don't know what to say to my mother. You can imagine her disappointment when she hears that I won't be returning by way of New York. In the meantime, I've written saying that you don't believe you will be able to come to Mexico. I still don't have the courage to tell her I'm not going to New York.

June 6, 1950

My dear, sweet love, after waiting four days I have received your letter. I find so much sadness in it. My dear, is it not you who always sends me on tour for that famous something known as pride? You know what I want to say, so there is no point in belaboring it . . .

I must confess I've been very ill in this damned Mexico from the moment I arrived. I haven't managed to be well one single day. Even in Italy I had begun to feel the weight of the past two years' work. In Naples it was a struggle to see it through to the end. I tried to persevere, but during the last performance of *Aïda*, because of nerves, the air conditioning, some annoyances, my voice started to give out; my morale was also low because of worry. Today, during the dress rehearsal of *Tosca*, I thought I was going to faint. The kiss of death is the fact that I am unable to sleep. I'm still awake at six or seven in the morning.

I pray to God that He helps me to see it through to the end of the contract. Then I will concentrate on regaining my strength. It is important, however, that I make it to the end, otherwise my colleagues will be overjoyed.

Dear Battista, I have to make a confession. I want so much for us to have a baby. I also believe a baby would be good for my voice and my bad skin. What are your thoughts? I send my greetings, my love, with all of my heart, which loves, desires, respects, and appreciates you, and declares that you are its god.

June 8, 1950

My love, this time I've broken my own record—8:30 in the morning and I've yet to fall asleep. I believe that I will go mad here in Mexico. They say it's difficult to sleep at this altitude. I find it difficult to fall asleep at home; you can imagine here. The only good thing about this trip is that I've lost weight. I hope to stay this way so when I return you'll find me more beautiful.

We did *Tosca* and it was a big success. The audience was cold during the first act and they hardly applauded, but they gave me an ovation in the second act. They went crazy after "Vissi d'arte." Five minutes of applause. The reception was even more enthusiastic than it was for the other operas. One consolation is that God always helps me.

Liduino wrote saying that Bing, of the Metropolitan, wants

me for [the Queen of the Night in] Mozart's *The Magic Flute*. He's crazy!

June 12, 1950

My love, I haven't written for several days because I've had so much to study with *Trovatore*. I cannot retain a thing. One becomes an imbecile here in Mexico. On top of that, I have a blemish on my face—the same problem as in Rome, only worse. And to think that I have a performance of *Aïda* tomorrow and will have to darken my face, with my skin in that condition!

My beloved, I cannot endure this any longer. I only look forward to the hour of my departure. It seems like a year since I last saw you, and it has only been a month.

My mother arrived and we are together. I'm feeling a little better, but of course I'm very nervous and that upsets her, the poor woman. I find myself in the most trying period of my life, but one must be patient.

Dear, I will return on the direct flight to Madrid, and from there I will take the connecting flight to Rome or Milan. Are you anxious to see me, Battista? I don't have any other news to tell you, other than the fact that I'm even thinner and my face is a mess. It was a triumph for me here, but I only want to recover my health and find myself enwrapped in your arms, as only you know how to do. My love, I am only well when I am with you. I adore you.

My mother sends you a kiss and I ask you to embrace your mother for me. I'll leave you now—I'm kissing you and squeezing tightly. Think of me.

Maria returned from Mexico in good spirits. Her mother was in much better health. The eye infection proved to be less serious than it had seemed at first. There also appeared to be a new truce between the two of them. The only point on which Maria quarreled was the divorce; her mother refused to heed her advice, and left George Callas. Maria became incensed once again and told me that under no circumstances was I ever to mention her mother again.

The rift was soon irreparable. Evangelia Callas eventually found herself in the hands of unscrupulous people who tried to use her to extort money from Maria. They persuaded her to grant interviews to newspapers and on television and to write a book disparaging to her daughter. Only once did Maria speak out about these matters, writing in her own hand: "It is true that around the end of 1950 my mother asked me for money and it is also true that I refused. Shortly before that, she was with me in Mexico, at my expense. I bought her a mink coat and many other things. I settled one of her debts in the amount of a thousand dollars. I then gave her another thousand for her personal expenses, urging her to make it last for a year. And she could have managed to do this, because she already had another fifteen hundred dollars which I had given her. In doing this, of the three thousand dollars which I had expected to take back to Italy with me from Mexico, I was left with only a few hundred dollars. But I was content. About eight weeks later, however, my mother asked for more money, and then I became angry. At that time I had been married a year and could not bring myself constantly to impose upon my husband. Moreover, my mother wished to divorce my father, who was old and infirm. It was then that I said 'enough!' "

Maria's rapport with Evangelia was tenuous, to be sure, but I am certain of one thing: Maria loved her mother and suffered greatly because of her.

Chapter 11

Toscanini Auditions Maria
for Macbeth

One of Maria's greatest dreams, never realized, was to sing under the baton of Arturo Toscanini. Maria worshipped this conductor and her face would glow at the mere mention of his name. She often referred to her brief meetings with him as among the most beautiful moments of her life.

Maria had begun to admire Toscanini as a little girl, when she was studying singing and piano in New York. She heard him conduct over the radio and even owned some of his old 78 rpm recordings, but her admiration for him reached its apogee after her arrival in Italy, when she began her main career. As she expanded her repertory and worked with new maestri, she became increasingly more fanatical in her search for perfection. She absorbed the best of what each conductor had to offer, but none totally satisfied her. Maria always craved something more, and was convinced that only Toscanini, "the grand old man," would be in a position to guide her to perfection. But to approach him seemed an impossibility.

Maria's dream remained for some time only a chimera. Unexpectedly, however, it became palpable and was soon to become a reality. This is a little-known chapter in the life of Maria Callas, but one that was of the greatest importance because of its ramifications. It was Toscanini, in fact, who opened for Maria the doors of La Scala, which until then had seemed hermetically sealed to her.

The three years 1948–1950 were perhaps the loveliest in the artistic life of Maria Callas. She passed from one triumph to another, astounding everyone. They were total successes, untroubled and serene. The great manifestations of envy were yet to surface, the "hissing snakes" which later often disturbed her performances. After each appearance, Maria's dressing room was invaded by fans who asked for autographs, brought her flowers, or simply wished to shake or kiss her hand.

Among these admirers was one person who followed her religiously. He was a handsome man, tall, always dressed in a blue suit, with a large carnation in his buttonhole. Wherever Maria sang, he was there. We would see him in the auditorium and, after the performance, without fail in Maria's dressing room, where he arrived with flowers or was accompanied by new admirers. He was charming, polite, and obviously adored Maria.

At first we spoke lightly of this man. I contended he was in love. Maria would ask how we could repay so many kindnesses. Eventually we learned that her admirer was an industrialist and landowner from Parma. His name was Luigi Stefanotti. He loved opera passionately and had been married to a singer who had died several years before. We became accustomed to having Stefanotti in the room and soon became friends. When Maria sang in distant cities, being unable to join us, he would send letters and telegrams. He had many friends in the musical world and often associated socially with performers. He was also one of the privileged few who frequented Toscanini's home.

Stefanotti later told me that in his conversations with the great maestro he often spoke of Maria Callas. He revealed that his secret dream was to introduce them, but I did not believe this could possibly happen. I thought that Toscanini was inextricably and historically linked with La Scala. Since the theater, in the person of Ghiringhelli, obstinately ignored Maria and her operatic activities, I was convinced Toscanini would follow suit. I was mistaken, however.

On September 10, 1950, Luigi Stefanotti wrote to Maria: "Dear signora, I must speak with you because I have some important things to tell you. I cannot put them in writing, but so as not to leave you wondering, I will say immediately that the subject concerns Toscanini, with whom I had a long conversation yesterday evening in his home in Pallanza."

When I telephoned Stefanotti, he told me that Toscanini had a project in mind; he wished to hear Maria. 1951 marked the fiftieth anniversary of the death of Verdi and he wanted to commemorate it in the town of Busseto with an opera mounted by La Scala. He was looking for suitable artists. I told Stefanotti we would be happy to see the maestro and he should fix an appointment.

About a week later, on September 22, a telegram arrived addressed to Maria and signed by Toscanini's daughter Wally: "My father awaits you in Milan, Via Durini 20, on whatever day is convenient to you before his departure the twenty-eighth. Cordially, Wally Toscanini." Maria replied with this telegram: "I will be in Milan Wednesday the twenty-seventh, at Maestro's disposal for the entire afternoon."

Maria was nervous during the trip, which was most unusual for her. I had accompanied her many times to important appointments and had always found her to be perfectly relaxed and calm. This time she was tense. Not so much because she was afraid to sing for Toscanini, but simply because of the fact that she was meeting this unique artist for whom she had boundless admiration.

We arrived at the maestro's home in Via Durini around noon. Toscanini was then eighty-three years old. He received us graciously, but without excessive warmth. He was not a man of many words. While waiting for some lunch, we spoke in the drawing room. The maestro asked precise, definite questions. He spoke exclusively with me, glancing at Maria with his flashing, penetrating eyes. He asked me where I had discovered this woman, and what operas she had sung. I told him of our first meeting in Verona, and then briefly summarized Maria's career. But Toscanini already knew all that. At each important stage of her career that I mentioned, Toscanini made some observation. "The *Tristans* in Venice were more important than the *Giocondas* in Verona," I said. "Yes, I remember," he interjected. "She sang it on the last day of the year." I made a reference to the performances of *I Puritani* in Venice which Maria sang alternately with *Die Walküre*, after having learned the Bellini opera in only six days. Toscanini replied, "Oh, that was a true *tour de force!*" He knew of her *Norma* in Florence, the *Parsifal* in Rome, and of the seasons in Argentina and Mexico. I told him that Maestro Serafin was very enthusiastic about Maria. To this he made a grimace and commented, "Serafin is good, but he thinks with his wife's head." For every name I mentioned, often of the most celebrated artists, he had some derisive, caustic remark. Some were downright cruel. His manner of speaking was less a reflection of his true professional judgment of the person in question than a manifestation of his rebellious, nonconformist nature.

At one point Toscanini asked me why we still had not made contact with La Scala. I made reference to the apathy shown by Ghiringhelli toward Maria in April of that year, when she had substituted for Tebaldi, and also Labroca's negative evaluation after her audition in September 1947. Toscanini had a contemptuous opinion of Ghiringhelli. "He is an ass who knows nothing," he said. His comment set me back on my heels, for I had thought that Ghiringhelli was a pupil of Toscanini's. However, as I was able to ascertain later, Toscanini did not have any ties with Ghiringhelli; it was the latter who sought the support of the maestro so that he would have greater prestige in the musical world. Of Labroca, however, he said, "That's strange, because he's a musician and should be a good judge of voices."

After lunch, Toscanini explained why he had invited Maria Callas to his home: "I have never conducted Verdi's *Macbeth* in my life, because I never found a soprano capable of interpreting the part of Lady Macbeth. This role was particularly dear to Verdi. He reworked it a great deal. He himself in a letter [to Neapolitan librettist Salvatore Cammarano] indicated how his Lady Macbeth should be—'I want Lady Macbeth to be ugly and evil; her voice should be hard, stifled and dark.' I have never succeeded in finding an interpreter with these qualities. From the reports I have heard, you may be the person for whom I have been looking. I have asked you to come here so I can hear your voice. If you are all they have told me, we shall do *Macbeth*. I do not want to die without having conducted this opera."

The maestro spoke as one inspired. His tiny eyes glowed like coals. There was a great silence in the room as we hung on his words. The maestro bolted out of his chair and walked to the piano. He opened the score of *Macbeth* and began to play. Maria was next to him. I have never forgotten what took place that afternoon in Toscanini's home. The maestro played, attacking the keyboard with relentless determination. Maria sang—her face mirroring the text—with a vocal coloration and power that were startling. They went on like that for almost the entire first act. Never have I felt such intensity, so much magnetism in the air. I was huddled in a corner, almost afraid. The others present also seemed insignificant.

Stopping abruptly, Toscanini said: "You are the woman whom I have hoped to find for such a long time. Yours is the voice I can use. I will do *Macbeth* with you. Tomorrow I will speak to Ghiringhelli and I will have him send you a letter of intent." The maestro was expansive and satisfied. His face was luminous now, instead of flushed. Maria's eyes were shimmering and I knew she was ecstatic.

Toscanini then said: "I know you have already had a meeting with Siciliani about doing *Macbeth* in Florence. You understand that my offer precludes your accepting that engagement." Maria replied, "To be able to work with you, I am prepared to renounce any other contract."

During the trip back to Verona, Maria said: "I don't know if this *Macbeth* will take place, but it doesn't matter to me. I am immensely happy because of what I experienced today in Milan."

There is no doubt that Toscanini was enthusiastic about Maria's voice and truly intended to do *Macbeth* with her. He showed this by the fact that he spoke immediately with Ghiringhelli and announced he had found the soprano to realize his lifelong dream. He had not said the singer's name and Ghiringhelli inquired, "Have you chosen Tebaldi?" thereby demonstrating he did not have the slightest knowledge of voices. Tebaldi, in fact, had been praised by Toscanini as having "the voice of an angel," and she was known throughout the operatic world by this appellation. For Lady Macbeth, Toscanini wanted a "diabolical" voice and Tebaldi was the least appropriate singer. Toscanini answered Ghiringhelli with an insult and told him to write to Maria Callas, asking her to remain at liberty for the period of August–September 1951.

In a letter dated October 2, 1950, Ghiringhelli wrote to Maria: "Dear signora, I have learned with great satisfaction of your meeting with Maestro Arturo Toscanini. In accordance with what he has already indicated to you, I ask you to please confirm your availability for the months of August–September of next year. If you have occasion to visit Milan in the next few days, please let me know, so I may have the pleasure of discussing this with you. Please accept my best wishes, Antonio Ghiringhelli."

This letter is a most significant document. It suffices only to call attention to its tone to see how things had changed after

Toscanini spoke of Maria Callas. Six months earlier, Maria had sung in the Milan theater as a guest artist and Ghiringhelli had been unspeakably boorish to her. Now that Toscanini had personally spoken on her behalf, Ghiringhelli invited her to telephone so he could "have the pleasure" of talking with her.

Maria replied to his letter, confirming that she would be available for the period indicated. She was full of enthusiasm and excitement over the forthcoming event that would certainly have made history. Maria's friends were also elated. But mysterious and vague difficulties arose, and the *Macbeth* was never given.

What really happened has never been clear. It was said that they were not able to present the opera because of the failing health of Toscanini, but that is not true. Both the maestro and Maria were victims of some internal machination.

After the initial letter of October 2, Ghiringhelli neglected to tell us anything further. On January 19, 1951, Maria telephoned him from Florence, seeking information, but Ghiringhelli was not to be found. She telephoned again the following day and managed to speak to him. Ghiringhelli told her he had just finished writing her a letter, which, however, never arrived.

Toscanini, who was now in New York, continued to make plans for his *Macbeth*. Stefanotti wrote us on January 23: "Maestro Toscanini is still firm in his decision to conduct *Macbeth* at Busseto. In the United States, where he is now, he is constantly informed about how things are proceeding. Unfortunately, various circumstances and misunderstandings at La Scala have delayed some decisions. I will explain it to you more fully in our next meeting."*

* La Scala's foot-dragging was probably not directed entirely at Callas. Ghiringhelli was a wealthy autocrat who was not accustomed to being insulted by Toscanini or anyone else. Long before 1950, the venerable conductor was a god to the Italian people, but as far as La Scala's administration was concerned, their allegiance was to conductor Victor de

Two weeks later, on February 7, Stefanotti wrote again: "Maestro, by way of his son Walter and his daughter Wally, has sent a long letter requesting precise details as to how La Scala is proceeding with the work of organizing the *Macbeth* for the tribute at Busseto. The financial support is guaranteed. From Milan, with the lawyer Riboldi, we have sent a telegram to the maestro assuring him of this. The lawyer followed this up with a letter containing all the details which the maestro asked for about the performances, including the assurance that the opera will also be broadcast."

Despite all the reaffirmations, exchanges of letters, and participation of lawyers, the Toscanini *Macbeth* never took place. Some envious people in the music world (the same who impeded the realization of the *Macbeth*) spread the rumor that the opera was not staged because Toscanini did not care for Maria Callas's voice. These insinuations were malevolent. If Toscanini had not cared for her voice, he would not have spoken with Ghiringhelli, instructing him to write the letter that was so unusually cordial in tone. There is also another example of the interest of the Toscanini family in Maria. A few years later, in the course of a long letter, Wally Toscanini mentioned to me that it was she who had prodded Ghiringhelli into engaging Maria for La Scala. If Toscanini had not spoken favorably of Maria's voice at home, Wally would not have bothered urging Ghiringhelli to give her a contract. Unquestionably, it was Tos-

---

Sabata, who had been a mainstay at the theater since 1929, and who was shortly to replace Mario Labroca as artistic director. De Sabata had an influential coterie of fans in Milan as vociferous as those of Toscanini. A Toscanini–Callas *Macbeth*, produced by La Scala at the town nearest to Verdi's birthplace, would have eclipsed the work of de Sabata and all other conductors during the "Verdi year." Toscanini had long singled out de Sabata for scorn, if only for the younger musician's political beliefs; the high-strung De Sabata, whom Callas had actually seen spit on the first violins during a Scala rehearsal, would have had every opportunity to exert his influence against the *Macbeth*, in conjunction with Ghiringhelli.

canini's enthusiasm for Maria Callas that afforded her entrée into the Milanese theater.

Maria's association with Toscanini continued amicably. A few months after their first meeting in Via Durini, Toscanini took it upon himself to recommend Gian-Carlo Menotti, a composer in whom he had a special interest. This musician was already very well known in the United States, even though he was still young. Toscanini admired his work and was interested in him at this time because one of his operas, *The Consul*, was receiving its Scala premiere. The production was slated for January 1951, and Toscanini wanted Callas to have the leading role. Maria, however, was not interested. She knew Menotti, respected him, and had read the score, but she did not feel her voice was suited to this music. "I'm used to Norma, Isolde, Turandot, Violetta, characters from the past, swathed in a romantic aura," she explained. "I wouldn't feel comfortable portraying a contemporary character." Despite the urging of Toscanini, she would not change her mind.

Maria had another brief but unforgettable encounter with Toscanini on September 19, 1952, when the maestro gave his last concert in Milan. Maria was already firmly established at La Scala by then. Ghiringhelli had put his hostility and indifference behind him, and had become one of her great admirers. All the musical world was galvanized by the announcement of that concert. Requests for tickets arrived at La Scala from all over Europe. Hundreds of people waited all night before the theater to buy tickets. Some fainted from the exhausting ordeal. We went as guests of Ghiringhelli, in his box.

The program consisted entirely of music by Wagner, including selections from *Tristan, Die Walküre,* and *Parsifal,* operas which Maria knew intimately from having sung in them. I will never forget Maria's emotional participation during that concert. She was unable to sit still and her facial expression changed continuously. It was a trial being next to her. At the conclusion she said to me, "One must acknowledge the fact that, just as there is no one like Toscanini today, there never will be his equal." She went backstage to pay her respects. The maestro was surrounded by friends and various distinguished guests. When he noticed Maria, he went over to greet her. Without saying a word, he took her hands and squeezed them affectionately.

Their paths crossed on two other occasions during the next two years. The first was at the end of November 1954. Maria was rehearsing Spontini's *La Vestale* at La Scala, directed by Luchino Visconti and conducted by Antonino Votto. Toscanini wanted to attend a rehearsal. He was escorted into the theater, where he sat in the empty auditorium for a while. At one point he wished to speak with Maria. There is a lovely photograph which preserves that historic moment: with the maestro are Maria, Victor de Sabata, artistic director of La Scala, and Antonino Votto, conductor for *Vestale*. They are conversing among themselves and all three maestri are looking at Maria.

They met for the last time about a month later, around January 1955. La Scala was preparing a production of *Carmen* [to be sung in French, with Simionato and Di Stefano] under the direction of Herbert von Karajan. Toscanini had been accompanied into the theater to observe the rehearsal. Maria also wanted to attend that particular *prova*, and she found herself sitting near the great maestro. Toscanini exchanged a few pleasantries with Maria, but he was moody and nervous. He followed the rehearsal with great intensity, but it did not seem to be to his liking. In fact, he continued to grumble and curse. Maria could not determine precisely what was annoying him, but suddenly he arose and left the theater, muttering. Arriving at home, he gave vent to one of his legendary outbursts of anger, smashing plates and glasses against the wall. Shortly afterward, he returned to the United States and we never saw him again.

Chapter 12

Success in I Vespri Siciliani; the Callas—Tebaldi "Feud"

Toscanini's interest in Maria Callas created something of a furor in musical circles. As the news was passed along, it was embellished with details which had nothing to do with reality. There were those who minimized the significance of it, and those who attached more importance to it than it warranted. Everyone, however, knew that the conductor was a human steamroller—when he decided to do something, no one was able to dissuade him. Thus, the public awaited something extraordinary.

Toscanini's enthusiasm encouraged the most fanciful suppositions. From the United States he continued to send letters to friends and family inquiring into the progress of the Busseto *Macbeth*. He spoke with such fervor about this project that everyone was wondering just what he found so unusual in Maria Callas's voice to throw himself so totally into the preparation of an opera which he had never chosen to conduct during his entire career. People wanted to know why a singer who had found such favor with Toscanini was not singing at La Scala, and these queries reached Antonio Ghiringhelli and his associates, who now were no longer able to ignore Maria and her achievements.

After so much waiting and torment, Maria suddenly found herself in the ideal position for her acceptance by the most prestigious opera house in the world. She was propelled by events, without having to ask favors of anyone. While waiting for this situation to run its course, Maria pursued her career assiduously, continuing to accept engagements. All of the theaters wanted her, for her reputation was now considerable. Even provincial theaters in the smallest cities clamored for her. Not one quibbled about the fee—they were prepared to pay whatever sum was necessary to obtain her services.

On September 22, 1950, Maria sang *Tosca* at Salsomaggiore. The two other principals were Rinaldo Pelizzoni and Giovanni Inghilleri; Angelo Questa conducted. A few days later she repeated *Tosca* at Bologna's Teatro Duse, again under the baton of Angelo Questa. Her colleagues on this occasion were Roberto Tuvini, Rodolfo Azzolini, and Giannetto Zini. From Bologna she went to Rome for *Aïda* at the Teatro dell'Opera, with co-stars Mirto Picchi, Ebe Stignani, Raffaele de Falchi, Giulio Neri, and Augusto Romani; Vincenzo Bellezza was the conductor.

On October 7 and 8 she sang *Tosca* in Pisa. The role of Cavaradossi was taken by the famous tenor Galliano Masini, at that time getting on in years, but still the possessor of a splendid voice. The theater in Pisa did not have the most efficient organization. Specifically, they had financial problems. They had not succeeded in finding all the money necessary to pay the artists after the first act, as was the practice at that time. Galliano Masini had retired to his dressing room and announced that if they did not return with his fee, he would not sing. I had to advance the balance for Masini from my own pocket, otherwise the performance would not have continued.

After the *Toscas* in Pisa, Maria returned to Rome for Rossini's *Il Turco in Italia*. She was pleased to be able to perform a role so different from the usual heroines in her repertory. Although her temperament was typically that of a dramatic soprano, she proved incomparable in this brilliant comic role, establishing conclusively that she was a complete, imaginative, and versatile artist. The orchestra was led by Gianandrea Gavazzeni; with Maria appeared Mariano Stabile, Cesare Valletti, Sesto Bruscantini, Anna Maria Canali, and Franco Calabrese. Maria's final engagement for 1950 was as Kundry in *Parsifal*, sung in concert version November 20 [Act I] and 21 [Acts II and III] in RAI's broadcast studio in Rome. The conductor was Vittorio Gui.

1951 was of major importance in Callas's career. She began the year in Florence with a stupendous *Traviata* conducted by Tullio Serafin, with tenor Francesco Albanese and baritone Enzo Mascherini. In the same month she sang in *Il Trovatore* in Naples with Giacomo Lauri-Volpi, again under the baton of Serafin. She then went to Palermo for *Norma* conducted by Franco Ghione, followed by *Aïda* in Reggio Calabria with Maestro Federico del Cupolo. This was followed by a broadcast concert from the RAI auditorium in Turin, with Wolf-Ferrari conducting. In March she sang *La Traviata* in Cagliari with conductor Francesco Molinari-Pradelli, followed by a concert for the Red Cross in Trieste in April.

Francesco Siciliani scheduled Verdi's *I Vespri Siciliani* and Haydn's *Orfeo* for the 1951 Florence May Festival, both to be conducted by the distinguished maestro Erich Kleiber. The *Orfeo*, in fact, was a world premiere, for Haydn's opera had never been staged. The production in Florence was warmly applauded, especially by the aficionados of Haydn's music, who had traveled considerable distances to attend the festival. I remember the excitement and enthusiasm of one young man from Venice, Nicola Cipriani, at that time a law student, who was familiar with all of Haydn's operas. Although it was financially prohibitive, he made the trip to Florence specifically to hear *Orfeo*. That young man went on to become an important magistrate, and even today, when we run into each other, he speaks of that extraordinary performance of *Orfeo*.

During the rehearsals of *I Vespri Siciliani* there was a serious dispute between my wife and Maestro Kleiber. One day Maria wanted to return to our home in Verona for the weekend. A rehearsal was scheduled for Monday morning, but it was one that did not really involve Maria. She notified Siciliani that we would be back in Florence Monday afternoon, and would he please tell Maestro Kleiber. "Don't worry, I'll take care of it," Siciliani said, but then he forgot all about it.

Erich Kleiber was a very precise and fastidious conductor. Monday morning he was annoyed not to see Maria at the rehearsal. He waited a little before beginning and then, muttering, resigned himself to proceeding without her. Siciliani was there and could have spoken up, but, unexplicably, he remained silent.

In the afternoon, when we arrived at the theater, Kleiber lashed out against Maria. It should be pointed out that Maria, scrupulously, was always the first to arrive at rehearsals, and she never missed one for any reason. She would say, "I don't want to be reproached by anyone, because I don't want to put that person in the position of receiving a rude answer in return."

It seemed as if Kleiber wanted to goad her into losing her temper that day at all costs. He began to make sarcastic references to the fact that she was not present at the morning rehearsal, but Maria did not give it much thought. She did not consider herself to be in the wrong, for she had spoken with Siciliani and assumed that he in turn had notified Kleiber. She did not understand, therefore, why the conductor was so angry. She kept her head lowered as she looked over the score. This infuriated Kleiber even more.

Finally he said, "I expect not only sensibility and artistic sincerity, but also basic education."

"Oh, my God, that's it," I thought. Maria, in fact, went off like a coiled spring at that remark. She put down the score and, turning to Kleiber, said calmly but with tremendous resolve: "Now, enough. You can sing *Vespri* yourself." She walked out of the auditorium and returned to her hotel.

Knowing her well, I realized immediately that we had a very

serious problem. Siciliani was more dead than alive. He came to me, repeating. "For God's sake, try to placate her, try to reason with her."

I followed her to the hotel. "Maria, forget about it, return to the theater," I said.

"I will return only if Kleiber comes here to apologize," she replied.

"Good Lord, you can't expect a conductor as famous as Erich Kleiber to come here and ask you to forgive him," I said.

"And why not? It was he who was disrespectful. Either he comes to me with an apology, or I will return to Verona."

The entire afternoon there was a feverish coming and going of people who tried to reconcile the two. After they labored to patch things up, Kleiber realized he had overreacted and apologized. Maria then returned to the theater.

Maria was touched by Kleiber's gesture, for she was responsive toward people who were capable of admitting a mistake. In a couple of days the incident was completely forgotten. There arose between the conductor and Maria a perfect understanding which evolved into a great friendship, in which Kleiber's wife and I participated. The four of us became inseparable. We spent all of our free hours together. Occasionally we were joined by Leopold Stokowski and his wife [Gloria Vanderbilt]. Those were marvelous days which I still recall with nostalgia.

I Vespri Siciliani was a triumph. This time the echo of Maria's success did reach Milan's La Scala. Ghiringhelli sent a congratulatory telegram in which he announced he would be visiting Florence shortly to talk to her. Ghiringhelli probably expected us to prostrate ourselves at his feet and welcome him with open arms. It proved to be very difficult, however, to persuade Maria to agree on a time for the appointment. There were various telephone calls and exchanges of telegrams. The meeting was finally set for June 2, after the third *Vespri*. Ghiringhelli attended the performance and then met with Maria in her dressing room. He paid her many compliments and invited her to open the season at La Scala on December 7 of that year, in the same opera. Maria thanked him, said his offer interested her, and promised to give him her answer the following day.

Maria was pleased to accept Ghiringhelli's offer. Even though the actual contract had not yet been signed, the news made the rounds in musical circles. Many people were pleased, others less so. In the world of opera, there are always hidden interests for which one must be on the alert. Those who were supporters of other singers saw a grave threat in Maria's arrival at La Scala. Thus began the gossip, the intrigues, the complaints, and the little vendettas. The first fruit of these maneuvers was the evolvement of an exasperating rivalry between my wife and Renata Tebaldi, who was the reigning diva at La Scala. Even more than the two singers, the rivalry involved their fans, who allowed themselves to go to the limits of fanaticism at times. There is no doubt, however, that Callas and Tebaldi themselves were caught up in the cabals of these fanatics on certain occasions. Thus was born the famous Callas–Tebaldi "feud," which was perpetuated in newspapers around the world for a decade and is still mentioned in books.

It is possible to write at length about the subject, but for the moment I will limit myself to the first skirmishes in that "war," which took place during the season in Brazil in September 1951, three months before Maria made her official debut at La Scala. Callas's contract for that *tournée* stipulated eight performances of various operas in São Paulo and Rio de Janeiro. The company consisted of principal conductors Tullio Serafin and Antonino Votto, and young but famous singers: Maria Callas, Renata Tebaldi, Giuseppe di Stefano, Boris Christoff, Tito Gobbi, Fedora Barbieri, Gianni Poggi, Mirto Picchi, Nicola Rossi-Lemeni, Elena Nicolai, and others.

The visit was organized by a certain Barreto Pinto, well known in Brazil, a member of one of the five wealthiest families, and a person very active in the politics of that country. Physically, Barreto Pinto was almost repellent: small, toothless, with his head set down in his shoulders, always giving the impression of being dirty. When he was seated, he looked like a frog. He was the director of various theaters in Brazil and ran the opera seasons like a dictator, according to his moods. Programs underwent continuous changes. It was he who decided which operas were to be given and who should sing in them. At times he decided at the last minute, and no one dared contradict him.

One evening *La Traviata* was scheduled, and the conductor was to be Antonino Votto, who already had an international reputation. A couple of Votto's friends arrived shortly before the performance. As the theater was filled to capacity, Votto found places for them in the back of Pinto's box. When Pinto arrived and found his box occupied, he began to berate the interlopers and Maestro Votto. They tried to explain, but Pinto did not give them a chance to utter a word. Finally, Votto lost his temper and began to shout at him. Then the Brazilian said, "You're fired, get out of here!" He summoned a replacement, the Veronese Nino Gaioni, and told him, "Take your baton and go conduct." And Gaioni had to comply.

This was Barreto Pinto, whom everyone had to endure. It was not possible to obtain excellent artistic results under his system, but the Brazilian public loved opera and they did not have high expectations. They packed the theater for every performance.

Callas and Tebaldi sang the same roles, alternately. In that way the public had the opportunity to enjoy two extraordinary interpreters, completely different, who were often the object of heated, passionate arguments between their respective fans. One of Callas's most unequivocal supporters was Serafin's wife, Rakowska. Even though Serafin, wise and sensible, admired and felt a profound affection for Maria, who was artistically one of his creations, he also loved Tebaldi.* In his conversations with his wife he would point out the merits of each of them, but Rakowska, impulsive and not the least bit tactful, openly and passionately sided with Callas.

"They have different voices and different repertoires," Serafin would say to his wife. "It's absurd to compare them."

"That's true," she replied, "but there is one small difference: Maria can sing whatever she wants of Tebaldi's repertoire, while Tebaldi will never be able to do certain operas that Maria sings."

When the discussions became heated, almost to the point of being laughable, Rakowska would cut him short. Looking at her husband with pity, she would say: "It's useless talking to you. You don't know beans about singing." The genial Serafin would smile and remain silent.

These conversations became more spirited and frequent when Tebaldi and Callas alternated in *La Traviata.* Both earned clamorous successes each night. Serafin was content. One evening, while we were dining with some other artists after the performance, he said to his wife, "You see, they are two dissimilar voices, each capable of certain effects which excite the public."

"Don't be ridiculous," Rakowska replied. "If you were a man of integrity, you would have the courage to turn to the audience before each of Maria's performances and say, 'Ladies and gentlemen, this evening *La Traviata* will be sung in tune.' But, instead, you are a clown and would never find the nerve to do

* In 1979 Tebaldi told interviewer Lanfranco Rasponi: "Tullio Serafin, a genius when it came to voices, kept after me for years to learn *Norma,* and I stubbornly kept refusing. 'Take no engagements for a few months,' he often repeated, 'and study it with me. I know you can do it splendidly.' 'Callas is wonderful in this part,' was my answer, 'and why risk such a formidable assignment, for which one must have a very special type of voice, temperament and style?' "

this; thus, nobody knows which one is singing *La Traviata* the way it was written."

Her comments were rather tactless and a few of them were probably passed along to Tebaldi, who took it badly. For days afterwards, Maria and I noticed that Tebaldi was rather cold, in fact, almost hostile, but we did not pay it much mind. On September 14, however, on the occasion of a concert, Renata comported herself in a manner which left us perplexed. Barreto Pinto, as usual, had asked us at the last minute to participate in a benefit concert. The visiting singers complied, but it was mutually agreed that everyone would sing only one aria, and there would not be any encores whatsoever. If I remember correctly, it was Tebaldi who made the proposal, which was accepted unanimously.

The concert proceeded normally, according to the arrangement previously agreed upon, until Tebaldi sang. After offering the "Ave Maria" from *Otello*, Tebaldi, to the shouts of *bis* from the audience, instead of withdrawing from the stage, as did her colleagues, sang "La mamma morta" from *Andrea Chénier*, followed by the "Vissi d'arte" from *Tosca*. It was obvious that her "joke" had been carefully prearranged. The other singers, including my wife, were mortified and incensed.

During the dinner following the concert, there was an animated conversation between Tebaldi and Maria, and the topic of discussion was La Scala. Tebaldi was complaining that she was never at her best at La Scala, and sought in every imaginable way to turn Maria against the Milan theater.

The incident of the *Tosca* occurred around the end of September. Maria was still to do a few performances of this opera in Rio de Janeiro, while Tebaldi had gone on to São Paulo for *Andrea Chénier*. The first *Tosca* went very well. There were a few scattered dissenters, who were immediately shushed by the others. The day afterwards, however, the gossip around the theater was that Callas would be replaced by Tebaldi. One had even heard that Tebaldi, before leaving for São Paulo, had ordered a set of costumes made for *Tosca*. "That's silly chatter," Maria said, and she chose to ignore the talk.

The morning of the day she was scheduled for her second *Tosca*, Maria and I left the hotel, and passing in front of the theater, we stopped to look at Barreto Pinto's poster. "Let's see who will be singing with you this evening," I said. But we realized with astonishment that she was the only member of the cast who was changed. Incredulously, Maria read the broadsheet without her name. After a couple of moments of silence, she said, "Let's see Barreto Pinto."

Walking with the stride of a Valkyrie, she set out for the office of the superintendent. I had to scramble to keep up with her. Seeing her with her head up and walking with that military gait, I knew what to expect. Maria walked straight into Pinto's office without knocking. Inside were other singers, including, I believe, Elena Nicolai. Pinto was behind his desk. Maria asked him, "Listen here, why have you replaced me?"

"Because you were lousy the other night," he replied.

"Ah, in your opinion I was lousy?" she repeated in a rage. On his desk was a large bronze inkstand and paper holder. It weighed over twenty pounds. Maria picked it up and, holding it in the air, said, "Repeat what you just said, if you have the nerve, and I'll smash your skull."

She had fire in her eyes. Limitless strength seemed to emanate from her entire body. I had never seen her so furious. I rushed forward to restrain her. The other people present also intervened and managed to hold her, but only with difficulty. Barreto Pinto, terrified, had sunk down into his chair. Maria continued to revile him with the most abusive insults. When Pinto was certain we had managed to remove the inkstand from her grip, he said, "Now I am going to call the police and have you arrested for threatening me."

He should not have said that. Maria pushed us aside, and

threw herself on Pinto, striking him in the stomach with her knee. It could have been a fatal blow. Maria at that time weighed more than two hundred pounds, was twenty-eight years old, and had the power of a young bull. I heard Pinto emit a moan, and then I saw him close his eyes and double over. "Oh, my God, he's just breathed his last," I thought. Asking the others to look after the unfortunate man, I took Maria by the arm and we hurried back to our hotel.

The situation was serious. Barreto Pinto had many friends in the government and he could have had us arrested; no one would have been able to stop him. I was extremely worried. Maria, however, was now very calm. She walked about the room humming, totally pleased with what she had done. "Don't you think you overdid it?" I asked.

"I only regret not having broken his head," she said with a smile. "I don't like that man and I will never again consider singing in this country."

Immediately after noon, the hotel desk announced that there was a person asking to speak with us. "There we are," Maria said. "It's the police. Now be good, don't open your mouth, for goodness' sake. Let me do the talking."

I had the visitor come up. It was not a policeman, but rather a messenger from Pinto. In one envelope he had the money for Maria's fee, including the performances stipulated in her contract but which she had not yet sung; in another envelope were two plane tickets for our return to Italy. "The plane leaves in two hours," the envoy said. "Barreto Pinto has already reserved your places. In front of the hotel is a car ready to take you to the airport. Barreto asks if he must send along another one for your luggage."

"Certainly," said Maria.

"One will be here immediately," the man said.

We hurriedly packed our bags. Two hours later we left Brazil, never to return.

That incident was certainly provoked by the despotic and disagreeable character of Pinto, but I am convinced that if Maria had made that *tournée* without Tebaldi, it would have gone as smoothly as on the other occasions. Rivalry was evolving between these two great artists, provoking fierce animosity in the operatic world, at times with unexpected consequences. What happened in Brazil in September 1951 was only the beginning.

Chapter 13

The Conquest of La Scala

On December 7, 1951, Maria Callas opened La Scala's 1951–52 season as Elena in Verdi's *I Vespri Siciliani,* conducted by Victor de Sabata. It was a triumph. The newspapers reported that Maria's characterization was history-making. With that opera she began her collaboration with the Milan theater, an intense and glorious artistic relationship that was to continue for more than ten years, during which Maria sang a total of 181 performances of twenty-three diverse roles, offering the public her greatest interpretations and contributing more than a little to the international prestige of La Scala.

Much has been written about Maria's success at the theater, pointing out how La Scala had plucked her from provincial theaters and had sent her forth into the great world of opera. This launching was attributed primarily to the genius and foresight of Antonio Ghiringhelli, the vaunted superintendent of the theater. This version of the facts has little to do with reality. Maria conquered La Scala alone, establishing herself there through her art and her personality. "Ghiringhelli did not want to hear about me," Maria wrote in 1958. "Many people have told me that, including Ghiringhelli himself."

Antonio Ghiringhelli was the administrator of La Scala for twenty-six years, from 1945 until 1972, when he retired for reasons of health. He dedicated his life to La Scala. The period of his directorship was so glamorous that it is still referred to as the Ghiringhelli era. Ghiringhelli certainly did much for the Milan theater, having assumed leadership immediately after World War II, when La Scala was half-gutted from air raids. He supervised its reconstruction from the beginning and contributed to the increase of its prestige and supremacy in the operatic world until the very end of his regime. All this did happen, but, in my opinion, it is incorrect to assert that this was due solely to his efforts. The credit rests especially with the great artists whom he had at his disposal.

I was friendly with Ghiringhelli, and worked with him during the years when Maria sang at La Scala. We used the informal "you"; we dined together; I came to know him well. He was a cold, capable manipulator of talent and circumstances. His greatest gift was knowing which way the most propitious winds were blowing, and then hurling himself headlong in that direction. Maria wrote in 1958: "If Ghiringhelli needed you, he became the most devoted shoeshine boy. If he no longer had use for you, he ruthlessly tossed you aside without pity. If all the artists who passed through La Scala after the war had the courage to speak out, how many incredible things one would learn."

Maria's words are unflattering and critical, but they do capture Ghiringhelli to perfection. He tried to comport himself in this manner with Maria, without taking into account my wife's granite-like character. After resisting her for years, he sought to bring her into the fold through cajolery, but he walked into a brick wall. From the very first days of Maria's arrival at La Scala, tremendous battles were waged between my wife and Ghiringhelli, which the director invariably lost, and which cost him a great deal of money.

Ghiringhelli knew very little about music. A noted critic said that he was incapable of distinguishing a bass from a baritone. I do not believe he ever remained in his box for an entire opera. He came from a family of leather manufacturers. At La Scala, he continued to work with the mentality of a contractor. His cultural background was nonexistent. One evening, after one of Maria's performances at La Scala, Ghiringhelli came to our house with Giuseppe Saragat. Saragat admired our home, especially the paintings, and was taken by a large canvas that hung in the drawing room.

"That's a Titian," Saragat said, approaching to see it better.

"Yes, it is by Titian," I affirmed. "It depicts Actaeon [in Italian pronounced *Ateone*] as he discovers Diana and her servant girls at their bath."

Ghiringhelli, who had caught only the last part of the name, said, "I didn't know that Titian was interested in Pollione." The only cultural associations which came to him were those suggested by operatic roles or singers. Observing my painting by Hayez of a beautiful woman of the eighteenth century, he asked, "Is that a portrait of Maria Malibran?"

He governed La Scala like a dictator. His underlings feared him. They referred to him as Tenno* the Emperor. He had neither regard nor respect for those with whom he worked. In letters to Maria he would often write: "Maria, you and I are La Scala. The other people don't matter."

His admiration for Maria was not prompted by respect, but only by financial considerations. He was forced to open the doors of Scala to Maria only when he realized that opera-goers insisted on hearing this new and major drawing card. Then he did not hesitate to sacrifice the artists whom he had supported until that moment, replacing those who had been in part responsible for Maria's exclusion.

Their first formal meeting took place June 2, 1951, at the Teatro Comunale in Florence. Ghiringhelli arrived with an elaborate, detailed schedule, a long-range prospectus which he

* "Tenno," literally heavenly sovereign, was the official designation of the Emperor of Japan. *Mikado* is the more popular form of the word.

had worked out at his desk. He had decided to win Maria over to his side.

Our paths had crossed on other occasions. In October 1949, Maria and I, while passing through Milan, stopped to have dinner with Maestro Serafin at Biffi Scala. Ghiringhelli entered and greeted only Serafin. There was no love lost between the two men. Serafin had been artistic director of La Scala immediately after the rebuilding. I do not know why he resigned: Serafin never spoke of it, but I do know that he did not get along with Ghiringhelli. In fact, he would not conduct there even during the period when Maria was a member of the company. Serafin was not overly cordial to Ghiringhelli and on this particular evening he tried to be pleasant, in order to turn the conversation to the subject of Maria, but Ghiringhelli pretended not to understand. At one point Serafin asked, "Did you hear what a historic triumph we had in Argentina with *Norma*?"

It was a topic which did not find favor with Ghiringhelli. The previous season he had mounted a production of *Norma* at La Scala which turned out to be a disaster. He went through three sopranos and three tenors without managing to put together a decent performance.* Stung to the quick, Ghiringhelli replied: "To do *Norma* is not as difficult as you think. You do not believe that La Scala can do a sensational *Norma* whenever it pleases? As a matter of fact, I intend to present one that will make history."

"Ah, yes?" said Serafin. "And how do you plan to do that?" The conductor was physically an unimposing little man. He wore his hat tilted to one side, and had a nervous tic which gave him a strange mien. His comments were always brief but incisive. He looked up at Ghiringhelli with a skeptical half-smile.

* Meneghini is correct in stating there were three tenors (Battaglia, Tasso, and Breviario), but Maria Canaglia sang the role of Norma in all four performances.

"You doubt, perhaps, that La Scala, the greatest opera house in the world, is in a position to stage a brilliant *Norma*?" Ghiringhelli queried.

"Good Lord, I did not intend to imply that," Serafin replied. After a moment he added: "I am from Rottanova di Cavarzere, from the environs of Venice. We have a famous rice dish in our area—*risotto alla pilota*. Do you know what you need to make *risotto alla pilota*?"

"What do you need?" asked Ghiringhelli, who could not see what this dish had to do with *Norma*.

"The rice," Serafin answered dryly. Then, nodding toward Maria, he said, "Only this singer is worthy of doing *Norma* today."

Ghiringhelli, without looking in Callas's direction, said, "Next year I will show you just what kind of *Norma* La Scala can do." Ghiringhelli could not have known that he would not be able to do his "brilliant" *Norma* at La Scala until 1952, when he had to use the recipe suggested by Serafin.

In April 1950, Maria sang *Aïda* as a guest performer at La Scala, stepping in to replace Tebaldi. In an interview given a few years before his death, Ghiringhelli said that he was very close to Maria on that occasion and after the performance took her to dinner. This is not true. As I have stated, he did not wish to acknowledge her Scala debut.

In the summer of 1950, upon returning from her season in Mexico City, my wife decided to spend a few weeks resting at home. We went to the Arena and various restaurants in Verona, every evening, like two tourists.

One night our guest was Elvira de Hidalgo, Maria's first important teacher. After the performance we stopped for dinner in the Piazza Bra, at an outdoor restaurant usually patronized by musicians and opera fans. Maria was famous by this time and people continually came over to our table to pay their respects. That evening the visitors, who included reporters and photographers, were even more numerous because of De Hidalgo. At one point, two tables from us, Antonio Ghiringhelli sat down with some friends. He was aware immediately of the presence of Maria and De Hidalgo because of all the activity, but he pretended not to notice us. De Hidalgo said to Maria, "I knew that he was ill-bred, but not to this degree."

In 1951, at the age of twenty-eight, Maria was now a thoroughly established artist. Ghiringhelli began to realize that Callas was becoming an important piece of artistic property: one either had to meet her terms or run the risk of finding himself cut off from the mainstream of operatic activity. Ghiringhelli belatedly realized that in collaborating with Maria he would in turn enhance his own prestige. He therefore decided to drop certain artists whom he had backed up to that moment, and ran to prostrate himself before Maria. The word "prostrate" is no exaggeration, but accurately reflects the manner in which Ghiringhelli finally approached Callas.

The superintendent visited Maria after a performance of *Vespri* in Florence and proposed that she open the forthcoming 1951–52 season at La Scala with the same opera. He also offered her three other operas for the same *stagione: Norma, The Abduction from the Seraglio,* and *Don Carlo.* Even at that time, Maria was particularly famous for her Norma, and had virtually no rivals in the role. But she also knew the part of Violetta was ideal for her, and wanted to be heard at La Scala as the Verdi heroine. It is a role which, while it exerts fascination upon sopranos, is exceedingly difficult. To execute it truly well, the singer requires agility in three different voices. Even Maria's most illustrious rival, Renata Tebaldi, had not been a total success in her *Traviata* at La Scala. It was obvious that Callas wanted to establish her reputation at that theater specifically in that opera.

Ghiringhelli, who had championed Tebaldi until now, felt he could not offer Callas the same opera in which Renata had had difficulties. Maria reiterated she was most interested in doing it. She would even like to sing it as her second opera, in place of *Norma*. She made it clear that, without *La Traviata*, the offer to open the Scala season did not interest her much. When Ghiringhelli left, he indicated this might be possible. We parted with the understanding we would meet again a few days later in Verona.

This second appointment never materialized. On June 23 Ghiringhelli sent Maria this registered letter: "Dear Signora Callas, I would have so liked to have been able to see you in Verona, but a recent series of obligations, none of which can be deferred, makes this impossible. I had intended to visit you so that we might continue the discussion initiated in Florence. In the meantime, however, to avoid misunderstandings in the scheduling of forthcoming performances, I would like to confirm that La Scala would like to have you from November 20 to December 26 for five performances of *I Vespri Siciliani* (the first opera of the season); from January 3 to February 2 for five performances of *Norma*, and then February 10 for a sixth performance; from May 8 until the first of June for four performances of *Don Carlo*, or another opera in our repertory to be agreed upon by mutual accord, if it proves to be too difficult to assemble a suitable cast for *Don Carlo*.

"I ask you, dear signora, to give me definitive approval, so that I can instruct the administration to go ahead with the relevant contracts. I am pleased that at last, in this coming season, you will find it possible to realize in our theater all of the artistic rewards which you so deserve. I wish to extend to you and your esteemed husband my warmest greetings. Antonio Ghiringhelli."

Maria notified him that the dates indicated were fine, but she stated again that she wanted to sing *La Traviata*. In July we went to Mexico and in August to Brazil. We returned to Italy at the end of September.

On October 2, without even an advance telephone call,

Ghiringhelli came to Verona to see us. Around four in the afternoon Maria and I were in the drawing room. I was reading, and she was going over a score at the piano. The doorbell rang. Matilde, our maid, returned and said that three gentlemen wished to speak with Maria Callas. She handed us the visiting card of Ghiringhelli. He was accompanied by Luigi Oldani, administrator of La Scala, and a lawyer. They had come to settle the contract.

Ghiringhelli opened the conversation by speaking of money, but Maria interrupted him immediately. "I am pleased with your offer," she said. "Singing at La Scala has been one of my goals, but without *Traviata* I am not interested, at least for the coming season. So, before addressing other subjects, let's resolve the question of this opera."

Ghiringhelli was dumfounded. I believe it was probably the first time that a singer offered specific objections to a proposal which included the opening night of the Scala season. Maria's attitude must have seemed unthinkable to him, but it should have alerted him to the fact that this artist was not one who could be wheedled.

After a brief silence he continued his conversation, trying to convince Maria to drop the subject of *Traviata*. Then Oldani, who was more persuasive, intervened. Maria listened quietly, pleasantly. After the two had exhausted their store of explanations, pointing out that what they were offering was a unique opportunity, one which she was going to accept even without *Traviata*, Maria said: "Fine, since you are not able to do *La Traviata*, let's continue this conversation next year. I know you all have a lot to do in Milan, and I don't want you to lose valuable time on my account."

They stood up. The three men, confused and incredulous, followed her to the door. They said goodbye, almost stammering, and left. When we were alone, I said to Maria, "I think you made a mistake not seizing this opportunity." She replied, "I want to go to La Scala on my own terms." She sat down at the piano and continued to study.

Not ten minutes later, the bell rang again. It was Ghiringhelli with his two associates. "We have been thinking it over," the superintendent said, "and we feel it should be you who opens this season at our theater. We will do our best, therefore, to present *La Traviata* also." They sat down and returned to discussing the terms of the contract.

Maria went to Milan at the end of November for the first *Vespri* rehearsals. She was obsessed with the idea of doing *Traviata* and asked about it constantly. Ghiringhelli would only say that they were working to overcome difficulties.

All of Milanese society was present for the first *Vespri*. Fans and connoisseurs had even come from the United States and distant European cities. The success was tumultuous, the applause unreserved, the reviews were glowing. Franco Abbiati, the most respected of all the critics, wrote in *Il Corriere della Sera:* "The miraculous throat of Maria Meneghini Callas did not have to fear the demands of the opera, with the prodigious extension of her tones, their phosphorescent beauty, especially in the low and middle registers, and her technical agility which is more than rare, it is unique."

Maria's triumph was repeated every evening for the seven performances. She had become the new queen of La Scala. Ghiringhelli assumed that with this success Callas would be more than satisfied and would forget about the *Traviatas*, but he was mistaken. Around the end of the month she again broached the subject, receiving from the superintendent the usual evasive answers.

At the beginning of January 1952, shortly before we were to leave for Florence, where Maria was to do *I Puritani*, she said: "Ghiringhelli thinks he can give me the runaround with *Traviata*, but he will regret it. If he does not give me a conclusive

answer, I will not sing in La Scala's *Norma* in two weeks. Write
to him in these exact terms."

I immediately sent a registered letter to Ghiringhelli saying
that Maria wished to see him to "discuss the question of *Traviata,* a matter that, if not quickly resolved, could unquestionably
compromise all her scheduled performances for the rest of the
current season, because these performances are based on the
fundamental and mutual understanding that she would do *La
Traviata.*"

Reading that letter, Ghiringhelli must have realized the situation was deteriorating. Nevertheless, rather than acquiescing, he
tried to skirt the issue. On January 9 he sent this telegram to
Maria: "I am confirming that the rehearsals with orchestra for
Norma will commence Friday the eleventh, at two. Best wishes."

I responded with another telegram: "I am sorry that my registered letter of January 5 has remained unanswered. I am informing you that my wife will not be taking part in any performances
of *Norma.*"

Ghiringhelli became panicky. He quickly sent another telegram: "I assume my special delivery letter has already reached
you in Florence. I strongly urge that Signora Callas take part in
Norma, if only because it is stipulated in our contract. I reassert
that every matter involving Signora Callas will always be settled
in a spirit of genuine cordiality."

The special delivery letter to which Ghiringhelli referred in
his telegram was a delayed reply to my original letter. Because
of the usual ambiguity, his response led one to believe that he
intended to keep the promises he had made. For this reason
only, Maria decided to go to Milan.

January 13, we were in Ghiringhelli's office. Maria said to
him: "*Caro* Ghiringhelli, it is pointless to waste time chitchat-
ting. You promised to let me do *La Traviata,* and only for that
reason did I agree to sing in *Vespri.* This *Traviata,* however, is

still up in the air. I am not going to sing *Norma* unless you tell me when we will be doing *Traviata*."

"You are absolutely correct," Ghiringhelli said, as he began to make excuses, "but you must understand my position. La Scala has many problems. If one cannot produce *La Traviata*, there are good reasons."

"And what are these reasons? Give me one," she said, persisting.

"For example, the unavailability of Enzo Mascherini," Ghiringhelli proffered.

It was a ridiculous excuse. Presenting *La Traviata* does not hinge upon the baritone, and he could undoubtedly find a substitute for Mascherini. The conversation became increasingly more heated. Ghiringhelli, pushed to the ropes by Maria's insistent questioning, began to crumble. "It is useless to continue with this," he said. "We cannot give *La Traviata*."

"But then you have been deceiving me from the outset," Maria said, rising from her chair and advancing belligerently toward Ghiringhelli. "Even in October, when you met with us in our home, you knew you were not going to present this opera. You lied to me to get me to sing in your *Vespri*."

She was cold and contemptuous. Ghiringhelli was white as a sheet. "Calm down, be understanding," he kept repeating. "I made a mistake. Tell me what I should do to rectify the situation."

If I had let her speak, Maria probably would have said, "Goodbye, Ghiringhelli; you can sing *Norma* and the other operas yourself," thereby causing a scandal and hurting her career. The schedule was already posted, and after the réclame of the *Vespri*, there was great expectancy surrounding her appearances in the two others for which she was announced. I therefore quickly stepped in and said to Ghiringhelli, "Since the error rests with you, then you yourself should suggest some equitable way to make amends."

Turning to Maria, Ghiringhelli said, "I promise to mount for you next season a grand *Traviata* worthy of you. For the performances not given this year, I will, nevertheless, pay your regular fee." Opening his large book of blank checks, he began to compute the total amount for the four nonperformances of *Traviata*. As Maria's *cachet* at that time was 350,000 lire per performance, the sum came to a total of 1,400,000 lire.

As he started to make out the check, Ghiringhelli stopped suddenly and said: "No, I cannot do it this way. It would be illegal. La Scala cannot pay for performances which have not been given. I must resort to some subterfuge. The amount will be dispersed among the fees for the performances of the operas which are actually sung, prorated accordingly." It was in this manner that Ghiringhelli squandered money on a *Traviata* which he had promised but did not produce, in order to avoid running afoul of certain other people.

That afternoon Maria took part in the rehearsal for *Norma*. Three days later she appeared on stage as the Druid priestess and earned another unqualified success. This was followed by an equally triumphant *Abduction from the Seraglio* in April. Maria had conquered La Scala, and Ghiringhelli was vanquished.

Chapter 14

How We Brought Visconti to La Scala

The years 1952–53 were among the most intense in Maria Callas's career. Having established herself at La Scala, the most prestigious opera house in the world, she no longer had any obstacles to overcome to be the leading prima donna of opera. Now it was she who made the decisions, and selected the operas to be presented and the artists with whom she would be working. She demonstrated an infallible intuition and instinct. The credit for various celebrated productions at La Scala during her tenure there is in large part due to Maria Callas.

When she was approached about an opera that was to be mounted, she familiarized herself with all the other artists in the cast, and evaluated them with extraordinary competence. "This one is not suitable, for the following reasons," she would say, and her observations were always valid. When she inquired who the conductor would be, she used a phrase which she had picked up from Serafin. She would ask, "Who is beating time?"

One day at La Scala they were discussing who would be the conductor for an opera by Gluck. "He is a good conductor but he's not ideal for Gluck," she said of the choice made by the directors of La Scala.* The reviews later corroborated her opinion.

After fulfilling her Scala commitment for December 1951 and the first months of 1952, Maria went to Rome for a broadcast concert from RAI's studios, and then to Catania in March for a *Traviata* conducted by Francesco Molinari-Pradelli, with Nicola Filacuridi (Alfredo) and Enzo Mascherini (Germont). In April she returned to Milan for the Scala premiere of Mozart's *Abduction from the Seraglio,* under the direction of Jonel Perlea. Her co-stars included Salvatore Baccaloni (Osmin), Giacinto Prandelli (Belmonte), Petre Munteanu (Pedrillo), and Tatiana Menotti (Bionda). At the end of April, she was in Florence for Rossini's *Armida.*

The composer from Pesaro had written this opera for Naples's Teatro San Carlo in 1817. After the first performances, mounted with great success, *Armida* slipped into neglect, for impresarios were not able to find singers equal to its demands. Maria was enthusiastic about it. *Armida,* conducted by Serafin, opened the Florence May Festival. The other singers included Francesco Albanese, Mario Filippeschi, Alessandro Ziliani, Gianni Raimondi, Antonio Salvarezza, and Marco Stefanoni.

After Florence, Maria went to Rome for *I Puritani,* where she appeared again with tenor Giacomo Lauri-Volpi. She then left for her third season in Mexico City. She returned to Verona in July for the outdoor season, where she sang *La Gioconda* and *La Traviata.* In the fall she went to London for *Norma* at Covent Garden. This was her London debut. The Bellini opera was conducted by Vittorio Gui. Maria's colleagues included Mirto Picchi (Pollione), Ebe Stignani (Adalgisa), Giocomo Vaghi (Oroveso), and, in the small role of Clotilde, a new soprano

* Callas was probably referring to Nino Sanzogno, a specialist in twentieth-century music.

Joan Sutherland. Callas received a warm reception from both the English public and press.

In December 1952, Maria returned to Milan to open, for the second year, the opera season at La Scala. The work was Verdi's *Macbeth*, conducted by Victor de Sabata. Callas's colleagues included Enzo Mascherini (Macbeth), Gino Penno (Macduff), Italo Tajo (Banquo), and Ivo Vinco (Herald). She once again had a triumph. Franco Abbiati wrote in *La Corriere della Sera:* "In the lyrical passages Maria Meneghini Callas projected her voice with purity and moderation of accent. In the more emotional moments she continued to mold the phrases and hold in check the impetuosity of the part, as Verdi wished it."

Another reviewer, less enthusiastic about Maria's performance, voiced reservations. On the occasion of Maria's first *Macbeth*, *Unità*'s critic Rubens Tedeschi commented: "Signora Meneghini Callas alternately had satisfactory moments and others less so, as is her wont. She, in particular, did not find that expression of nobility without which one does not have a Lady Macbeth."

Teodoro Celli of the *Corriere Lombardo* was of a different mind, however: "Perhaps no other opera can be considered as tailor-made for Callas as *Macbeth*, for which Verdi turned down a soprano with a lovely voice in order to use another, Barbieri-Nini, who was a great actress capable of emitting 'diabolical' sounds (according to the adjective in one of Verdi's own letters). This should have been remembered by those two or three who, with prearranged whistles, tried to harass the singer after the great sleepwalking scene, thereby transforming what would have been enthusiastic applause into a triumphant, interminable ovation."

Immediately after the *Macbeth*, Maria sang *La Gioconda* at La Scala with Giuseppe di Stefano, Ebe Stignani, Carlo Tagliabue, and Italo Tajo, under the baton of Antonino Votto. This was followed by *La Traviata* in Venice and Rome, *Lucia* in

Florence, one additional *Gioconda* at La Scala, and, immediately after, at the same theater, *Il Trovatore* with Gino Penno (Manrico), Ebe Stignani (Azucena), Carlo Tagliabue (di Luna), and Giuseppe Modesti (Ferrando), again with conductor Antonino Votto.

Another important event in Callas's career was Cherubini's *Medea*, which she sang for the first time in Florence at the 1953 May Festival. This opera was suggested to Maria by Siciliani. Composed around 1797, *Medea* was quite popular in the nineteenth century, particularly in Germany. It was then almost totally forgotten. In fact, there had been only a single performance in Italy in this century (in 1909 at La Scala, with Ester Mazzoleni in the title role). Maria's success was even greater than that of the *Armida* of the previous year. The conductor was Maestro Gui, who was now very old. My wife was in the full splendor of her youth. She felt that great Greek tragedy so intensely that she had violent clashes during rehearsals with Gui over the proper interpretation of certain passages. But despite the wrangling, the outcome was most felicitous.

The press was unanimous in hailing Maria's extraordinary interpretation. Giuseppe Pugliese, *Il Gazzettino*: "Maria Callas has surmounted a challenge which today perhaps no other singer would even be able to attempt. Entrusted with a role ideally suited to her excellent gifts, she displayed a vocal generosity that was scarcely believable for its amplitude and resiliency."

Giulio Confalonieri, *La Patria*: "On stage, Maria Meneghini Callas was a marvelous interpreter because of her musical security, her understanding of the character, and the sheer intensity of her singing. Her voice, rather rebellious by normal standards, was perfectly suited to Cherubini's remarkable declamation."

Leonardo Pinzauti: "One can describe Maria Meneghini Callas as the heroine of the evening. With an artist of this magnitude there is no need to enumerate her gifts as a singer and an actress. It is enough to say that her musicality at certain moments was such to make one forget the voice itself, in order to transport the state of mind of the public to a loftier dramatic level of mythical power, such as that of the event being narrated."

Teodoro Celli, *Corriere Lombardo*: "The viability of *Medea* depends on the singer who has the tremendous burden of the title role. Yesterday evening Maria Meneghini Callas was Medea. She was astonishing. A great singer and a tragic actress of remarkable power, she brought to the sorceress a sinister quality of voice that was ferociously intense in the lower register, and terribly penetrating in the high register. But she also had tones that were heartrending for Medea the lover, and touching for Medea the mother. In short, she went beyond the notes, directly to the monumental character of the legend, and she handed it back with devotion and humble fidelity to the composer."

The continuing presence of Maria at La Scala had created tension and jealousy. Tebaldi felt that she had been pushed aside. Her fans protested. Ghiringhelli did not wish to antagonize anyone, and sought to please both prima donnas.

In the fall of 1953, Ghiringhelli visited us and said to Maria: "You have already opened La Scala two seasons in succession. Permit me to give the honor of opening night this year to Renata Tebaldi. Toscanini would like us to open with *La Wally* by Catalani, with whom, as a young man, he was friendly. 1954 is also the centenary of Catalani's birth and we wish to remember it with a staging of his masterpiece. You will sing the second opera of the season, Alessandro Scarlatti's *Mitridate*."

Maria's contract was signed October 28, just a little more than a month before opening night. The preparations continued amid the usual doubts, uncertainties, and contretemps. Ghiringhelli and his associates were dissatisfied with the projected repertory, which struck them as being too inconsequential. After *La Wally* and *Il Mitridate*, they planned to do *Rigoletto*—none of which would cause a stir or attract attention, especially in the press.

It suddenly occurred to someone to make a dramatic substitution. Remembering Maria's success with *Medea* in Florence, they decided to mount Cherubini's opera instead of Scarlatti's *Mitridate*. Ghiringhelli telephoned my wife and asked her if she would be interested in doing *Medea*. "It's fine with me," Maria replied. "But how will you manage to put together a cast and take care of everything else, with so little time left?" The most crucial point was to find a conductor, since this opera demands a maestro of great temperament. Vittorio Gui, who was familiar with the score from having conducted it in Florence, was unavailable. Victor de Sabata, who would certainly have been outstanding, was also busy. Ghiringhelli could not come up with the name of anyone he could rely on. It was then that Maria said: "A few nights ago I heard a concert broadcast over the radio. I don't know who was conducting, but I was thrilled by his work. I'm positive he would be ideal for *Medea*."

Ghiringhelli pursued the lead immediately. He was informed that the concert had been conducted by Leonard Bernstein, a young American who was almost unknown in Italy. Because he was unknown, Ghiringhelli did not want to engage him, but Maria was insistent. Ghiringhelli then sounded out the conductor by telephone. Bernstein told him he was unfamiliar with the opera and was therefore not interested in the assignment. "Let me talk to him," Maria said. I don't know what they discussed, because they were speaking in English, but I could tell that at one point they were talking about Rossini's *Armida*. By the end of the phone call, Bernstein had accepted.

With *Medea* making its bow on December 10, only three days after the official opening of the season with *La Wally*, starring Tebaldi, a competitive atmosphere arose around the two prima donnas. Comparisons were inevitable, and there were lively discussions as to which one had the greater triumph.

The evening of December 7, Maria and I were in Ghiringhelli's box, applauding Tebaldi, who sang truly well, even though the opera itself did not exactly set the stars spinning. Three nights later it was Maria's turn to dominate the stage, and I looked to see in which box Tebaldi was sitting. She was not with Ghiringhelli. At the conclusion of the first act, Maria had a tumultuous ovation. When the lights were raised, I noticed that in the box above Ghiringhelli's there was a woman, alone, who was preparing to leave the theater. I could not make out who she was. Curious, I walked over to the box. As I entered the loge I found myself face to face with Tebaldi, who seemed to be disconcerted at seeing me. I paid my respects, she said something, and left. Shortly after that, she went to the United States. She herself said in an interview that she had left La Scala because, after the arrival of Maria, she felt there was no longer a place for her in Milan, and that she preferred to sing in theaters offering her more opportunities.*

With the *Medea* at La Scala, Maria surpassed the success she had had in the same work in Florence. This production received international press coverage. From that moment, she became the uncontested star of the company. Everyone wanted to work with her. I have saved numerous letters from famous conductors who wrote inviting her to collaborate with them on various projects.

Celebrated stage directors also sought her out. One who had a genuine adoration for her was Luchino Visconti, who is now part of theatrical history and legend. There have been biographies written about him which do not do him justice and which are not entirely accurate. For instance, virtually all that has

---

* Between 1955 and 1972, she was to sing over 250 performances of fourteen roles with the Metropolitan Opera.

appeared in print about the rapport between Visconti and my wife is, for the most part, based on the writer's imagination or on gossip. No one denies the fact that Visconti was a great stage director who had unique insights in the world of opera. It is also possible that he was infatuated with Maria. But I deny categorically that Maria was in love with him, as is commonly stated. My wife admired Visconti's artistic talent, and for this reason she agreed to work with him, but she was never able to get along with him on a personal level. His ideas, life style, and especially his vulgar language, irritated her enormously.

Visconti's infatuation with Callas began in 1949 when Maria sang in *Parsifal* in Rome. Visconti, an ardent Wagnerite, went mainly to see the opera, but he was most impressed by the woman who was singing Kundry. I believe he sent Maria a congratulatory telegram. He made a mental note of my wife's name and from then on he went to hear her every time she sang in Rome. He also saw her in Rossini's *Il Turco in Italia,* in which Maria appeared at Rome's Teatro Eliseo in October 1950. Visconti was one of the financial backers for that production.

After Maria established herself at La Scala, Visconti intensified his courtship. Lengthy telegrams arrived punctually after each performance. His compliments were now followed by requests to work with her. These invitations began December 8, 1951, the day after her Scala debut in *Vespri*. He sent the following wire. "Most happy about your new triumph. All my warmest congratulations after having heard you with the greatest pleasure on the radio yesterday evening.* I hope to see you again very soon and be able to work with you at last."

If he was in the theater for her performances, he would stop by her dressing room to say hello. There were brief encounters of little importance, but they were frequent. One evening Maria

* This historic performance, combining the talents of Callas, Boris Christoff, Enzo Mascherini, and Victor de Sabata, is the only Callas broadcast from La Scala which does not seem to have been preserved in sound.

and I were at Rome's Hotel Quirinale; my mother was with us. Visconti arrived in the lobby with Anna Magnani and other friends. The actress was wearing a low-cut dress which revealed most of her bosom. My mother, a lady of another generation and very proper, was indignant. As Visconti started to introduce Magnani, my mother turned to me with a look of disgust and said, "How vulgar!" Her comment was overheard and this encounter quickly ended.

Visconti later became our friend. We began to see each other socially and we would use the informal "you." Maria respected his intelligence, but she could not abide his language. Visconti's conversations were always full of obscene words, coarse expressions, and scurrilous epithets. Maria frequently said to him, "When you talk that way, you turn my stomach." He would exonerate himself by saying: "People are fools. They don't understand anything. You have to be explicit."

When he was working, his language became even earthier, especially if his comments concerned women. This made Maria seethe. She would say to me, "If he dares apply one of those terms to me, I'll give him a slap that'll send his teeth flying." Perhaps Visconti read Maria's mind, for he never showed her the slightest lack of respect.

Ghiringhelli also did not care for Visconti. Despite all that has been published, I do not believe that Toscanini was enthusiastic about him. In fact, it does not appear to me that it was he who recommended Visconti to La Scala's administration. Much has been published about a projected *Falstaff* which Toscanini, at this point very old, wished to conduct at La Scala, and for which he had requested Visconti as stage director, but Visconti never made any mention of their collaboration to me, not even in his letters.*

* Luchino Visconti told Gerald Fitzgerald, for the book *Callas* (1974): "At that time the small theater—the Piccola Scala—was under construction. The plan was for Maestro [Toscanini] to inaugurate it with *Falstaff*, which

Visconti and La Scala

The only people who were truly concerned that Visconti should work at La Scala were Maria and myself. We often spoke of it to Ghiringhelli, who, perhaps tired of hearing us recommend Visconti, decided to use him. His first assignment was slated for the season of 1953–54. He was responsible for the mise en scène of the ballet *Mario and the Magician*, for which he wrote the scenario, based on a story by Thomas Mann. The music was composed by Visconti's brother-in-law, Franco Mannino. A few days before the premiere of the ballet, La Scala had presented a modern opera, *A Drive in the Country*, by Mario Peragallo, to a libretto by Alberto Moravia. In one scene an automobile was brought on stage, in which the two protagonists sang while they executed a striptease. The audience whistled loudly and booed, reportedly because of the automobile. The directors of La Scala knew that Visconti planned to use bicycles in the ballet *Mario and the Magician*, and they canceled the production so as not to incite the public further. Visconti took it very badly, but by May 1954 he asked me in a letter sent to Verona to continue to support his candidacy at La Scala.

May 1954

Dear Maria and dear Battista (I am also writing dear Battista because I know too well that Maria will not even read the letter, and if anyone answers, it will be Battista):

I shall close this overlong preamble and come to the point. Where are the two of you? I'm supposing you're in Verona and it's there that I'm sending these lines. Has Maria already sung [*La Forza del Destino*] in Ravenna? It went well? I can easily imagine the triumph Maria had there! I hope you are resting now, or do you have some other recordings? I seem to recall you

---

he wanted me to stage. Often I went to his home for lunch to discuss this, and one day he expressed the wish to watch one of my [*Vestale*] rehearsals. I was delighted and when he arrived I put him in the best box . . ."

have to sing Margherita [at the Verona Arena] in that tedious and ugly *Mefistofele*. I remember that only a year ago in Verona, though, we were enchanted by a marvelously Oriental *Aïda* with Maria. This year who knows where I will be during that period.

What news of La Scala? I will tell you mine. The ballet was withdrawn, as you know, and we were a little at loggerheads with that honorable collection of bunglers, but then everything was resolved as I had requested. And these gentlemen settled the matter both financially and artistically in a manner satisfactory to us. The incident still annoyed and disgusted me, though, because I do not think that they should be able to meddle with impunity or engage people if they do not have their thoughts together, especially if they are incapable of presenting a serious program worthy of respect.

In short, I came away from the experience somewhat resentful. You can easily imagine what I wanted to tell them. Even so, I didn't hesitate to speak my mind at every opportunity, and rather bluntly at that. Despite all this, Ghiringhelli did not let me go off before he made a lot of grand promises, which are, essentially: a production of *Norma* for the opening of the season; or (and this, however, was only a hope on their part, for I don't know on whose authority they mentioned it) the opening of the season with *Un Ballo in Maschera* conducted by Toscanini.

That's all! How much of it do you believe? I believe hardly any of it, at least right now. But here is the main reason for my letter. If I am to begin working at La Scala, be it with the one opera or the other, I would naturally like to begin with Maria. What do you know of these propositions? Do you know of this *Ballo*, and if Maria is to do it? And if they do decide on *Ballo*, then there would be no *Norma*. In that case, would Maria do *Sonnambula*? And with whom . . . Giulini? Would he want me as the director of *Sonnambula*, if ever? And when? And what of

Traviata? Is it just to disappear, or could it be worked in between March and April 1955? (Ideally, April, the period when I would be in Milan anyway with the theater company, for which the dates are now set.)

Please excuse this long series of questions, but these are points about which I would be happy to receive your ideas, of course if it is possible for you to give them to me. Right now I am settling my theater and film contracts, and I always keep in mind the prospect and possibility of working with Maria. To go to La Scala without Maria doesn't interest me a whit. Okay? Please respond to my letter, if convenient. In the meantime, I wish you a pleasant, restful summer and many beautiful and joyous things. As always, faithfully, Luchino.

From this letter it is evident we were Visconti's only link with La Scala. He also had an obsession about *Traviata*. He had seen Maria in the opera and from that moment his dream was to be able to direct her in it. He realized that with an artist such as Maria he would be able to create a masterpiece, a great work that would remain a milestone in the history of opera. But there were other directors of the same mind, including Franco Zeffirelli, who wrote various letters to Maria trying to persuade her to do *La Traviata*. Visconti was jealous. He feared that someone else would bring this project to fruition before him.

One day I wrote a letter to Visconti in which, among other things, I mentioned that Maria had had some offers from certain television producers to do *La Traviata*. I should never have done this. Visconti replied with a long letter in which he expressed the greatest concern over what I had told him, imagining the worst if the project were initiated.

June 19, 1954

Dear Battista, I thank you for your long letter so full of news and important details. I see that, notwithstanding the fact that we are in the vacation period, Maria continues to toil away without rest—recordings, recitals, etc. Viewing it subjectively, I am pleased because our record shops will soon be rich in stupendous Callas recordings (even *Pagliacci*, which I detest; but even Leoncavallo, when sung by Maria, becomes Wagner).

Who knows if I will be able to flee to Verona in August to hear *Aïda* again, which lingers in my mind as some enchanting memory from *A Thousand and One Nights*. Perhaps my trip to northern Italy for the screening of my film at the festival in Venice will be during the same period, and then I will also be able to hurry over to Verona for the opera.

I was dismayed by one piece of news which you passed along —that of the television offer. How can Maria allow herself to be seduced by a project so absurd and fraught with danger? I am not speaking from selfishness and envy. Envy, yes, in that Maria is doing *Traviata* with others (because I would certainly not want to work for television!). But have you ever seen a theatrical presentation on television? And even worse, an opera? My God! My God! In my opinion it is the ugliest, most disagreeable anti-artistic and counterproductive display one could possibly see now.

First of all, there are the current technical conditions of the medium of television: a horrible picture, the ugliest cinematographic results, and an unrelieved grayness without soul, without vitality. And let's not speak of the performances . . . performances where pseudo-directors, in their quest for boldness and originality, mix theater with cinema, drama with documentaries. Just imagine that stew! And what is worse, to obtain a wearisome liveliness of interpretation (which they consider clever) they move their cameras in a way to make you seasick.

Besides, do you know that they do opera with a pre-recorded sound track? The opera is sung first and recorded, after which the singers (I can see Maria!) go through the entire opera again (the acting part of it) just moving their lips! This is fine for dilettantes, but not for a true artist.

And Maria would offer her *Traviata* in such a barbaric and compromising fashion, an important and eagerly awaited *Traviata*, having it televised (what a beautiful word!!), badly photographed with close-ups that would be arranged, well lit, thought out, studied, with Violetta's stage business set a couple of days in advance, so that she looks like a goldfish in a bowl.

Please excuse this outburst, but I cannot see how Maria could hope to profit from such a risky venture. You can say to me, "Stick to your own business, and we'll tend to ours." But I, stubborn man that I am, persist with the true sentiments of a friend and admirer of Maria, discouraging her from undertaking such an enterprise which could only turn out to be unflattering to her as an artist.

The medium is still so rudimentary. You should at least wait for color, and let them employ the services of artists for their (so-called) spectacles only when they are not, as they are now, still in experimental stages. And then, what a *Traviata*! To allow that work, which should represent for Maria, in my opinion, her goal, her interpretive masterpiece, her artistic culmination, her Ninth Symphony, to go up in smoke! Tell me to go to hell, but I would not consider myself a friend if I did not offer my opinion. And now I hope and flatter myself to think that perhaps you will seriously consider my advice in theatrical matters. I will terminate this buttonholing about *Traviata* on television. I have been rather overbearing.

The rest of your letter tallies with what I wrote previously. With *Norma*, everything is . . . moving along, at least judging by what they've told me. *Ballo in Maschera* was a possibility, but it was specifically tied in with Toscanini. If Maria's engagements for *Sonnambula* and *Traviata* are projected for somewhere between March and April, perhaps it would be possible to combine them. I mentioned before that I would be able to find time during that period for one or the other. *Sonnambula* interests me enormously and the idea of Bernstein as conductor is most attractive. Maria in Bellini (and what Bellini *Sonnambula* is) has appealed to me for quite a long time (or *Norma*, of course; Maria, don't misinterpret what I'm saying!). *Traviata* is *Traviata*. Enough has already been said about that one.

Speak to Oldani about this, and then we'll see. There is still time, it's true. But, in my opinion, to think things through adequately, there is never sufficient time. Subject closed. You are right. That's how things are in Italy now. Have you seen *The Barber of Seville* on television? Pity. That would give you an idea. I had a stomach ache from it. Many warm greetings to Maria. And to you a cordial and friendly handshake. Luchino.

Visconti continued to write to us during the summer of 1954. The chief topic was always *Traviata* at La Scala. Eventually I was able to inform him that Ghiringhelli was disposed to his working there with Maria. Visconti was to begin with Spontini's *La Vestale* for the opening of the 1954–55 season, to be followed by *Sonnambula* and then the *Traviata*, which was so important to him. Visconti was pleased, but he was also concerned because no one at La Scala kept in touch with him personally. He feared that the promises made by way of Maria were a ploy to get him to stage the other operas. However, on the evening of December 7, 1954, Milan's opera season opened with Spontini's *La Vestale* with Maria Callas, directed by Luchino Visconti. Thus began the association between these two great personalities, a collaboration which yielded extraordinary artistic fruits, even if some of the critics at that time seemed to be unconvinced and perplexed.

Domestic

Archivio Meneghini

Callas in New York at age eleven, with her sister Jackie
and unknown friend

With her father, New York airport, 1956

With her mother and sister, Athens, 1938

Maria in June 1947 on the ship to Italy

With Meneghini before their marriage, Verona, 1948

At a restaurant in Venice, 1956

The Meneghinis at home in Milan, 1953

Backstage at La Scala during *Fedora*,
with Silvana Zanolli, May 1956

The Meneghinis at Lake Garda, probably summer 1955

Backstage at *I Puritani*,
Florence, 1952

Maria in Frankfurt, 1959

Convalescing at her hotel on tour

With her chauffeur, Paris, 1976

Chapter 15

Visconti and Callas

Maria and Visconti worked together on five operas at La Scala. After the *Vestale* of December 1954 came *La Sonnambula* and *La Traviata* in March and May of 1955, respectively; in the spring of 1957 they collaborated on Donizetti's *Anna Bolena* and Gluck's *Iphigenia in Tauris*. Each of these productions was an epoch-making event, cited in books on the history of music as examples of the ideal presentation of opera. The *Traviata* is especially remembered as the supreme masterpiece of the series.*

Working together and enjoying clamorous successes, Maria Callas and Luchino Visconti became "an item" among the chic set. Newspapers and illustrated magazines took an interest in them, writing a lot of rubbish and fiction. It was said they were in love, inseparable. It was also stated that, upon meeting Visconti, Maria began to dress elegantly, have rarefied tastes, wear superb jewels, admire fine art, and decorate her home with

---

* One of the most tantalizing of the projected Callas–Visconti collaborations for La Scala, which unfortunately never occurred, was a production of Zandonai's *Francesca da Rimini*, announced in the press for spring 1957. Callas was never to sing the role of Francesca, a part which should have been ideal for her at that period of her career, both vocally and temperamentally. When it finally reached the boards two years later, Callas was no longer a member of the company. The roles of Francesca and Paolo were sung by Magda Olivero and Mario Del Monaco; Carlo Maestrini was the stage director.

antique furniture. It was even published that Maria, one evening during a performance of *Traviata*, was so overcome by the desire to embrace Visconti that she left the theater during the second intermission wearing her costume and make-up, and joined the director, who was dining nearby at Biffi Scala. These are absurd statements, not one of which is accurate. These stories, which still find their way into print, are pure fabrications.

My wife and Visconti came to know each other better as they worked together. Visconti's admiration and affection increased. With Maria, however, the opposite occurred: the better she came to know Visconti, the more she avoided him. She always retained the greatest admiration for his keen mind and spirited artistic sense, but she never succeeded in being truly close to him or in fully appreciating him as a person. She absolutely did not want to see him outside their professional relationship. Maria had an unusual mentality when it came to evaluating things or people. She followed her instinct only, which often precluded her being objective. She could never associate with a person who possessed some trait that offended her sensibilities.

As a child she had suffered because her parents did not get along. She lived in fear of the dissolution of their marriage. Because of this she hated conjugal separations and divorces. She had a rigid, puritanical concept of matrimony. She could not accept, for any reason, that two married people could be unfaithful or even less that a legal separation would come to pass. Recalling how she herself behaved later in her relationship with me, leaving me to go off with Onassis, it seems impossible that she would have this concept of marriage, but that is exactly how she was.

My housekeeper, Emma Brutti, who was with me even when I was living with Maria, remembered the following incidents very clearly. When Maria learned that one of our friends had been unfaithful to his wife, from whom he was now separated, she no longer wished to see him. Once Emma admitted someone to the house who had often come to visit us and who now had left his wife. Maria made a scene and refused to speak with him. "Now that he has left his wife, he is no longer our friend," she declared.

Ingrid Bergman and my wife were good friends. One day we ran into Ingrid, who had just been separated from Roberto Rossellini. Ingrid greeted us with her usual warmth, while Maria was rather cool. Later, as we chatted, the subject of the recent separation came up. My wife reproached Bergman and said that from that moment they could no longer be friends in the way they once were.

Maria judged people who cultivated her friendship with this uncompromising, intransigent attitude. When someone told her that Visconti was a homosexual, she refused to believe it. But then Visconti himself mentioned it to her, for he did not make a secret of his sexual preference. From that moment, Maria began to dislike him. Her aversion was obvious, extreme, and at times almost maniacal. She said that she did not want him near her, that even his scent and breath annoyed her. Other than the times when they were working together, Maria never associated with Visconti, nor did she ever want him to come to our home. We went to his home in Via Salaria in Rome on only one occasion.* We went out together for dinner a few times.

Visconti adored Maria. He would telephone, he would write, but as far as she was concerned, it was as if all this never happened. It was I who responded to his letters and phone calls.

* According to William Weaver, Meneghini's "memory here was at fault: I remember meeting Callas and Meneghini at Visconti's on at least two occasions and my impression was that they were regular guests . . . If Maria loved [Visconti]—and she surely did, at least while they were working together—it was that kind of possessive friendship or devotion that often surrounds an electric, creative personality." Quoted from his review of the Italian edition of Meneghini's book in *Attenzione*, May 1982.

Visconti became resigned to it, and usually addressed his letters to me. Visconti was more my friend than Maria's, and I felt honored because I always had the greatest respect and admiration for his talent.

In rehearsal, Visconti found it difficult to make Maria accept his ideas. He was a tyrant with other artists, but when it came to my wife, he had to resign himself to giving in to her. He himself stated that he would allow her to work out her movements according to her own inspiration. It is not accurate to state, as many have, that Visconti "created" Maria Callas the actress. He *used* her well, suggesting certain ideas which improved her interpretations. This also applies to their famous *Traviata*. Maria always asserted that her Violetta was taught to her by Serafin, implying with this statement that in order to interpret an opera well, one must, above all, study the score. One day an entire afternoon was taken up by a search for a specific parasol for a scene in the Scala *Traviata*. Maria was furious. She could not tolerate losing so much time because of an object which, in her estimation, contributed nothing to Verdi's music.

She and the director squabbled over Violetta's death scene. He wanted Annina to help the sick Violetta get dressed in chic clothes, including a bonnet, for her lover's visit. Maria said this was absurd: a woman who is preparing to die does not think about hats. I had to intervene and convince Maria to do as Visconti asked, otherwise there would be trouble. For him, the hat in this scene was of fundamental importance. "All right," she said to me finally, "but I will do as I please when I'm on stage."

During the *prima*, they reached the portentous scene with the hat. Maria allowed Annina to place it on her head, as dictated by the director. Then, while she was singing, with an elegant gesture she tossed it in the corner. Visconti, who was watching the performance with me in Ghiringhelli's box, said, "Oh, my God, she lost her hat."

"You didn't notice that she threw it away intentionally," I said.

"Ah, that miserable woman, she will pay for this," he muttered. After the final curtain Visconti went backstage to voice his objections, but to no avail. In each performance of that production, Maria refused to sing the death scene wearing the hat. She would not allow anyone to impose an interpretation unsuited to her style. If she had agreed to do something of which she was not convinced, it would have turned out badly. She was totally sincere, both on stage and in life.

At the beginning of July 1955, Maria and I were in Rome, where she had just made some recordings and had also taken part in a studio broadcast [of *Norma* with Mario Del Monaco and Tullio Serafin]. She had fulfilled her engagements, and we were about to leave. Visconti knew we were in Rome and he sent a telegram saying he would like the pleasure of visiting with us. A few hours later he telephoned inviting us to dinner and asked what kind of food we were in the mood for. "I would very much like to have fish," I said.

"Then we'll go to Ostia with some of my friends," he replied.

I had an Alfa 2000 and for the long trips home I preferred to drive at night. We put our luggage in the car, because after dinner in Ostia, Maria and I planned to continue driving north. It was a lovely evening. Visconti was in wonderful spirits, and the fish was superb. Maria and I gorged ourselves so much that I was concerned. My wife suffered from car sickness and I feared that, after that abundant meal, the trip would be hell for her. Instead, it was I who was to become ill.

At first, everything went smoothly. We sped along through the night, illuminated by the moon. Suddenly I became aware of stomach cramps which became increasingly more severe. Around daybreak, the pain was unendurable. I realized I was no longer capable of driving. We had reached Siena, and I said to

Maria: "Let's stop here and go to a hotel and call a doctor."

I was limp as a rag. Perceiving how sick I was, Maria was very worried. We were treated very well at the hotel. They recognized my wife immediately. They telephoned for a doctor. Count Chigi Saracini, founder of the famous Accademia Chigiana, also came to the hotel. He was a great admirer of Maria's. Finding himself face to face with the famous soprano Maria Callas and Siena's distinguished count, the doctor panicked and did not know what to do. He said that he had to consult with a professor of medicine at the university, who was a specialist. They went to fetch him. He also seemed to be in a state of confusion. He examined me and concluded that I had an acute inflammation of the urinary tract. "It's necessary to get you to a hospital and operate immediately," he said.

Maria leaped forward like a tigress. "Operate? But on no account will I permit it. We're going to our doctor in Milan."

She telephoned to Verona and summoned our chauffeur. She then telephoned Visconti. She was furious with him. She blamed him for my illness—he, who had nothing to do with it whatsoever. She accused him of having made an attempt on my life. And when he, over the telephone, did not seem to be unduly concerned about my illness and did not offer to rush to Siena to be at my bedside, Maria was mortally offended and decided then and there never to see Visconti again. She told him this and put it in a letter.

Later, when I had recovered, Maria realized she had overreacted and she wrote to Luchino asking him to accept her apology. He responded, explaining why he did not come to Siena. "It was not possible for me to come to Siena," he wrote on July 22, 1955. "My contractual obligations kept me here in Rome. And then, consider the matter a little dispassionately: I should chuck everything here and race to Siena to do what? Even Battista would probably have been annoyed by this rather melodramatic gesture. One must consider things in their true perspective, dear Maria. A sense of proportion is a great yard-stick in life, including personal relationships. You yourself would have deemed my intervention excessive. So, your decision never to see me again after my, shall we say, abstention, was disproportionate to my . . . offense. Do you not agree? I am certain that you do, and I am happy that you have modified your harsh decision."

After that dinner in Ostia, Maria did not see Visconti again until the spring of 1957 when they combined their talents for Gluck's *Iphigenia in Tauris* and Donizetti's *Anna Bolena*. In the intervening two years, Visconti continued to write to me. He complained of never managing to see us. He would arrive in one place and find we had just left, or we would arrive somewhere shortly after he had departed. Sadly, he wrote: "It's destiny . . . it's fate." It was Maria, in fact, who did everything she could to avoid him.

Visconti spoke openly in his letters to us, discussing his projects and soliciting our conversation and friendship. I always answered his letters, and he appreciated this. In the summer of 1955 he wrote of his frustrations and disenchantment involving his film work. He had been awarded the Silver Ribbon and was very pleased, but it did not sit well with him when he learned he had to share the honor equally with two other film directors. "The satisfaction of receiving the Silver Ribbon has been com-promised somewhat by the hypocrisy [*tartuferia*] of the jury which assigned it also to Fellini and Leandro Castellani," he wrote. "Thus, there were three directors who won the same prize. The whole thing annoyed me and I didn't go to the pres-entation ceremony that evening. But I sent a telegram, cleverly worded so that it was gracious but also subtly tongue-in-cheek, which entertained those in the audience who knew what was going on. This evening, however, we are going (all us Ribbons) to visit the President of the Republic, who wishes to congratu-late us. What fun!"

In the same letter he spoke of Rossellini, who had directed Verdi's *Otello* at the Verona Arena that summer. The production, which starred Mario Del Monaco and was conducted by Antonino Votto, had not been a success. There had been dissension between Del Monaco and Rossellini. At the end of the second act of one performance, Del Monaco did not want to continue. Visconti, who never minced words, wrote in a letter to me: "Did you see that *Otello* business in Verona involving Rossellini, Del Monaco, and Votto? Rossellini is a fool, but so are those other two! What is unfortunate is that Rossellini, with his incompetence and superficiality, succeeds in debasing stage direction in opera."

Maria never answered Visconti's letters and he often made reference to that fact. On August 2, 1955, he wrote: "It is true when Manzoni said that 'one does not discuss the happy moments . . .' One sees that you are in a peaceful, happy period of rest and now you no longer respond to letters from distant friends."

Visconti's chief topics of discussion in his letters concerned his métier, which was the mainstream of his life, and specifically the *Traviata* that he staged with Maria, which he always considered his masterpiece. In August 1955 I informed him that EMI had decided to record *La Traviata* with Giuseppe di Stefano and a soprano other than Maria [Antonietta Stella]. The news infuriated him. He railed against La Scala, Di Stefano, and the recording company. After the triumph of the Scala *Traviata* in May, he viewed this as an unacceptable affront to Maria and himself.

"I am absolutely shocked," he wrote, "by the underhanded trick, certainly instigated by someone, that His Master's Voice would like to play on Maria. And I refuse to believe that La Scala did not have a hand in it. Apart from that, even more than bad faith or cowardliness, this could be a case of stupidity. One is never aware of the true extent of people's imbecility until you're hit over the head with it! Maria should respond incisively

(but one need not bother giving her that advice, isn't it so?).
The dirty trick seems to me to be obvious, offensive, inconsiderate, petty, lacking in gratitude, and more that cannot be set
down here.

"It's probably a shabby, underhanded trick on the part of Di
Stefano, who thinks that in this way he can avenge himself for
the ridiculous figure he made in the theater this past May.*
Maria has in her hands the cards and weapons to rebuff this
despicable attack, and she has only to draw upon them to spread
panic among the Scala ranks. And I do hope she will use these
weapons.

"It seems absurd to me that Ghiringhelli knows nothing of
this! Who knows? In short, it all appears so unclean and cow-
ardly to me that the whole thing stinks. To record *Traviata* with
someone other than Maria—if it were not such a serious matter,
one could die laughing. But, once again, from this episode
emerges the impression of prearranged hostility, organized
against Maria and against the entire *Traviata* of last May.
Against a performance which, in its totality, was a thorn in the
side of the mediocrities, the obtuse, the jealous, those who sense
and foresee the collapse of their comfortable world of intel-
lectual poverty, of routine, of mental sloth. Let Maria send them
all to hell! She should threaten not to sing at La Scala again,
threaten, if she can do it, to sing elsewhere. And then we will see
them all beshit themselves. Hurrah!"

In September 1955, Visconti returned to the subject of
Traviata because it seemed that La Scala did not want to offer it

---

* Giuseppe di Stefano was irritated by the length of Visconti's painstaking
rehearsals for the new production of *La Traviata* at La Scala. He began
showing up late for rehearsals or not at all. At the conclusion of the
opening-night performance, conductor Carlo Maria Giulini urged Callas,
during the course of the curtain calls, to take a solo bow. Di Stefano,
enraged, walked to his dressing room, changed, and left Milan. He was
never to work with Visconti again, though he did of course sing with Callas.

two years in a row, as they had promised. In December of the same year, he contacted us when he learned that the opera had been announced. "I will certainly come for *Traviata*," he wrote. "It was the only true satisfaction I derived from my association with La Scala. Just imagine my not coming! To have this *Traviata* seen again is for me a joy, not only because I believe in what I have done, but just to hear you sing it again and to see the critics have new bile attacks! What a delight!"

On August 13, 1956, Visconti wrote me a long letter, seven pages, which are very lovely. He remained alone in Rome while everyone else went off on vacation, and he spoke freely of his views on stage direction in opera and the reasons for his admiration of Maria's art. It is a lengthy letter, but one worth reading in its entirety, for it constitutes a valuable document, both artistic and human, from a great director.

Dear Battista, Gnam Penati forwarded your regards by telephone. This was shortly after I received your much appreciated letter. I know, therefore, that you are in good health, that Maria is busy at work, and that, fortunately, it is not sweltering in Milan as, on the contrary, it is here in Rome, where in the past few days we thought we were all going to cook like eggs in their shells.

Nevertheless, and despite the great heat of San Lorenzo (who did not finish up on a grid for nothing like a steak *alla fiorentina*, or those filets at Biffi Scala which Maria loves so much), I have decided not to budge and instead remain here to enjoy a little rest, shut up at home like a mole, or like a Christian in the catacombs. To go away . . . in order to go where? Where at this moment everyone, believing they have fled the city, gather *en masse* in a thousand places and thus re-create, without having intended to, the congestion of the city, which now, however, remains deserted, like an abandoned ship, like the *Andrea Doria* just before it sank. Perhaps right here in Rome one can take pleasure in isolation, a semblance of solitude, almost as if it were a vacation. It also allows one to "draw the oars into the boat," as the saying goes, to mentally sort out imminent projects, to focus on a program of work for the coming seasons. And that is exactly what I am doing.

You asked about La Scala. I had told you that, for the time being, they had proposed *Aïda* for the opening production of the season. After considering it for a month, I finally said no. I just could not bring myself to tackle such a problematic work without a compelling personal interest. Perhaps if I were to put myself on the line with this *Aïda* (with all the pointed rifles and submachine guns, which we both know), I would have done it only with the understanding that I could throw all conventions to the wind, and eradicate errors and bad taste. But, as always in Italy when one reexamines an opera, a text, conscientiously and with a sincere desire to clean it up, one courts a scandal. *A priori*, irrevocably.

A scandal is fine if the spectrum of the task assigned to you is of interest. If, in other words, it is worth the trouble to take the plunge. Now, this is the package I was offered: Votto, Antonietta Stella and Di Stefano!!! I really did not feel like expending one gram of mental energy on that troika. That is why I turned it down. And I am not the least bit remorseful. On the contrary, I am pleased. When it happens—if it happens—that La Scala comes forth with a combination of particular interest (as it was with Maria: an artist such as Maria in *Traviata*), then I will devote myself anew (and I believe not unworthily) to pursuing the task of *rethinking* Italian opera of the nineteenth century, of which it has great need.

And, let us imagine if it were to have been Maria in that *Aïda*. Then my outlook would have been different, not to mention my zeal for work and enthusiasm. Because, you see, *La Traviata* will remain (despite the Johnny-come-latelies and blockheads who say it cannot be salvaged), and it will remain because that certain rethinking is now an artistic fact, achieved through the art of a great actress such as Maria. And note what I say: all the *Traviatas* of the future, soon, but not immediately (because human arrogance is a fault eradicated only with difficulty), will contain a little of Maria's *Traviata*. Only a little, in the beginning. Then (when they feel that enough time has passed so as not to run the risk of direct comparisons) much. Then all of it.

Future Violettas will be influenced by Maria's Violetta. It is fatal in art when one *teaches* something to all the others. Maria *taught*. But does it seem to you that I should set out to teach or suggest something essential, or some improvement, to Stella? What could she ever do with it? What influence can it have on her? And that conceited Di Stefano. If I were to live to be a hundred, I would not waste a single minute of my time to suggest a single comma to him. His lack of professional seriousness of purpose galls me. He thinks he knows more about it than anyone. Good for him. He can do it himself. I don't lose anything at all by it, nor does he. He will have the same successes, of that I am certain. But my discourse is on another level. I speak of art, and not of vulgar, easily won approval, of ham acting, etc. All that does not interest me, nor will it ever.

For that reason I am grateful to Maria when she had you tell me, as in your last letter, that she recalls with nostalgia the great work we did together. And even if circumstances of work, of life, of our professions, have for now prevented the resumption of such a happy collaboration, I do not give up hope that this will again come to pass in the future. At any rate, I appreciate her having remembered it, for having *differentiated it* from the other productions of which she has been a part. And I assure her that I also recall my work with her with a sense of satisfaction, of artistic joy, of the loftiest pleasure, as has rarely been my good fortune to experience. These are precious, indelible memories.

You wrote that the Scala *Traviata* will be going to Vienna, but will be conducted by Herbert von Karajan. I am dismayed by your news. I thought of Giulini who, through so much love and dedication, personally contributed to the success of this production of *Traviata*. Does it not seem to you to be a great slight to this maestro—unfair and tactless? My affection for a serious, conscientious artist, so unjustly cast aside, can only deepen. Giulini is a noble, refined man and, as a conductor, dignified, scrupulous, enthusiastic. The matter displeases me very much because of him. I am as impervious to the whims of those at La Scala as I am to changes in the weather. One fine day they take someone who has served decently, give him a boot in the behind, and "good night." That is why, after all, I rely on them neither a lot nor a little. First and foremost, cards on the table and a clear understanding.

As the saying goes, he who speaks last speaks best. At the moment their faith in Karajan is boundless. Karajan at breakfast and lunch. We will soon have an Austrian Scala, as in 1848. And one day it will come to pass that the martial "Guerra, guerra" chorus from *Norma* will once again incite the upper galleries, just as it did during the Austrian domination.

I don't have any other news to relay. I was invited by the Teatro San Carlo to work there, but, as usual, nothing has come of it as yet. I am working on two productions for Paris for '57, both of which are close to my heart, as much for their importance as for the fact that they will open new horizons of work for me in Europe. More than ever, Italy is the land of the dead as far as film and theater are concerned, at least for now.

I will be leaving for Venice soon, after the fifteenth of this month, where I will be a member of the jury for the film festival. Ten straight days of watching films will manage to turn me away from cinematography forever. And then I will take up cultivating flowers. Tell Maria that if she will hire me as her gardener, I will come with the greatest pleasure. In that way I will at least hear her sing from an open window.

In September I will be at the lake with my sister Nane. Then I will come to visit and gossip with you two and I will drive you both crazy, isn't it so? Now, I'm afraid I have been sewing on a button [*i.e.*, buttonholing you] for a rather long time, and I'll leave you before I snap it off.

Please convey to Maria my affectionate and always devoted thoughts. And for you, a handshake. Luchino.

Chapter 16

Franco Zeffirelli

One of my wife's great fans was Marlene Dietrich, with whom we spent various evenings together in the United States. Elsa Maxwell, the well-known American journalist who was a staunch supporter of Renata Tebaldi for a while, decided to become Maria's inseparable friend after hearing her sing—too inseparable, for my taste. During the height of her fame, Maria was feted by royalty, heads of state, and celebrities from the world of letters and the performing arts. Italy's ex-king Umberto was one of her great admirers, and he made long, taxing trips to hear her in the theater. At the conclusion of the performances he would come to Maria's dressing room to congratulate her; at times he would be accompanied by his children, who were also enthusiastic about opera. In London, Maria was received by Queen Elizabeth at a performance. In Mexico, we were accorded honors normally reserved for heads of state.

As for her professional milieu, theater directors wanted to have a monopoly on her and made very advantageous offers. After her first triumphs at La Scala, Ghiringhelli began to write her little love notes: "My dear, good Maria, I am sending you a surfeit of hugs."—"Maria, you are truly the lioness. My heart is proud and bursting. What do you deserve, Maria?—all the happiness in the world. I embrace you."

Francesco Siciliani in Florence suffered from seeing her slip from his grasp as she became increasingly more involved with La Scala. He wrote: "Dear Maria, I will be 'nice,' as you say, and will no longer persist in pressuring you about your decision. I would not be sincere, however, if I did not tell you that this leaves a deep wake of sorrow and disappointment. Apart from considerations of a formal nature, whom do you hope to punish by this act? Certainly not him who will be able to see an economic justification for your absence! The only one who has been almost humiliated in this matter is myself. La Scala will be pleased by this (another organization which, behind a rather formal propriety toward you, was certainly never overjoyed by your successes) and, ultimately, other singers, critics and people in the music world who all envied and feared our collaborations."

The only enemies Maria had were among her colleagues, especially some of the better singers who felt themselves eclipsed when they appeared on the stage with Maria; they sought to avenge themselves by speaking maliciously about her. That my wife was submissive and had a sweet temperament is something no one will claim; but the little tales spread by her colleagues to slander her, tales which were subsequently picked up by the newspapers, were inventions.

Mario Del Monaco complained that Maria had kicked him in the shins to keep him from holding a high note; Di Stefano maintained that she wanted to take solo bows after her performances. He used this excuse, after the first night of Visconti's *Traviata* at La Scala, to refuse to participate in all later performances of this production. Denying these accusations, Maria wrote: "It is not true that I have tried to take solo curtain calls after my performances. On various occasions I myself have sent colleagues out alone, even when it normally was not permissible. For example, Di Stefano during the first night of the new *Lucia* at La Scala; Luigi Infantino during a performance of *Lucia* in Venice; Del Monaco in his last performance of *Andrea Chénier* at La Scala [before he left for his season in New York]. If these three colleagues are sincere, they can corroborate what I am saying."

Maria had a strong character and specific ideas about her vocation, and she often clashed with her co-workers and directors. The only director with whom she was always in agreement was Franco Zeffirelli. Maria respected him and enjoyed being in his company.

We made his acquaintance in 1950, when Maria sang in Rossini's *Il Turco in Italia* at Rome's Teatro Eliseo. The opera was presented by a society [the Associazione Anfiparnaso] which folded immediately afterwards, leaving various personnel unpaid. Not even Maria received all her money. Luchino Visconti was also involved in this bankrupt organization; I seem to recall that it was he who arranged for his friend and protégé Franco Zeffirelli to assist Gerardo Guerrieri, who was the stage director.

Zeffirelli was young and likable. He had almost a veneration for Maria, who said of him: "I like that fellow, all fire and nerves. He'll go far." A mutual esteem was to develop between Zeffirelli and my wife. Franco followed all her new endeavors and sent enthusiastic letters and telegrams. In addition to his intelligence and cleverness, Maria admired his humility. Visconti was grand: he always spoke of himself and made you aware of his presence and culture. Zeffirelli, on the other hand, was unpretentious, reserved, sweet, kindly. Maria enjoyed conversing with him because he spoke with deliberation and his language was "clean," in contrast with that of Visconti.

Zeffirelli's working relationship with my wife was somewhat hindered by Visconti, perhaps out of jealousy. Zeffirelli was a product of the school of Visconti, who taught him how to be an actor, designer, and director. Zeffirelli had already made a name for himself as a set and costume designer, working on productions which received unqualified praise from the critics. Now this young man from Tuscany was displaying the same flair for directing, and this annoyed his mentor. It may have been that Visconti feared Zeffirelli would become greater than himself, or perhaps there were other reasons; I do not intend to comment on these tangled matters, simply because I am ignorant of the details. The fact remains, though, that Zeffirelli had wonderful insights and ideas and wanted to work with Maria, but the opportunities to collaborate rarely presented themselves.

In April 1955, Zeffirelli directed Rossini's *Il Turco in Italia* at La Scala, with Maria in the leading soprano role of Fiorilla; Gianandrea Gavazzeni was the conductor. The other interpreters were Mariano Stabile, Cesare Valletti, Nicola Rossi-Lemeni, Franco Calabrese, Jolanda Gardino, and Angelo Mercuriali. The production was enthusiastically received.

This was during the concentrated period of Callas–Visconti productions. The Scala *Vestale* had been four months earlier, followed by *La Sonnambula* in March 1955, and then *La Traviata* two months later. Despite being so closely associated with Visconti, Maria was also enthusiastic about working with the younger director. On one occasion, when a difference of opinion arose between Visconti and my wife, followed by harsh words, Maria made a comparison in which she candidly expressed her preference for Franco's quiet, relaxed mode of working.

Maria's attitude did not sit well with Visconti. Easily offended, he decided to put his young protégé in his place. "A designer yes, director never," Visconti decreed, and he threatened to wage a ruthless battle against anyone who thought of assisting or siding with Zeffirelli. By the middle 1950's, Visconti was a god in the fields of theater and film. No one dared antagonize him intentionally. He was surrounded by an entourage of loafers, gossips, yes-men, and sycophants who distilled insinuations and slander in Milanese society, and manipulated opinion in the theater world. If they spread the word that Visconti was enthusiastic about a young actor or actress, a career was assured, but, conversely, a negative evaluation could be the kiss of death.

Franco Zeffirelli

In the summer of 1955, Franco Zeffirelli was blacklisted. The word from the Visconti clan was that the young director no longer existed, and woe to anyone who helped him or extended him credit. Maria was caught up in this disagreeable business because she had indirectly contributed to Zeffirelli's prestige when she appeared in his production of *Turco in Italia*.

At that time, Maria was very influential in her own right. Being Callas's friend in opera was at least as important as being in Visconti's good graces in the world of stage and film. It was imperative to divorce Zeffirelli from Maria's protection, and to this purpose Visconti's vicious friends began to circulate negative observations about Zeffirelli, attributing them to Maria.

These remarks reached Zeffirelli, who took it badly. He knew Maria very well, he was aware of her respect for him, and he had come to learn that she was incapable of lying. He could not understand how she could be so two-faced. He was especially perplexed because the comments had come from people worthy of the greatest respect.

After mulling over the situation, Zeffirelli had the courage to respond to this calumny. Instead of letting these people get the best of him, the good Tuscan decided to bring everything out in the open. He penned a long letter to my wife in which he expressed his concerns and asked for an explanation.

Dear Maria, . . . Let's come to the point of this letter. I want to assure you I am telling you all these things in absolute loyalty, and with all the friendship which I have always and sincerely felt for you. It is a question of some remarks which have reached me from various sources (normally I am not accustomed to collecting gossip) concerning a purported aversion you have for me. This situation has truly upset me, and since I do not intend, even for a moment, to give credence to what is being said, I think I should pass it along to you just as I heard it.

We have known each other for several years now, and you

know how much admiration and genuine affection I have always had for you. Even more so during the past few months when we worked together, at last, in a production that had such a fine success. We shared experiences which cement a friendship rather than weaken it, at least in my opinion. I recall with how much kindness you went to meet my father and sister after the opening night of *Turco*, even though you had a dressing room jammed with enthusiastic admirers. It was a gesture which touched me deeply, and that is how I will always remember you.

That is why these absurd statements anger me and I wish only to dispel them immediately. Or have I, perhaps, offended you in some way? I have often seen you irritated, even enraged, because of colleagues who have in some manner insulted or frustrated you, but it was always because of a very specific reason, even if, I must admit, I sometimes felt your reactions were disproportionate to the circumstances. But, however that may be, you have always accepted full responsibility—with your head back—in the face of your adversaries. "I cannot stand him," you would exclaim in rage. "It's him or me!" That's part of the Callas make-up, your strength, your fascination. But in this instance, nothing like that has happened . . .

My wife read this letter with indignation. She instructed me to respond to Franco reaffirming her admiration, friendship, and the high regard in which she held him. Zeffirelli immediately wrote another touching letter.

Dear Battista, you cannot imagine how happy your letter made me. I awaited it, day after day, with confidence and also with some anxiety. Now it has come, thank heaven, and I can breathe more easily. Now I ask myself, what kind of punishment is prescribed in the statute books for those who disseminate lies such as the one according to which Maria harbored this great dislike for me? Is it possible that one can make people pay for actions of this sort? Fortunately, there is a confidence and trust which exists between us; otherwise, just imagine, this situation could have worsened, irreparably, and would truly have resulted in enmity.

Now, however, my unhappiness is not totally at an end: I reproach myself for having listened too readily (even if I did not believe it) to these dishonest and injurious voices. I should have had more faith and a greater store of common sense. A considerable amount of time will have to pass before I am able to forgive myself for these doubts.

But, you see, I found myself defenseless in this atmosphere. The source of confusion is that someone speaks with you, tells you lies, and then goes away, smiling; and already the poison is in you. He speaks with a sincere regard for you and even enthusiasm, and in his heart he is only waiting for you to make a mistake, no matter how small, so that he can immediately tear you to pieces . . .

The discord between the two directors did not last very long. It was apparently dissipated one evening that winter during a rather acrimonious argument; the two ran into each other in front of Milan's Teatro Piccolo. Zeffirelli confronted Visconti and heatedly demanded some explanations. The older man, annoyed, replied with blistering insults. Things went from bad to worse, and some said that punches were exchanged. It was a purging quarrel. From that moment, they became even closer than they had previously been.

That March, Visconti accompanied Franco on a brief vacation in southern Italy, from which they sent us Easter greetings. Upon returning to Rome, Visconti wrote to Maria: "My Easter telegram worked its way up from Potenza. I had left with

Franco and Danilo for a brief excursion by car through lower Italy. I wanted to visit some cities with which I was yet unfamiliar, such as Matera, Altamura, etc. Passing by Potenza, I took time out to send some Easter greetings to friends so that they would arrive on time. The little automobile trip was pleasant and we returned to Rome Monday evening of the holiday."

That summer Visconti decided to take another vacation with Franco. He had been invited to Madrid by Lucia Bosé for the baptism of her son Miguel. Zeffirelli was in Holland staging a *Falstaff* conducted by Carlo Maria Giulini. Visconti left from Rome with his friend Gnam Penati, and they picked up Zeffirelli. Then, in leisurely tourist fashion, they proceeded on to Madrid.

They sent postcards or letters to Maria from every city they visited. Zeffirelli wrote from Madrid, July 15, 1956: "Dear Maria, this most beautiful trip through Spain with Luchino and Gnam is more protracted than I had anticipated . . . The pretext of our trip was, as you know, the baptism of Lucia's son, which was last Thursday. A beautiful, memorable day. We visited Toledo yesterday and today and we even went to a bullfight. Tomorrow we're heading toward Andalusia, and I'm holding my breath in anticipation. The specter of *Carmen* hovers there . . . Luchino and I talk about you often. Are your ears burning? While driving, we always hope to repeat that electrifying experience of last year when, during a violent storm in the north of France one night, the radio bestowed on us your broadcast of *Norma*."

Visconti wrote to Maria upon returning to Rome: "Spain is a country of mystery and of an extraordinary fascination that would please you enormously. I believe it is the most fantastic country I've seen and I'm very happy to have been there. Moslem and Arab blood courses through the veins of the Spanish like some precious enrichment which over the centuries has altered and beautified the race. It is a little as with you—that hint of exoticism which adds to your temperament as an artist and woman so much mystery and strength . . ."

In August 1956, Zeffirelli wrote a rather curious note to my wife: "Dear Maria, yesterday evening Marlene Dietrich, one of your rabid admirers, spoke constantly of you. She says that in American hospitals they play your records continuously because they have discovered that your voice helps those who are ill, giving them confidence, calming them, and helping them to recover from what ails them. That is not surprising—we have known that for quite a while. La Dietrich also told me that she reserved her tickets for your Metropolitan Opera debut over seven months ago, and she managed to do that only because she knows Rudolf Bing very well. It is obvious that that evening you will not have a triumph but an apotheosis."

Zeffirelli, like Visconti, had an obsession about doing *La Traviata* with Maria. Franco was convinced that no other soprano in the world could render Verdi's masterpiece as well as she, but he did not long to direct it in a theater, for that had already been done magisterially by Visconti. He dreamed of a filmed version of *La Traviata.*

One day in Dallas he spoke with us about this project for three hours. He had already secured the financial backing and organized a corporation. On the musical side, the sound track would be recorded by the London Philharmonic under the baton of Victor de Sabata. For textual and musical advice, he was considering Susi Cecchi d'Amico and Fedele d'Amico. Lila de Nobili [designer of the Scala *Traviata*] was his choice for visual effects and color consultant; for the photography, Giuseppe Rotunno. He had even scheduled a period of time needed for the filming.

In his letters and whenever he ran into Maria, Franco continued to speak of this project. Maria was always indecisive. He resorted to every conceivable argument to realize his goal, as evidenced by this letter, written from Rome on June 26, 1958:

Dear Maria, I did not wish to upset you during these times by speaking of the film.* I do not know if I have done it well or badly: however that may be, it was impossible to do otherwise given my inherent reluctance to do what all other directors do, in general, and that is to lay siege to the stars whom they desire to interest in their business projects. You know what I have on my mind and what I wish to do. And you know that I have too much affection and respect for you to propose undertakings which are not absolutely worthy of you.

You must believe that I understand all the reasons for your uncertainty and caution. I know that you are inundated with offers and that you painstakingly examine them because of the responsibility which you feel toward your work. I also understand that nothing is ever sufficiently enticing for you, nothing can ever entirely satisfy you. And this is not because you are disenchanted or difficult to please, as one might superficially surmise, but because in knowing you a little I understand that each new professional engagement represents for you, more than the others, a herculean creative effort. It is understandable that a new experience, as the cinema is for you (new and full of unknowns), puts you in a position of being wary, even if it basically appeals to you. Can you imagine that I do not fully understand this!?

Nevertheless, I feel that our project of filming *Traviata* is a very serious undertaking and it is for this reason I have labored such a long time so that it might become a reality.

Personally (but perhaps this is only my problem), I believe

* In 1958 the tension was so great between Callas and Antonio Ghiringhelli that, in May of that year, Callas formally announced her departure from La Scala. When Zeffirelli wrote this letter, Callas was completing a triumphant series of *Traviatas* at London's Royal Opera House.

that for the rest of my days I will reproach myself if we do not succeed in capturing now, on three thousand meters of film, your *Traviata*! Because the justification for the existence of this film—and I will never tire of reminding myself—is born from this moral exigency: to have a living and perfect documentation of one of your greatest interpretations, a documentation of the spectrum of your possibilities as a great artist, in the years of your splendor as a woman.

I want this film to go around the world, to distant or almost forgotten places, from the Congo to Patagonia, so that everyone can see it, and so that tomorrow (when we are no longer here) you will remain and generations to come will have what neither Eleanora Duse nor Sarah Bernhardt was able to leave—the preservation on film of this remarkable creature with which you have shaken, moved, ennobled, and enraptured theater audiences and individuals in this afflicted half of the twentieth century!

Dear Maria, I do not know if you need to see me and talk this over with me before making your decision. As I have said, I detest badgering you, but I am more than prepared to join you at any sign from you. And if you have any reservations about meeting, please tell me what they are, with that familial frankness which is one of the most endearing sides of your nature. I am in Rome during this period and I do not have any obligations calling me away. It is pointless to tell you how anxiously I await your final decision. An affectionate embrace for you and Battista from Franco.

Despite the alluring promises and entreaties, Maria never decided to accept Zeffirelli's proposal. In my opinion, she made a mistake. I am certain that together with Franco she would have achieved something extraordinary, and far superior to that cinematographic experience [*Medea*] which she undertook years later with Pier Paolo Pasolini.

Chapter 17

The Strange Story of
Maria's Weight Loss

When Maria made her formal debut at La Scala in December 1951 she weighed 210 pounds; three years later, when she opened the 1954–55 season, she had dropped to 144 pounds. Her physique had undergone a drastic change which in turn influenced her entire way of life. She seemed to be another woman with a different personality. One could say that this change was fundamental for Maria Callas's life and for her artistic activity.

Her shedding of all those pounds made operatic history. From a kind of clumsy, encumbered whale, Maria was transformed into an elegant woman with the figure of a model. Rapid weight losses generally leave a person's skin loose and flabby. Maria, however, had reduced without any complications. Her skin remained taut, smooth, and glowing.

A few months afterwards, our doctor prescribed a series of vitamin injections for my wife, and Maria asked our housekeeper Emma to give them to her. Emma was concerned, fearing she would do it badly. As she said later, she thought that Maria's buttocks would be too sensitive for the needle because of the change. Maria insisted and Emma had to give her the shots. After the first injection, our housekeeper said to me in amazement, "It's incredible, your wife has the firm, little backside of a young girl."

Maria's transformation was discussed in the newspapers and fashion magazines, and she was interviewed by doctors and dietitians. In the middle 1950's, especially among women, Maria was more famous for her mysterious weight loss than for her singing. Every day she received dozens of letters from women begging her to reveal her secret.

Clinics and firms that manufactured various products offered her astronomical sums for an exclusive patent on "the Callas formula." Not even I, who lived with her day and night, managed to discover precisely how she did it. The newspapers invented theories and absurd hypotheses. It was written that in her desperate desire to have a perfect figure, Callas underwent terrible fasts, brutal diets, secret therapy. Someone went so far as to write that she visited a famous doctor in Switzerland who advised her to ingest a tapeworm. Maria agreed, drinking the "slimming" parasite in a glass of champagne. These are examples of the most ridiculous stories.

My wife was always tormented by problems involving her physical appearance. She was a proud, intelligent woman who loved beautiful and elegant things. To see herself condemned to having a heavy physique which precluded her wearing lovely clothes or enjoying in full her youth and the fame that went along with her career was a very sad thing for her. She tried every imaginable diet, but without ever obtaining appreciable results.

When I first met Maria, her weight was a little over two hundred pounds. Because of her size, she had poor circulation, especially in her legs. If she had to remain standing on her feet for a few hours, her ankles would swell enormously. She was also plagued by a variety of skin problems. I was concerned and had her visit different specialists immediately. I was not particularly worried about her plumpness; Maria had a very lovely face and I find fleshy women attractive. I was worried, however, about the swelling of the legs, the poor skin condition, and all the other complications related to her excessive weight.

Upon the advice of Elena Rakowska, we went to a famous doctor, Professor Coppa, who was recommended to us as a miracle worker for problems of this kind. After thoroughly examining Maria, Coppa said: "You are healthy. You do not have any disorder and therefore do not need curing." Then he added, smiling: "If you are sick, it is in your head. You artists are all a little crazy. You are more of an artist than the others, so you can be a little crazier than the others."

The truth of the matter was that many of the doctors were afraid to prescribe medicine, or advise Maria to diet, because they did not know what the consequences would be for her voice. There may have been certain medicines which would have yielded results, but none of the specialists wished to experiment on such a famous singer. As my wife's reputation for her artistry grew, the problem of her obesity became increasingly more pressing. She was featured more often in the newspapers, meeting important people, being invited to receptions, mingling with elegant women, and she often felt ill at ease.

I gave her jewelry and urged her to buy some beautiful clothes, but with limited success. I often accompanied her to the boutiques. She would pause and admire certain ensembles with feminine curiosity, but she would walk away unhappy and frustrated, believing that they were inappropriate for her. She always dressed modestly, in dark colors which made her look older than she was, and she resisted having herself photographed. When she traveled she would carry her scale in her luggage because she was afraid either that one would not be available in the hotel or that it would not be accurate.

At the end of 1953, her weight plummeted unexpectedly. We

were in Milan, staying at the Grand Hotel. Our room was close to that in which Verdi had passed away. One evening I went to La Scala to see a performance which interested me. I rarely went out alone, and that was one of the very few exceptions.

I was sitting in the first row. About thirty minutes into the performance, an usher came to me and said: "Commendatore, your wife telephoned. She said that you must return to the hotel immediately." It was not unusual for my wife to try to locate me when I went out; she was always doing it, often for the silliest reasons. Sometimes it would concern something to eat. She would telephone and say, "They gave me this and I want to share it with you." Other times she would simply say, "I want you here with me, come back right away." They were almost childish actions, but I understood her well and would hurry back.

That evening, the "urgent" part of the message worried me. My mother, who lived in Verona and was very old, was sick at the time. I thought that Maria might have had a telephone call from Verona concerning my mother. Therefore, before leaving La Scala, I telephoned the hotel, asking the main switchboard operator if my wife had received a telephone call from Verona.

"No, the signora has not spoken with anyone, but she's very upset and she's driving everyone crazy," the operator informed me.

"Please connect me with her room."

Maria was indeed in a highly excitable state. "What? You haven't left the theater yet?" she shouted. "You must not leave me alone. Battista, Battista, please come immediately, I've killed it!"

"What?" I asked.

"Come, come, do it quickly," she said, and hung up the phone.

At that point I found myself in a tragicomic situation which was stupid in one sense but which caused me to pass a harrowing quarter of an hour. Maria's remark "I killed it" frightened me and triggered my imagination. Maria had an impulsive nature. In a moment of rage she was capable of irreparable actions.

An incident that had happened when we were in Brazil came to my mind. One morning I had gone out to buy the newspaper, and Maria, who was alone in the room, had her breakfast brought up. The waiter, finding her in a dressing gown that was perhaps a little revealing, tried to touch her breasts. Maria became as enraged as a wild animal. She grabbed the waiter, opened the door, and flung him through it with such force that the poor miscreant slammed into the knob of the outer door and gashed his head. It was necessary to have him taken to the hospital. The police came, there were questions and much unpleasantness, and we decided to change hotels.

The memory of this episode made me fear the worst.* With my heart pounding, I left La Scala at a gallop, entered the hotel, and raced up the stairs. I listened for a moment outside the door. Not a sound. I entered. Maria walked out of the bathroom. She was wearing a blue dressing gown. "Battista, I killed it," she said.

"What have you killed?" I asked, feeling myself become dizzy. She saw what a state I was in and burst out laughing. It was a rather indelicate matter. While she was bathing, she had removed a rather long section of a tapeworm and had killed it. She was distraught.

---

* Steven Linakis in his biography *Diva* (1980) gives another vivid example of Callas's volatile temper. When she returned to New York after her years in Athens, Callas moved in with her father and his housekeeper-mistress, whom Callas openly detested. "One night, just after a Sunday dinner," Linakis recalled, "Maria was accompanying herself at the piano and Alexandria went around holding her ears, saying that all the noise was shattering her eardrums. Maria . . . got up from the piano, still singing, took a heavy oval spaghetti platter . . . hit her high note, and without any pause whatsoever, brought the big platter right down on Alexandria's head, shattering the dish . . ."

"Don't worry," I reassured her. "It's a very common parasite, especially among people who eat uncooked meat, the way you do." We telephoned our doctor in Milan, Gerardo de Marco, who confirmed what I had told her. He added that it was necessary to eradicate the tapeworm totally and he prescribed some medicine. In a couple of days Maria had rid herself of it.

It was assumed that this incident was closed and forgotten, but during the next few weeks Maria sensed that something within her was changing at a startling rate. Her life proceeded as before, but she felt like an entirely different human being. The various troubles which regularly tormented her simply disappeared. She was more agile, more unconstrained, and, miracle of miracles, in one week she lost over six pounds. What was the reason for all of this? With the help of the doctor we arrived at the conclusion that the change was due to the expelling of the tapeworm. While in the majority of people this parasite causes a drop in body weight, in Maria it was having the opposite effect. Once she was free of it, the pounds began to melt away.

Her nutritional regime remained the same: no bread or pasta, grilled meats or steak tartar, great quantities of unseasoned vegetables, little water, and only a drop of wine. She continued to have massages daily. For years this routine had not been particularly beneficial, but now it worked wonders.

Even Maria's temperament changed: she became calmer and more cheerful. Her stamina increased and she no longer felt weak or drowsy. She began to work at a greater pace than previously.

I personally felt this weight loss was excessive. She went from ninety kilos to sixty in one year. "You are no longer my other half," I would say, "but my other quarter," and she would laugh. Eventually, though, I told her I was worried that she would lose too much weight. She became furious and we had a battle royal.

Now that she was slim, Maria began to wear jewelry, furs, and elegant clothes. She felt she had earned the right to wear them.

She had herself dressed by the best couturiers and wore only original creations. I had the custom of marking the first performance of each important role by presenting her with jewels, to which I gave the name of the opera. On the occasion of her first *Lucia* I gave her a set of diamonds, consisting of a necklace, bracelet, and ring; for *La Traviata* it was a set of emeralds—a necklace, bracelet, ring, and earrings; for *Iphigenia in Tauris*, a ring with a *navette* diamond, so named because of the cut of the stone, which gave it the appearance of the hull of a ship; for *Medea* a set of rubies; on other occasions I gave her a pair of clip-fastened diamond earrings which could be worn together or separately; then a ring with an emerald of singular beauty—it is said that only the Queen of England had a similar one.

When Maria began to appear regularly at La Scala, we stayed at a hotel in Milan, but often, at the end of the performance, she would say: "Battista, please, let's sleep in our own bed, in our house," and we would drive to Verona. These trips were wearisome and dangerous, especially with the fog in the winter. I decided to take a house in Milan. I sold our home in Verona and bought one at 44 Via Buonarroti. It was a little villa with large trees in the front and a garden in back. I had it furnished by the designer Tamaglini, who, not surprisingly, found himself following Maria's instructions. From Verona we brought the piano and paintings. My wife wanted the sixteenth-century Madonnina by Caroto in the bedroom. On her dressing table she placed the little oil by Cignaroli, which I had given her the day we met and which she considered her "mascot." Once, when she was in Vienna for some performances of *Lucia*, she realized she had left her little painting behind, and she felt she could not sing without it. It was necessary to telephone a friend in Milan and importune her to go to our home and then fly to Vienna with Maria's talisman.

Life between Maria and me was blissful in our Milan home. I

cannot believe that two people ever lived together so serenely. Maria would not allow me to leave her alone. I always woke up early and I could go for the newspaper, but I was expected back by nine because, even before the maid brought her coffee, she wanted to see me. After her "good morning," she would ask: "How are you today? What should I wear? Do you have any plans for us to go somewhere?" I would run down the schedule for the day and she would select something suitable for the appointments. It was I who always helped her dress. I brushed her hair and even did her pedicures.

We ate lunch at one. Maria never sat down at the table before I was seated. She would say: "Battista is the master of the house and one must show him great respect." She had a rigid and traditional concept of family life. She wished to live honoring old-fashioned values, which she respected intransigently. As she was disciplined and meticulous in her musical preparation, so it was with her domestic habits.

We had several servants in Milan: housekeeper, cook, maid, gardener. In order to maintain "perfect harmony" and "perfect order" (to use her expressions), Maria set down a list of rules which they all had to observe scrupulously. It is interesting to read through these eleven points because one gains an insight into her way of thinking and her character:

RULES OF THE HOUSE

1. The utmost respect for each other.
2. Absolute cleanliness *always*, and without excuses from anyone.
3. Everyone, including the housekeeper, will wash and iron their own garments, especially intimate items.
4. Uniforms will be washed and ironed and kept in perfect condition by the maid. The staff will try to keep them as clean as possible and shall never appear in a soiled uniform.
5. Before entering any room, even if it is presumed empty, it is necessary to knock and ask permission to enter.

6. One must address the master and mistress of the house with utmost respect and never with annoyance. Voices must never be raised for any reason.

7. When speaking with the master and mistress of the house, I insist upon exaggerated courtesy and maximum respect when referring to friends of the family. Never, for any reason, should one lose patience or use only the first name of a friend or acquaintance of the house.

8. When you are summoned by us, you will come immediately, and always perfectly dressed.

9. One will never say no to what has been asked, and no more of that "Yes, sir" "Yes, ma'am" nonsense.

10. Chores will be done well, thoroughly, and quietly, without exchanges of ideas or gossip, or comments of any kind.

11. Everyone will do his own work and whoever shirks his duties will be reported to the master and mistress of the house by the others.

Maria, as one can see, insisted upon an adherence to Prussian guidelines, but contrary to what one might think, the servants always got along so well with her that we had very little turnover in staff. Along with this rigid sense of propriety, Maria also had wonderful human qualities and she knew how to make herself loved.

Chapter 18

Callas Disagrees with the Pope

By the beginning of 1954, a few months after she had rid herself of the tapeworm, Maria had already lost about twenty kilos, or forty-five pounds. Some friends and relatives spoke of it with concern, fearing she was the victim of some bizarre malady. But seeing that Maria continued to be in good health—as a matter of fact, she felt much better than when she was heavy—we began to consider the change providential.

Journalists were among the first to notice the loss of weight, and the news began to circulate. There were also those who hoped to exploit it for publicity purposes. A story was trumped up that absolutely infuriated Maria and gave impetus to legal proceedings that, with lawsuits, petitions, and conciliatory attempts, lasted five years and involved noted personages of the Church and the world of politics.

The idea of turning Maria's slenderizing into an advertising scheme was the work of Gino Coen, president of the board of directors of the firm of Pantanella Mills and Pasta Factories of Rome. This man was a friend of my brother-in-law, Giovanni Cazzarolli, who was a doctor on the staff of Verona's hospital. Cazzarolli was the only one of my relatives whom I allowed to frequent my home. He was a kind person, something I look for in friends. When I fell in love with Callas, he did not turn his back on me, as did the rest of my family. Thus, I never harbored any resentment against him; when I married Maria in 1949, he was my best man. Although Cazzarolli was not our family doctor, he was our medical advisor. Maria and I always turned to him with little problems such as colds, the flu, or things of that nature. He always made himself available to us.

It was my brother-in-law who introduced us to his engineer friend Gino Coen and had us visit the Pantanella mills. We became friends of the Coen family and sometimes, when Maria was singing in Rome, we went to dinner at their house. As we learned later, the firm of Pantanella Mills found itself in economic difficulties. I remember very well when, during one of our visits, Maria was asked to do something to publicize Pantanella pasta. My wife, who never ate pastasciutta, started laughing. "To ask me, of all people, to endorse that kind of thing," she said.

It was probably when the papers began to comment on Maria's slimming down that the idea came to Coen for his publicity gimmick. I don't know what he said or promised to my brother-in-law; the fact is that he succeeded in convincing him to collaborate with him. In February 1954, specifically on the eighteenth and twenty-first, an announcement appeared in two weekly publications stating that Maria Callas had lost weight after a treatment based on eating "pasta from the Pantanella Mills." The incredible thing was that the announcement carried with it a testimonial signed by the presumed doctor treating Callas, my brother-in-law Cazzarolli.

The advertisement was rather grand. A caption at the bottom proclaimed: "*Physiological pasta—dietetic foods from the great Roman industries of nourishment—the Pantanella Co. of Mills and Pasta Factories.*" Under the caption "certificate," was the photo of a letter written on the stationery of Dr. Giovanni Cazzarolli, and signed by him. It stated: "In my capacity as the doctor treating Maria Meneghini Callas, I certify that the marvelous results obtained in the diet undertaken by Signora Callas (she lost about 20 kilos) was due in large part to her eating the physiological pasta produced in Rome's Pantanella Mills. Giovanni Cazzarolli."

Maria couldn't believe her eyes when she saw the advertisement. She immediately began receiving telephone calls from people wanting information about the "miraculous pastasciutta." She nearly went crazy. It was impossible for Maria to allow herself to be exploited. She would never have agreed to say such a thing under any circumstances and now, seeing herself taken advantage of, she was furious. She gave me instructions to telephone our lawyers and take action against the guilty parties; she also wanted an immediate, clear, and precise retraction.

Every claim was a lie: it was not true that Maria had dieted, that Cazzarolli was the doctor treating her, or that she had eaten Pantanella pasta. But Maria was especially indignant for another reason. Even if everything that Dr. Cazzarolli had written were true, Maria would never have allowed her name or some personal experience to be sold for publicity. "Now the public will be able to think that I'm even doing business with my body," she said.

Contact was made with my brother-in-law and Coen, who were astonished at my wife's reaction. I told them they must publish a retraction immediately. They replied that that was impossible, as it would cause great harm to the Pantanella industries. Upon hearing their excuses, my wife said: "Then they'll spit blood in court. I'll see this to the end." And so began the lawsuit.

At the beginning, it seemed to be a matter of little consequence. We expected it to be resolved quickly, for everything was in our favor, but we soon realized there was a major complication. The Pantanella company had ties to the Vatican. The firm's president was Prince Marcantonio Pacelli, a lawyer and nephew of Pope Pius XII. Many newspapers banded against it. Deputies, senators, and monsignors involved themselves in the effort to impede the lawsuit. They offered us money not to pursue it, but it would have been necessary to leave the advertisement unchanged and forfeit our demands for a retraction. "Not on your life," said Maria. "I want the truth about this fraud to be told." And she refused to speak on the telephone with any of the various people who tried to placate her.

In 1953 my wife and I received an invitation to meet the Pope. Audiences are generally solicited by those who wish to visit the Pontiff, but in our case it was the other way around. It was Pius XII, through his functionaries, who informed us of the invitation for a meeting. We accepted with pleasure. Maria was very religious, even to the point of being obsessive about it. In her conversation and letters, God's name was frequently invoked. Maria attributed her success, health, the weather, and all the beautiful things in her life to God. She had a rather unusual concept of God: "her" God always sided with her. He defended her from her enemies, and vindicated her. When she heard that a colleague—one from whom she had met rudeness—didn't have a success, she would say, "God has avenged me." And she said it with conviction and true faith. She also accredited her triumphs to the justness of God. "He saw my sacrifices and my suffering," she would say, "and I have been treated fairly."

She prayed often, in her own fashion. In each city, before going on stage she went into a church and knelt for a long time, immobile as a statue. When she sang at La Scala, I would accompany her to the Cathedral before each performance. She knelt before the statue of the Madonna just inside the church, and remained there praying for as long as a half hour. To while away the time, I would visit the various altars and study the statues.

Despite having married a Catholic, she remained Greek Orthodox, and was closely bound to her Church. She forced herself to follow our liturgy, but she preferred that of her own religion. Faithful to her beliefs, Maria wasn't very sympathetic toward Rome's Pope. To her he was only a bishop, and even an inimical one because, according to the dogma of the Catholic Church, he was the first bishop of all bishops. As with all Orthodox people, she had acquired a certain coolness in her attitude toward the Roman Pontiff. Thus, when the invitation arrived to go visit Pius XII, Maria accepted willingly, but without excessive enthusiasm.

The morning of the appointment I woke her and told her to begin getting ready so we wouldn't be late. Rolling over lazily in bed, she said, "I don't want to see the Pope this morning. It's raining, it's a gray day, and wearing black would irritate and depress me. We'll go some other time." I tried to make her understand that an appointment with the Pope was different from an appointment with one's dentist or lawyer. "A person gets to see the Pope once in a lifetime, and not everyone is even that fortunate," I said. There was no way that I was able to persuade her, however, and the audience went up in smoke.

A few months later I received a letter from Monsignor Callori di Vignale on behalf of His Holiness, Pius XII. The prelate referred to our tactlessness in not attending the audience. He said that the Pope rarely expressed a desire to meet people, as he had done in our case. He repeated that an invitation from Pius XII was always honored and he asked me to indicate during what period we would be free. We chose spring of 1954.

This time my mother also wished to come with us. Being very religious, she considered the Pope to be God on earth, and for her this audience was the most precious moment of her life. She prepared for it with an enthusiasm that seemed to rejuvenate her. She went to Rome filled with emotion; for several days she had hardly been able to sleep. I thought that the audience would be the way it was described in the newspapers: you find yourself in a large room with a lot of people in the middle. The

Pope arrives, blesses the group, says a few words, walks among those present, and stops to talk to each person who is presented to him.

On my invitation it was written that I should wear white tie, that is to say, formal dress. I had two sets of formal attire in Milan, but one of them was too tight. I instructed my housekeeper to examine both of them carefully and send the larger one on to me. Unfortunately, when I began to dress the morning of the audience, I discovered that she had sent the wrong one. At this point it was too late to find another and I had to make the best of it. It was like trying to get into a plaster mold. My mother was beside herself and almost in tears. Maria, however, was laughing like a madwoman.

With incredible effort and the assistance of the chambermaid, I managed to get into my suit. I looked ridiculous, but there was nothing that could be done. I had to be careful, though, not to make extreme movements, so as not to burst the seams of my trousers. Upon arriving at the Vatican, we were led into a room where other people were already waiting. Presently the door opened and a monsignor, wearing a small violet cloak, appeared. Reading from a paper, he called, in this order: "Signor Commendatore Giovanni Battista Meneghini, Signora Giuseppina Meneghini, Signora Maria Callas." In Vatican protocol, the order in which people are summoned has its significance. Normally, my wife should have been called after me, but instead she was preceded by my mother. Later I learned that this was because Maria was Orthodox. The Vatican also makes distinctions in the matter of religion.

We entered another large room in which there was no one except the prelate who had escorted us. After a few moments, Pius XII appeared from a small side door at the back. He was a most moving sight to behold. I still have the image before my eyes. Tall, white-haired, austere, that man who came toward us with his hands raised in benediction exerted an extraordinary fascination. My wife and my mother went forward to meet him. I remained motionless, as if transfixed.

The Pope blessed us, and then he placed his hand on the head of my mother, who was certainly the most worthy of the three of us. "Let us bless the mother," he said. "And then also Commendatore Meneghini and his wife, whose musical art we know from having heard her with admiration on the radio." He looked at Maria and smiled. The Pope continued to speak with Maria. He said that he had heard her in Wagner's *Parsifal*. "You moved me very much," he said, "and it is for that reason that I have wished to meet you." They began to exchange opinions about Wagner's operas. "I am sorry," the Pope continued, "that you did not sing *Parsifal* in German, in the original version. Wagner loses much in Italian translation."

"The broadcast was done for Italy," Maria replied. "If we had sung it in German, few would have understood it."

"That is true," said Pius XII. "But it is inappropriate to separate Wagner's music from the words which he himself wrote. The music was born together with the words, and they are inseparable."

"I do not agree at all," replied Maria. "The opera is undoubtedly more complete in the original version, but in Italian translation not that much less. In order to know the depths of the music, it is indispensable that one understand the sense of the words."

The conversation became more animated, especially since Maria was not accustomed to giving in easily. My mother was obviously distressed and certainly looked upon Maria as a sinner because she was contradicting the Pope. He, however, seemed amused. Maria was actually becoming too animated and I feared she would blurt out some impertinent remark. I intervened, trying to shift the topic of conversation. I asked the Pope if he had read a certain article that had appeared in the papers at that time, and added, "I don't know if you read the papers or if you see only the most important pieces which your aides prepare for you."

Fixing his gaze on me, the Pope said, "I read the papers from beginning to end. Nothing escapes me. Not even your legal fight with the Pantanella company. Our nephew is president of that organization, and the newspapers do not miss any opportunity to have a field day with the Pacelli name. We would be grateful if you could arrive quickly at an agreement, in a manner in which the Pope could be left in peace."

"Your Holiness, we will do our best to settle everything as quickly as possible," I said.

The visit was over. The Pope presented my mother and Maria with a rosary and little religious pictures. He blessed us once again and we returned home.

Arriving at the hotel, Maria said to me, "Remember that I myself did not make any promises to the Pope. Besides, this has nothing to do with the Pope. Even his nephew isn't involved. As president of the company, he was unaware of the dirty dealings initiated by your brother-in-law and Coen. The blame rests with them. They were the ones who behaved badly and they are going to pay for it. I don't intend to let them go unpunished as a favor to the Pope. I want this lawsuit to follow its course to its conclusion; I insist that the truth be known about this matter."

The suit against Pantanella continued on its legal course. There were various hearings throughout 1954, and a few in 1955. Each time, there were newspaper articles in which the Pacelli name was prominent. Remembering the promise I had made to the Pope, I urged Maria to arrive at a settlement, but all my endeavors were futile.

The first judgment was handed down at the beginning of '57. Maria was satisfied, for her opponents were found guilty. In addition to having to pay legal expenses and damages to my wife, they were ordered to publish a full retraction. The latter they did not want to do, because it would have been injurious to the company. I still had legal recourse, but they made a fresh attempt to arrive at an out-of-court settlement that would not oblige them to publish the onerous declaration. "This has been going on for three years," I said to Maria. "The court decision was in your favor. Don't you think it's best to conclude this?" Finally, she was agreeable to this, and our lawyers received appropriate instructions.

Another year passed. In October 1958, when we were in the United States for some concerts, I had just left the hotel one morning when I saw a man reading a newspaper with a large headline announcing the Pope's death. I bought several papers and returned to the hotel. We followed the radio and television coverage the entire day. The Pope was very special to us. We recalled with emotion the audience we had had with him and the kindness which he had shown us.

Suddenly Maria said, "Battista, now that the Pope is dead, there is no longer any reason for that favor you promised him. Telephone our lawyers and tell them not to pursue that out-of-court agreement. We're going back to court with this." I was upset by this decision she made the very day the Pope died. Instead of thinking of his death, Maria was thinking about her lawsuit. I told her as much, and said, "I'm doing this for you against my will. You know how much I hate deception and intrigue. This sordid business offends me. Nevertheless, we'll abandon private negotiations and let the law take its course."

I telephoned the lawyers and the proceedings continued. In July 1959, Rome's Court of Appeals handed down the definitive sentence which corroborated the condemnation of the Pantanella company and Dr. Cazzarolli. The letter from the lawyers informing us of the conclusion of the case arrived at our house while we were on the notorious cruise on the *Christina* of Aristotle Onassis. We learned of the legal victory only upon our return, but now it no longer mattered. Maria was totally absorbed in other matters.

Chapter 19

Debut at the Met; Elsa Maxwell

After having established herself at La Scala, my wife set her sights on the United States. She was already famous in Argentina, Mexico, and Brazil, but some of the most prestigious theaters were those in the United States, especially New York's Metropolitan Opera, which had been run since 1950 by Rudolf Bing, the well-known English impresario of Austrian descent, who had worked in Vienna, Darmstadt, Berlin, and at Glyndebourne. Authoritarian and commanding respect, somewhat on the order of Ghiringhelli, Bing had become all-powerful at the Met. He was convinced that all singers should feel honored if he took them under consideration.

Bing had heard mention of Maria Callas when he was still in England, before succeeding Edward Johnson. Shortly after arriving at the Met, he initiated negotiations to have her join the company. As was his custom, he went about it as if Maria were duty-bound to say yes: it was unthinkable to him that he might encounter any resistance. Our first contacts were made through our Milan agent, Liduino, who outlined our conditions for going to New York: $600 a performance plus traveling expenses for two. Bing replied that our demands were absurd. He was disposed to concede $400 a performance and airfare only for Maria. "They're not interested," I had Liduino tell Bing.

Word of Maria's successes in 1950 and 1951 began to reach

the United States. Toscanini had spoken highly of her and it was known that she had been chosen to open La Scala. American opera fans began to ask why she was not on the Met roster. Rudolf Bing realized that her presence was important for his own prestige. In order to prevent another American opera company signing her up first, he decided to act. In May 1951 he went to Florence, where Maria was singing in *I Vespri Siciliani*. He listened to her and then came to negotiate with us. There was a lengthy discussion about a contract for the 1952–53 season in New York, and we reached a mutually satisfactory agreement. The financial side of it was good, but in the end we were unable to go to the United States because the American ambassador turned down my request for a visa. By then I had left my family business to devote all my energies to my wife. I was, therefore, "unemployed." The American authorities feared that, accompanying Maria to the United States, I would remain as "an immigrant searching for work"; the risk of this was greater, I was told, because my wife was an American citizen! Maria refused to go without me, and the contract went up in smoke.

During 1953 Maria began to lose weight and by 1954 she was a svelte woman. Some American periodicals ran stories about her, and she started to become known in her own country. Bing made new attempts with letters, telephone calls, and suggested projects. He was now very anxious to have her, and he was offering $800 a performance. He was not alone, though, in wanting her services. Other theaters had the jump on him, and their offers were invariably more attractive. In the summer of 1954 we signed a contract with the Lyric Opera of Chicago for two seasons, with a fee of $2,000 a performance for the first season, and $2,500 per performance for 1955. When Bing learned of it, he almost had a stroke. He said that the sum paid by the Chicago Opera was insanity, and that I, because of my avarice, would soon destroy my wife's career by demanding so much money. I notified him that if he could not afford Callas, he should put her out of his mind, but Callas did not need the Metropolitan.

Even though he hated me to death, Bing was obliged to swallow his pride and negotiate with me. We finally reached an accord in the spring of 1955. Maria would open the 1956–57 season with *Norma*, after which she would sing two additional roles, for a total of twelve performances. I did not haggle over the fee: I wanted to show that I was reasonable, and we accepted $1,000 a performance, as had been agreed on the previous year. Thoroughly pleased, Bing had the contract drawn up and he gave it to Maria, asking her to sign and return it as soon as possible. I said to her: "Let's make him a little anxious for it. He should understand that the Metropolitan has not become what it is because of him but because of the artists who sing there."

Bing, in the meantime, notified the press he had engaged her. Newspapers began to run feature articles about my wife. It was obvious that Maria's Met debut was going to be an event. It was then that the polemics began. Tebaldi was firmly entrenched at the Metropolitan. The old rivalry which had originated at La Scala began to surface in New York.

As the weeks passed, not yet having received the signed contract, Bing became increasingly nervous. Without that piece of paper in his hand, he could not sleep peacefully. He bombarded us with telegrams and phone calls. We went to Chicago at the end of October 1955 for Maria's second season there. Bing, with his court, arrived by plane to plead with Maria. It was a rather pathetic scene. The great impresario said he had never done such a thing for anyone. Maria, with much graciousness, turned the embarrassing situation into a pleasant meeting and gave Bing the anxiously awaited signed contract.

Callas's Metropolitan Opera debut took place on October 29, 1956, in *Norma*, with Mario Del Monaco, Fedora Barbieri,

Debut at the Met; Elsa Maxwell

Cesare Siepi, and James McCracken; Fausto Cleva was in the pit. The days preceding the event were dreadful. My wife was surrounded by an atmosphere of hostility. It seemed as if all her enemies had converged there to insure that she would not have a success in New York, and every day something unpleasant occurred.

Maria was involved in a disagreeable legal matter in the United States during that period. A would-be impresario [Eddie Bagarozy] claimed that she owed him $300,000, even though he had never done anything for her. We were pursued by sheriffs who wanted to serve us with summonses, and by functionaries who wanted to sequester Maria's earnings.

Two days before her debut, *Time* magazine came out on the stands with a cover story devoted to Maria, which included a lengthy biographical piece containing inaccuracies and defamatory opinions. They had sent their correspondents to Greece, Italy, and Buenos Aires to interview everyone who had known Maria before she became famous. The end result was an article in a style and with a point of view which were almost scandalous. My wife was beside herself. She wanted to return to Italy without singing. Bing was frantic.

Members of the press had also thrown themselves at Maria's parents, insinuating that the rich and famous soprano left her family to suffer in poverty. Maria's father refused to support this story, but her mother did. She told reporters, with tears in her eyes, that she at least wanted the opportunity to see her daughter on stage, but she did not have enough money to buy a ticket. Americans, always sensitive about one's family, especially one's mother, received a very negative impression of Maria Callas.

To sing before such an indoctrinated audience was an arduous task. Maria, however, had an unusual personality. Instead of being disheartened by hostility, she tended to be inspired by it. When she smelled the scent of battle, she planted her feet and took on everyone. That is exactly what happened at her Met debut, and that evening, which could have been stormy indeed, ended in triumph.

But the debates did not subside. As I have said, there was some antagonism on the part of the press. One of the most vituperative of these journalists was Elsa Maxwell, the popular Hollywood gossip-columnist who exerted a great influence on public opinion in the United States. In addition to her syndicated articles, she was also known through her regular radio and television appearances.

Elsa Maxwell, at that time seventy-three, was the ugliest woman I have ever seen. She had become a partisan of Renata Tebaldi, and she never passed up the opportunity to attack Maria. She had even written unflattering articles about my wife when she first sang in Chicago. After the first New York *Norma*, Elsa Maxwell struck out at Maria. "The great Callas left me cold," she wrote in her sarcastic review of the debut. Her attacks continued when Maria sang *Tosca* and *Lucia* at the Met. "We have to shut her up," I kept saying to Maria, but I didn't know how to go about it. One day Maria said, "Leave it to me." A Greek millionaire had organized a great ball for the benefit of the American Hellenic Fund during the period we were in New York. A lot of celebrities were to be there, including Elsa Maxwell.

That evening Maria decided to go into action. She had someone introduce her to the "witch of Hollywood" and she remained with her the entire evening. I don't know exactly what they said, but Maxwell seemed to be very happy to have made the acquaintance of the famous soprano who showed such respect and seemed interested in her, despite all that she had written. *

---

* Spyros Skouras introduced them. The opening remarks, as retold by Maxwell in her column: (Maxwell) "Madame Callas, I would have imagined myself to be the last person on earth that you would have wished to meet." (Callas) "On the contrary, you are the first one I wish to meet because,

The next day Maxwell again mentioned Callas in her column, but in entirely different terms. "When I looked into her amazing eyes, which are brilliant, beautiful and hypnotic," she wrote, "I realized she is an extraordinary person."

From that moment, Elsa Maxwell became a fan of Callas. Her articles now had a singleness of purpose: to defend and publicize Maria, and to extol her artistry. The gossip's friendship proved to be invaluable. The damaging articles disappeared from the various papers as if by magic, giving way to others which were positive and favorable. Maria was invited to appear on television programs and to attend balls and important receptions.

In January 1957 Elsa Maxwell and Maria attended the famous annual costume ball at the Waldorf-Astoria. Guests included the ten most famous and beautiful women in America. It was organized by Harry Winston, the New York jeweler, who allowed fabulous pieces from his collection to be borrowed. That year, everyone was dressed as some famous person from history. Maria went as Cleopatra, and she was the most beautiful of all. Her jewels were valued at a million dollars. She had an enormous success, and photographs of her arrival [with two strong men holding her train] were published in newspapers around the world.

At the conclusion of the Met engagement, we went to Chicago, London, and then to Milan. Maxwell followed us everywhere with telephone calls, letters, and telegrams. She even telephoned during the night. It was obvious that she had a crush on my wife, and Maria was aware of it. It was a rather onerous courtship. There were serious and unfair insinuations about my wife and Elsa Maxwell at the time. Some people, aware of Maxwell's proclivities, assumed that Callas also shared these tenden-

---

aside from your opinion of my voice, I esteem you as a lady of honesty who is devoted to telling the truth."

cies. It is a topic which I have never discussed, but since this subject surfaces periodically, I think the truth should be set down.

There is no question about the fact that Maxwell was infatuated with my wife. She pursued her for months with sad, oppressive letters overflowing with affection and often full of the most grotesque inanities. Maria was nauseated by them. It reached the point where she no longer read them, and would pass them along to me unopened. Her instinctive reaction would have been to sever all relations with the old gossip, but Maria knew how influential she was, and she feared a vendetta. She chose diplomacy. Calmly, without being blunt, she let Maxwell know that the interest was not reciprocated. Everything was resolved within the year.

Maria's initial silence and her procrastination probably encouraged Maxwell, who for a while imagined that perhaps her affection would be returned. Because of this she began writing those intimate letters, full of allusions which often involved other very famous people. Pages and pages were taken up by phrases such as: "Maria, the only thing that sends me into ecstasy is your face and your smile."—"My dear, when I telephoned you the other night I almost did not dare disturb you, but upon hearing me speak, happiness emanated from your voice."—"I want to contribute as much as I can to your joy in life, so that you continue to create new and stupendous interpretations."—"I do not dare write all that I feel, or you would consider me mad. But I am not that at all: I am only a person different from the others."

In September 1957, Elsa Maxwell organized a great party in Maria's honor. We spent several days together at the Lido, and Maxwell was beside herself with happiness. She followed Maria around as if she were her shadow. "How can you stand it?" I asked my wife. That November, Maria went to Dallas for a concert, and the old woman followed her there. By this time my wife had finally had it with her, and she was certain she now had the upper hand. During the return flight to New York, there were heated words between the two which generated considerable surprise.

Reporters learned of it and the news that the friendship between Callas and Elsa Maxwell had gone up in smoke was circulated as if it were some big event. The press had a field day with it. It was also at the time when Maxwell was writing obviously prejudicial articles in favor of Maria and unnecessarily hostile to Tebaldi, who had just lost her mother. All this contributed to escalating the matter out of all proportion.

Maxwell was concerned and she cabled me from New York: "Tell Maria that if *Time* magazine asks if our friendship ended in Dallas, as they asked me, she should deny everything categorically, as I did. I wanted to discover the origin of this gossip which has been picked up by all the American television networks, and I learned that it began with an indiscreet remark on the part of a member of the crew on the plane we took back from Dallas. This news item must be stopped. There have been some misunderstandings because of my last article, which was not complimentary to Renata Tebaldi. Her mother passed away today, and I saw her this afternoon. She understands and forgives everything . . . They have just published an article I wrote that is very favorable to Maria, and it includes a photograph. I think this is enough to put a lid on this gossip."

In the middle of December 1957, Elsa Maxwell sent Maria a long letter, a kind of pathetic "farewell letter," not marking the end of their friendship, but rather the termination of that rapport which Maxwell now realized existed only in her mind: "Maria, while Christmas is around the corner, our first thought should be 'peace on earth and good will.' I must write to you and thank you for being the innocent victim of the greatest love one human being can have for another. Perhaps one day the two of us will understand this love and we will look back on it with regret or joy. Who knows, perhaps it is over already. It was I who ended it or, more precisely, you who helped me to end it, scarcely born and marvelous as it was. It did not bring you any happiness and, after a few wonderful moments, it brought me only a profound sorrow.

"Your place in life, at least in my opinion, is in the theater. It does not matter if I do not see you again, except on the stage, where you, a genius, know how to interpret parts never before attempted by common mortals. You destroyed my love that day on the flight from Dallas. Making me comfortable, the steward said: 'Miss Callas will be next to you.' But you, my friend Miss Callas, did not even say one word to me for several hours . . . And yet I think I almost touched your heart once or twice. But I am over it now. I am turning my back on a foolish and perverse interlude which now fills me with loathing. I do not reproach you for anything, except for the fact that you could have crushed these feelings before it was too late. But that is forgotten now. It is something in the past. If we ever run into each other, we should be friendly and cordial, otherwise people will wonder what happened between us. I have honored the promise I made to you: I was your most eloquent defense lawyer, and I will remain so. I took on your enemies, Maria, of which you have many!"

After this declaration, Maxwell tried to demonstrate how great her devotion was for Maria. She recalled an episode concerning the concert in Dallas which I, however, do not believe is true, at least in the way she described it. "When I arrived in Dallas," Maxwell continued, "Miss Miller telephoned to inform me what I had already suspected—that only fifty percent of the tickets for your concert were sold. It appeared that you might be singing to a half-empty house. Miss Miller asked me, almost desperately, if I could do something. So for the entire day I spoke of Callas, on the radio, on television, and in interviews. I did it willingly, because I loved you. It is never difficult to talk about the person one loves. It is difficult *not* to. But since nothing was happening for that evening, I personally offered to buy $2,000 worth of tickets to be distributed to students, teachers at the conservatory, people who truly loved music but were daunted by the high ticket prices.

"I am not seeking to take credit for anything. I am an independent person, and if I choose to buy tickets for some artist, I am doing it of my own volition. But obviously these things do come to light, even though I would have asked for maximum discretion. It seems that the incident is now in public domain. Thus, when various friends *angrily* confronted me with this, all I could do was joke about it. *You* were the only person who, I had hoped, would never learn about this. With that immense dramatic sensibility of yours, all Greek, which dominates your entire being, you would have been offended."

It seems that Elsa Maxwell had not succeeded in convincing herself that it was entirely over between them. She informed Maria that she would be in Rome for *Norma* at the Teatro dell'-Opera in January. She wrote that she would not try to see her or bother her, but at the same time she said that she would be there and hoped that Maria would ask to see her.

"I will be in Rome for the first *Norma* of the series. You should not think that I am coming to get in touch with you. This is not the reason. The Duchess of Windsor has asked me to join her and stay with her from December 27 to January 1. Since I have eight days free, I am thinking of accepting her invitation. I will come to Rome January 2 to see *Norma*. Oh, I do hope that you are good, because I am now in a state of such detachment that no friendship, past or present, would tempt me again to lose my integrity as a critic. I probably will not see you during my stay in Rome. You will be very busy, and I also have some things to attend to. If you sing *Anna Bolena* in April, I'll come to Milan; if not, I'll forego it.

"I refused to speak with Wally Toscanini after she told me

that Ettore Bastianini was better than you in *Ballo in Maschera* at La Scala. I insisted that she admit that you are a greater artist. She had a letter that Battista had written to her which included a somewhat unflattering reference to her father. I told her I was not interested in the least in what Battista had written; the fact remains that you are the greatest and most stimulating artist I have ever known."

Her lengthy letter ended with mention of the [benefit] *Traviata* which Maria was to sing in New York in February 1958. "*La Traviata* is almost sold out. The lower priced tickets went like hot cakes. I have given several interviews about you, one to *Cosmopolitan* magazine in particular. First, though, I had the editor promise they would publish exactly what I said and wrote. Wherever I go, I say and reiterate that we were only acquaintances for a couple of weeks and that you are not the kind of woman for friendships or affection of any kind, except with your husband. This seems to me rather clear now, and it makes everything easier for the both of us."

This is the true story behind the friendship between my wife and Elsa Maxwell. I am certain that Maria was never influenced by the ambiguous feelings of the "Hollywood witch." Her relationship with that woman was not, however, without its adverse effects, for it was she who introduced my wife to a certain circle of people who were rich but deceitful, without purpose in life, and involved in questionable business pursuits (among them, Onassis), all people whom she had not known previously. The change in Maria which caused her to leave me in 1959 probably started after her introduction to that witch, who was even then an extremely intelligent woman and, for that reason, fascinating.

Offstage

Maria curtsies to the Queen after the Covent Garden
centenary gala, 1958

Greeted by King Umberto of Italy, Lisbon, 1958, with
Maestro Ghione, Alfredo Kraus, and others in *La Traviata*

Visconti and Callas
rehearsing *La Vestale*,
La Scala, 1954

With Zeffirelli for his
new production of *Tosca*,
Covent Garden, 1958

With Marlene Dietrich and Meneghini after her Met debut
in *Norma*, 1956

With David Webster
after *La Traviata*,
Covent Garden

With Rudolf Bing after
Tosca at the Met, 1958

Curtain call after *La Sonnambula*
at the King's Theatre, Edinburgh, 1957

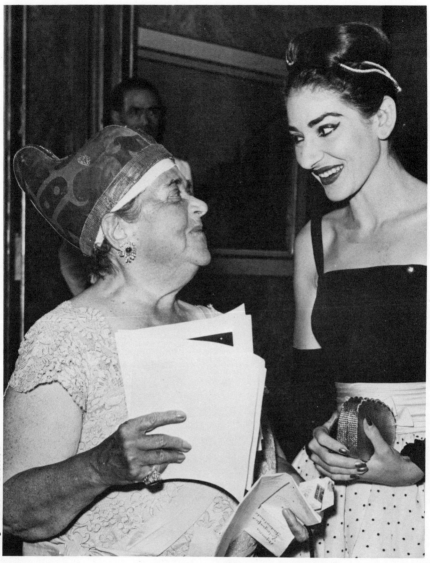

With Elsa Maxwell in doge's hat, Venice, 1957

With Lady Churchill, Tina Onassis,
her husband, and others, Greece, 1959

The Meneghinis and Elsa Maxwell with Onassis aboard his yacht, 1959

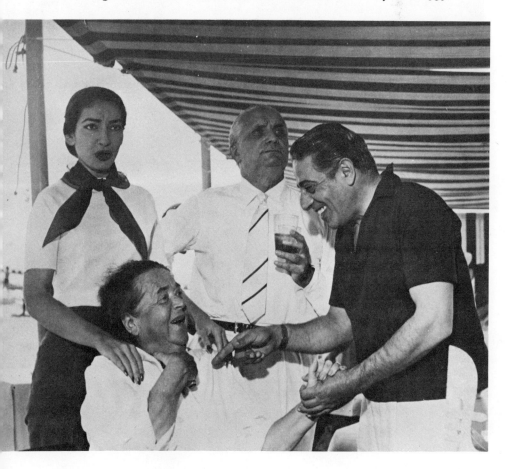

The author at work on his book

During recording session of *La Gioconda*, Milan, 1959

Leaving the stage after *Anna Bolena*, La Scala

Chapter 20

The Bagarozy Lawsuit

With my wife's international successes also came the tribulations. During her career she attracted the most devoted admirers as well as rabid detractors, who seized every opportunity to denigrate her. This happened in Italy, but especially in the United States, which actually was her own country.

Callas's United States debut took place in Chicago in November 1954, where she sang in three operas that season: *Norma, La Traviata,* and *Lucia,* all under the baton of Nicola Rescigno. She had tumultuous successes. Our visit to Chicago was to have ended with the performance of *Lucia* on November 15. We had plane reservations for the next day for our return to Milan, where Maria was scheduled to open the new Scala season with *La Vestale.* Because this was a totally new production, La Scala wanted her in Milan as soon as possible for rehearsals, but the directors of the Chicago Lyric Opera did not want her to leave. The furor over Maria was so great that they were flooded with requests for additional appearances. My wife eventually agreed to one extra performance: she would sing November 17, and we would leave the next morning.

The theater was sold out for the nonsubscription performance and the applause that night was interminable. Everything proceeded magnificently and it was impossible to imagine that the evening could end badly. At the conclusion of the opera, while

Maria was returning to the footlights to acknowledge the ovation, the county sheriff arrived behind the curtain with ten policemen. He intended to serve my wife with a summons. According to the law, it had to be delivered personally to the accused to be considered valid.

The sheriff, document in hand, blocked Maria's way while the ten policemen encircled her. A battery of photographers and reporters materialized unexpectedly. Maria was surrounded. Exhausted from her performance, emotionally drained by the curtain calls, unnerved by the unaccountable presence of these strangers, she began to shout. Chaos ensued. The other singers and theater personnel tried to come to her aid and escort her to her dressing room, while the police attempted to block her path. In the confusion she was mauled and bruised. Thus began one of the most mysterious chapters in my wife's life, one which I never managed fully to understand. This incident resulted in four years of legal maneuvers and brought to light strange quirks in Maria's character, as well as costing her a fortune.*

What had happened? A lawyer, Richard ("Eddie") Bagarozy, probably of Italian descent, claimed to be Callas's sole personal manager. He stated that he had a contract signed by her in 1947, before she went to Italy, which entitled him to ten percent of all her subsequent earnings. He accused my wife of not honoring that agreement and he asked for the sum of $300,000 for his fee in arrears.

---

* This famous incident with the process server is placed a year too early. Callas's second and last Chicago season ended on November 17, 1955, with an extra performance of *Madama Butterfly*. She was to leave the following day for rehearsals for the opening-night production of *Norma* at La Scala. At the conclusion of the Puccini opera, U.S. Marshal Stanley Pringle made the contact with Callas required by law. Lawrence Kelly, one of the founders of the Chicago company, firmly believed up to his death that his co-director, the late Carol Fox, for reasons of her own allowed the process servers to come backstage, despite stipulations in Callas's contract that she was to be protected from them.

It was an absurd demand. The carefully arranged serving of the summons clearly demonstrated that it had been organized with the collaboration of the local authorities and the Chicago Lyric Opera. It was a conspiracy against Maria. We had been in Chicago for three months. We knew that the county sheriff wanted to give my wife the summons and we did everything we could to avoid him, because Maria did not have time to spend in the courts. Up until that moment we had managed to avoid this encounter with the law, but just because of that fact, he probably selected the time and place most favorable for the maximum publicity: inside the opera house on the eve of our departure from Chicago. But more than a judicial controversy, the people involved wanted a scandal that would discredit my wife's reputation in the United States. The following day, in fact, as we were leaving for Italy, the papers exploited the affair to the hilt with photographs and commentary, all but ignoring her artistic triumph. They even wrote that Maria had fled the country.

When we arrived in Milan, I turned the matter over to our lawyers. I was familiar with the story of that contract. It belonged to the sad period in Maria's life when, young and without friends, she had tried to make a career for herself in the United States. In 1946 she was signed by impresario Ottavio Scotto, who for many years had been at the Teatro Colón in Buenos Aires. Scotto was organizing a company of singers. The administrator was Richard Bagarozy, a person assumed to be reputable. He was the husband of Louise Caselotti, who was also a singer. As mentioned earlier, the enterprise failed before they even gave one performance.

Richard Bagarozy must have been a very astute individual because, despite what had transpired, he still managed to maintain a certain hold over some of the company's artists, particularly Maria Callas and Nicola Rossi-Lemeni. They remained in New York and continued to be on good terms with him, believing in his promises of assistance in their careers, at least for a while.

When Giovanni Zenatello told Callas he had chosen her to sing *La Gioconda* in Verona, she, with incredible ingenuousness, ran to inform Bagarozy of the engagement. Knowing the importance of singing in Italy, especially in the Verona Arena, he sensed that this engagement could be the beginning of a very important career. He persuaded Maria to sign a contract in which he was declared her sole agent for ten years.

The most curious thing is the fact that his contract with Maria was signed on June 13, 1947, only three days before she signed with Zenatello. It is obvious that she signed over some money to Bagarozy, even though the man had nothing to do with securing the engagement. Why did Maria do this? At the beginning of our relationship I queried her about it on several occasions, but she never gave me a precise explanation. She said that she had signed without thinking, and because she was ignorant of contracts and legal matters. I was only to learn the truth as a result of the Bagarozy lawsuit.

When Callas arrived in Italy in the summer of 1947, she was accompanied by Bagarozy's wife, a singer who hoped to make a career herself. I even recall trying to find something for her, but without success, because she had a modest voice. Bagarozy was not mentioned again. Although I was thoroughly versed in contractual matters and the ins and outs of judicial proceedings, I never attached any importance to the contract Maria had signed. In her opinion, it was so absurd as to be deemed invalid.

In it Bagarozy was designated the personal representative and sole agent of Maria Callas, who was not to accept any engagement without his approval, not only for theaters, but for eventual recordings, radio and television appearances, films, etc. Maria promised to turn over ten percent of any and all gross earnings, and his fees were to become due and payable upon receipt of money received by her.

The contract began with a statement in which Bagarozy credited himself with having secured for Maria the engagement at the Arena. "I state that I acted as personal representative so that the Artist could sign a contract according to which she will take part, as principal soprano, in the 1947 summer opera festival in Verona, Italy. Moreover, at the representative's expense, the Artist has the benefit of the appropriate publicity so that she can make the proper contacts in the career which she has chosen." All of this was a lie, and Maria was aware of that fact even as she signed the agreement.

This was the story of the contract. As Bagarozy never did anything for Maria, I considered her obligation terminated. When he involved the sheriffs in Chicago in 1954, I was worried about the harmful publicity which could have resulted, not thinking for a moment about the possible validity of the contract. It remained for my attorneys to open my eyes. After examining the situation, they said that we should not be too confident. According to American law, everything about the contract was in order. We began our countersuit. We had to find some good lawyers in the United States. There were hearings, postponements, inquiries, the usual procedures.

In the meantime, the newspapers busied themselves following and reporting the progress of the suit. Maria was highly indignant. She felt that she was being treated unfairly. She wrote her own personal defense for the courts. She had hard, contemptuous words for the man who was suing her. "The court has accepted the word of this man regarding the contract in question," she wrote, "and no one has considered inquiring whether it is valid or not. I know it is not, because I was compelled to sign it . . . This man should prove that he is as esteemed and respected as he claims. He was responsible for the disastrous season that was to have taken place in Chicago in 1946. He even has a record of having been accused three times of fraud."

Earlier in the course of her long defense, my wife revealed a detail that was unknown to me concerning her departure from the United States. Bagarozy had left her without a cent at the last minute. "I accuse him," she wrote, "of having totally abandoned me, embezzling much of the thousand dollars which I had borrowed from my godfather for the trip to Italy. Bagarozy took the check to change it at a bank and then to purchase my steamship ticket, saying that he knew people who could give me a large discount. I never saw that money again. I do not know how much my ticket cost, but surely it was much less. He purchased, with my money, a ticket for me, his wife, and another woman. They put the three of us in the same cabin in a horrible Russian freighter. I almost died of hunger. They only gave us buttered potatoes. He promised to send the money to me, but I never saw it again. When I arrived in Italy I was expected to get by on fifty dollars . . . I know I was stupid to place my trust in Bagarozy, but I was young and I imagined he would feel sorry for me after the collapse of the season in Chicago."

Maria's defense generated a certain interest in the courts. The litigation ran its course and it seemed that the judgment would be in our favor, but in the summer of 1956, while Maria was preparing for the important New York debut, there was a new revelation. We were vacationing on the island of Ischia when our lawyers in the United States wrote to us saying that it was imperative for us to come to New York immediately. The case had been turned upside down and a scandal was about to break. Decisive action was necessary.

In order to discredit what Maria had said about him, Bagarozy had turned over to the courts three letters which Maria had written to him after she was in Italy. They were dated August 20, September 2, and October 25, 1947. The last one had been written by Maria about four months after her arrival in Italy, during the period when we were already close. In these letters (including the final one) Maria expressed herself in an open and familiar manner, as one does with an intimate friend. She asked advice not only about her career but even about her personal life. "If what Callas now says about me were true," Bagarozy told the presiding judge, "and if it were also true that I forced her to sign that contract, once she was in Italy, far away from me and with another man who was interested in her career, she would have completely ignored me. Instead, she continued to write to me affectionately, referring to me as her manager and taking the initiative to ask my advice."

From those letters it transpired that Maria and Bagarozy had been fond of each other. She had been in love with him for a while, and it had certainly been because of her personal feelings for him that she signed a ridiculous contract. He had treated her badly and perhaps never even helped her, but he took advantage of the situation and persuaded her to sign the agreement. Despite all that, she had not forgotten him.

She continued to think about him even after she met me and had fallen in love with me. On August 20, 1947, she wrote: "Dear Eddie, this morning, after two months, we have finally received a letter from you. Naturally I say 'we,' because Louise and I are now like one person. I am happy to hear that you are pulling yourself out of the difficulties you were in, Eddie, and I wish you the best with all my heart, as I always have and always will, more than you have *ever* realized.

"Dear, I know you are displeased because I don't keep in touch, and you're right, but you don't seem to understand that there could have been another reason. In fact I did start to write a very long letter with all my news, but for reasons which I'll tell you later, I decided at the last minute not to write to you.

"But this doesn't mean 'out of sight, out of mind!' I refuse to acknowledge that saying, and I beg you not to believe it either, even if someone told you this; and enough said. I believe you are intelligent enough to read between the lines . . ."

In the course of the letter Maria spoke of me in loving terms, but she asked her friend for guidance in our relationship:

"Thank the Lord He has given me this angelic person. For the first time in my life I don't need someone. As far as how much this concerns my eventually marrying him, I will give that a lot of thought, I assure you. But the truth is that one very rarely finds a kindred soul. You who know me well, my character and everything, must know that I am happy with him, that he must be everything I desire. He's a little older than I am, quite a bit, to tell the truth—he's fifty-two, but he's in good shape, from every point of view. And *so am I.* We are the same person. He understands me perfectly and I understand him. After all, that's what counts most in life: happiness and love. A deeply felt love is worth more than a lousy career that leaves you with nothing more than a name.

"For the first time I have found *my* type. I should leave him and be unhappy for the rest of my life? He has all that I could possibly want and he adores me, and there you have it. It's not love, it's something more than that. Please write me and *tell me what to do.* You are intelligent and unselfish, answer me.

"I'm happy I wrote this letter because it seems as if I were talking to you. It's almost as if I had had you near me, much nearer. I'm as bad as you are, and don't be egotistical and don't misunderstand me: *I still feel for you what I felt when I left you.*

"I would like you to write to me immediately, clearly and with humor, not as my *manager*, but as Eddie, my friend. My treasure, I'm so tired after this long letter. Try to read it without becoming annoyed, all of it, and force yourself to remember the beautiful moments we shared, and not the ugly ones, the way I do. I am always happy to have someone like you for a dear friend. Believe me, I never tire of loving you both. Kiss your family for me and our friends, and shit on all our enemies for both of us.

"In anxious anticipation of your letter and in the hope of always being considered your Maria."

On September 2, before receiving Bagarozy's reply, Maria wrote to him again and returned to the subject of our love: "My dearest Eddie, since writing to you I have changed my mind. I thought about it and rethought about it and I finally arrived at the decision not to get married. It would be foolish if I did it right now, even if I love him. I still have him here with me: I have a rich and powerful man by my side and I can choose to sing when and where I please.

"Barcelona has offered me *Norma* and *Forza* in November. I think I should accept, don't you agree?

"My treasure, what are you doing? I am happy for you. Continue to work and don't think I've forgotten you or will ever forget you. Only circumstances force me to behave differently. When I see you again one of these days I will tell you everything! But remember one thing—Maria does not change the way other people do. Even though you treated me very brusquely in the months before my departure, I didn't say anything, and I continue to be faithful to you.

"Dear, I'll leave you now and I wish you the best. Please write to me immediately and answer everything regarding my career and tell me if I'm doing well. Please excuse the change in my nature, but Battista doesn't like it when I tell jokes. I miss your funny remarks. Certainly even I deserve to raise a little hell, and why shouldn't I?

"One other favor, please: do not go around talking about this and the other business and my private life with our friends, because I wouldn't like that at all."

The third letter, of October 25, begins: "Ciao! My dear, I'm receiving so many of your letters that I truly don't know which one to read first, you skunk! And then you even have the nerve to ask me to answer them . . ."

After talking about me, Maria added: "Isn't he a sweetheart? Oh, he's so full of these lovely little gestures that are so nice. These are the things that I wanted, which you couldn't understand. Dear, these things are not expressed, they happen naturally. The two of us are made for each other, and that's how it is. The tragedy of the matter is that he is on in years and I am stupidly young, *stupidly* because you know that I am much older mentally and emotionally . . ."

The letter ends jocularly: "Okay, I'm ending this long, long letter with a big kiss on both cheeks and . . . perhaps one on your sweet, tempting mouth, but I'm afraid I would be unfaithful to Battista, for that would be too dangerous! So I'll control myself: no kiss on the mouth, but on the forehead. Ciao and please, Eddie, don't forget me."

These surprising letters did not deeply upset me. It is true that Maria never told me about her involvement, but I didn't over-react or make anything of it. I was aware of how much she had suffered in New York during that terrible period, and I could understand this sentimental reaching out toward someone who might help her.

It was obvious, though, that if these letters found their way into the newspapers on the eve of my wife's Met debut, it would have been a serious blow to her reputation. After the harsh statements she had made to the press about Bagarozy, these letters would have been an embarrassing refutation, and who knows how fancifully the journalists would have "interpreted" what Maria wrote to her old friend and her subsequent marriage to me. It was necessary to take the most expedient route. We had to come to terms with Bagarozy; we finally arrived at a settlement.

Chapter 21

The Canceled Performances

1957 was the year of the scandals. My wife was at the height of her popularity, and everyone felt qualified to sit in judgment on her and to comment on her every action. She was no longer free to do anything without first considering the possible reactions of the public and press. Whatever she said appeared in the newspapers. If she stated she was unable to sing because of illness, no one believed her. She was publicly tried by everyone, from doctors and sociologists to the man in the street who speculated about the "real" reason for her run-down condition.

Maria, who was a restless person anyway, felt caged in. She was inwardly seething with indignation. Her nerves, subjected for years to the pressures of her work, were nearly shattered. Her doctors prescribed absolute rest, but she found it impossible to extricate herself from the morass of her professional activities. Nobody believed she was truly ill when she said she was. Everything was attributed to caprice, mania, publicity stunts. Throughout that year, the slightest thing could set my wife off.

This trying period began at the end of 1956 with her successful first season at the Metropolitan. It was the last important theater in which my wife was yet to establish herself, and she wanted to conquer it at all costs. She prepared herself with zeal and she had a genuine triumph, but it was there that the ugly international polemics began. The old rivalry between my wife and Tebaldi was stirred up. It is understandable that there was some professional jealousy between the two women, but Maria never made the deprecating remarks which were attributed to her in the papers and which rightly unloosed such indignation. Tebaldi had become a great favorite in the United States. She sang frequently with the major American companies and her many recordings for London Records contributed to making her enormously popular. There were various Tebaldi fan clubs; the one in New York boasted over five thousand members. In Philadelphia they had even renamed a plaza Renata Tebaldi Square. She was, in short, one of the leading sopranos in the United States.

When my wife joined the Metropolitan Opera Company, it occurred to *Time* magazine to exploit this rivalry between the two prima donnas, pitting one against the other. They sent two journalists to interview my wife and then published a malicious article, full of half-truths. One gross inaccuracy had my wife saying: "Renata Tebaldi is an artist without a backbone." Maria never said this. I was always present at her interviews. It is true that they were conducted in English, a language which I do not speak, but I understand it well enough to follow the conversation. I heard the reporters address some questions to my wife concerning Tebaldi, and Maria answered them properly. The "backbone" remark was someone's invention, but it contributed to the rekindling of the feud between the two women.

After reading the *Time* article, Tebaldi wrote a letter to the editor which was published in the next issue and reprinted in other periodicals, even in Europe: "Sir, I am truly astonished at the statements made by my colleague Signora Maria Meneghini Callas regarding me. The signora admits to being a woman of character and says that I have no backbone. I reply: I have one great thing that she has not—a heart." Her letter added fuel to the fire, and the American opera public continued to choose sides. One paper wrote: "Callas has a greater technique and stage presence than Tebaldi." Another asked rhetorically: "Who does this Callas think she is? An Elvis Presley with longer hair?"

During her first season at the Met, Maria had words with baritone Enzo Sordello. They were to have sung together in five performances of *Lucia*. The incident occurred during the second *Lucia*. At the end of their duet, Sordello held his final high note after Callas had released hers, thereby encouraging applause for himself. Maria, who hated these vulgar displays, snapped at him indignantly: "You will never sing with me again."

"And I will kill you," Sordello replied.

He was a cocky baritone. He had a lovely voice and he had been praised by the critics. He probably wanted to issue a challenge with that retort, but Maria would have none of it. She flew into a rage and told Bing, "It's him or me."

Rudolf Bing did not take her seriously, but when *Lucia* was repeated four days later, he was forced to believe her. Maria, in fact, did not show up, and there was chaos in the lobby. The people were demanding refunds, and eventually the police had to intervene. Bing had to give in and he had Sordello replaced at the next performance. The baritone protested, he insulted Bing, and his contract was terminated on the spot.*

The firing caused an uproar in the press, with international repercussions. All the blame redounded on Maria. The papers wrote that she had engineered the firing of the baritone, who apparently was allowed to insult her. The press took up Sor-

---

* The audience for the *Lucia* of December 11 was not informed that Callas would not be singing until they were inside the theater. When it was announced from the stage that she was indisposed and that Dolores Wilson would be singing the title role, much of the audience stormed the box office which, they discovered, had a no-refund policy. Approximately forty-five minutes elapsed before the performance could begin. Frank Valentino was the baritone for Callas's two remaining *Lucias*.

dello's defense, and he took advantage of it to garner free publicity. He had himself photographed in front of the Metropolitan as he tore up a photograph of Callas.

December 22, when we arrived at the airport to fly to Milan so that we could spend Christmas in our home, we found Sordello waiting for us. He was accompanied by a battery of photographers. He said to Maria that he had come to make peace with her, and he wanted to shake her hand.

"Okay," my wife said, "but first I want you to apologize publicly for everything you've said about me these past few days."

"I cannot do that," Sordello answered.

Maria shrugged her shoulders. The photographers, who had come to immortalize this exchange of olive branches, had to be content with a picture of Sordello extending his hand, while Maria looked down at it disdainfully. This photo was more successful than the picture-shredding one, and it was even published in Europe. When we arrived in Italy, Maria was besieged by reporters asking her about Tebaldi and Sordello. We were obliged to spend our Christmas barricaded at home.

Shortly afterwards we were received by Monsignor Montini, Archbishop of Milan (later Pope Paul VI). It was an appointment that had been scheduled for quite a long time. At the end of the visit, Maria offered a million lire for the poor of the city. Her donation was mentioned in one of the Curia's publications. The newspapers picked up the story and reworked it for their own purposes. Tebaldi had recently given a benefit concert at the Manzoni in Milan and someone took it upon himself to write that Maria had made the contribution so as not to be shown up by her rival.

On January 12 we left for Chicago, where my wife was to take part in a concert led by the great Austrian conductor Karl Böhm. There was considerable publicity surrounding the pairing of these two musicians, and the expectancy was enormous. There was friction during the very first rehearsal, however.

Maria offered her views on the execution of a certain passage. Böhm, of a different mind, stood by his interpretation. Neither was prepared to acquiesce. The atmosphere became tense and at a certain point Böhm said, "I am a conductor and not an accompanist." He refused to conduct the concert and left the orchestra in the lurch. The incident received the usual attention on the part of the press, especially in Europe, where Böhm was particularly famous. Maria's "caprices" were cited as the reason for the disagreement.

As a replacement for Böhm, my wife asked for Fausto Cleva, who had been her conductor for *Norma* and *Lucia* at the Metropolitan. Cleva, however, was unpopular in Chicago, where [for three years] he had been artistic director of the Chicago Lyric Opera. He had failed to please the Chicagoans in this capacity. Maria wanted him, nevertheless, thus creating new tensions. It was a difficult situation, but it was also the ideal emotional climate to trigger in Maria that impetus she craved for big events. The concert itself was a resounding success. The auditorium was completely sold out, even though tickets were very expensive because it was a benefit by the Alliance Française for Hungarian Relief.

At the end of January we went to London, where Maria participated in two enthusiastically received *Normas*.* The critic for *The Times* of London wrote of Callas: "No one in the world can sing with so much power and intensity."

After London we returned to Milan, where Maria had three important new operas awaiting her—*La Sonnambula, Anna Bolena* (which was being revived after 127 years) and *Iphigenia in Tauris*, all to be directed by Luchino Visconti. These new productions kept her in Milan for three months. It was a period of intense work but also one of enormous satisfaction.

---

* During the first *Norma*, after the Norma–Adalgisa duet "Mira o Norma," Callas and Ebe Stignani were obliged to give Covent Garden its first encore in a quarter of a century.

At the beginning of May, there was another brouhaha, this time involving the Vienna Staatsoper and Herbert von Karajan. First the Austrian and then the Italian newspapers blew everything out of proportion, saying that Maria, simply to be perverse, had broken her contract for seven performances of *La Traviata* in Vienna, a series which had been announced for some time. The reason was reportedly the soprano's demand at the last minute for an unrealistic increase in her fee. Karajan refused and Maria was supposed to have replied: "Sing it yourself."

That is not, however, what happened. The fault was not with Maria but with the administration of the Staatsoper. Although my wife had great respect for Karajan, at times he wanted to play dictator, and Maria would not stand for it. In 1954 she had taken part in an extraordinary *Lucia* at La Scala, staged and conducted by Karajan. In September 1955 the production was taken to Berlin and in June 1956 to Vienna, always to great acclaim. It was on the occasion of the Vienna *Lucias* that Karajan had suggested *Traviata*. My wife accepted his invitation. When Karajan spoke of her fee, she said that she would like more than what she had received for *Lucia*. Karajan replied that her request was granted.

Nothing further was said about the Verdi opera. In May 1957 the contract arrived for her signature. Maria was surprised to see that the indicated fee was the same as that which she had received the previous year for *Lucia*. She protested and Karajan (despite his promise) said that he was not disposed to give her one schilling more. Maria didn't sign the contract.

She should not have done that. One would have thought it was the end of the world. The newspapers claimed that she was greedy, that she was concerned only with money, that she was ruthless. There was an outcry in the press against what they considered to be the scandalous *cachets* that Maria exacted. They wrote that few Italian theaters could allow themselves the luxury of engaging her without running the risk of bankruptcy.

The Canceled Performances

It is not true that Maria was greedy. She was precise, she would not permit someone to go back on his word, and she did not accept compromises. When it came to money, however, she was not as meticulous, and sometimes she threw away great sums without realizing what she was doing.*

One day the photographer Luisa Dalwolfe came to Milan to do a series of studies of Maria for *Harper's Bazaar*. The photographs were to be taken in the room in which Verdi had lived at the Hotel Milan. The jeweler Faraoni had loaned an antique necklace of emeralds for the session. Because of the great value of the emeralds, he had engaged a detective to keep an eye on them. Maria was annoyed by the presence of this interloper and she asked that he be sent away. "He must protect the necklace," Faraoni explained.

"Okay, I will buy it. Now it's mine, both of you get out," she replied indignantly. Standing there, she had made out a check for almost twenty million lire.

That was during the period when we always had Elsa Maxwell at our heels. She had come to see the Scala productions and had been a guest at our house. She wanted to organize parties in Maria's honor, but my wife never found the time to go. Elsa Maxwell threw a party in Paris at the end of June 1957. We were invited, but we didn't attend it. The old woman was offended. Maria then promised that she would go to the one Maxwell was planning for September, in Venice.

One of the countries that had been asking insistently for Cal-

---

* Meneghini was, of course, referring only to the period of their marriage. After Callas and Onassis ended their nine-year affair, Callas often mentioned in interviews that she and Onassis enjoyed discussing the stock market and other business matters for hours. In her last interview, given in her Paris apartment a couple of months before her death, Callas told Peter Dragadze: "I'm careful with money, but I'm not tight. The fact is that I have always been afraid of spending my old age in poverty, or dying in poverty. I have worked so hard in order to live without worries. I don't see why I should throw my money away now" (*Gente*, October 1, 1977).

las for some time was Greece. We had been in contact with Greek impresarios in the United States, and Maria promised to sing there. Early in 1957 the Greeks asked Maria to participate in the Athens Festival. Maria had only one free week, at the beginning of August, and she had already put it aside for a short vacation at the beach, but she happily renounced this brief period of relaxation because of her love for her compatriots.

When it was time to sign the contract, Maria expressed the desire to contribute her services. The organizers were offended and refused, saying that the Festival was not in need of subsidization or charity. Now it was Maria who was offended. Her act of generosity, sincere and spontaneous, was misunderstood. She then retorted by quoting the steep fee she was accustomed to receiving only in the United States. The men blanched, but they didn't have the temerity to protest.

Just as she was to leave for Greece, her health gave out. I took her to her doctor, Semeraro, who examined her and said that she was exhausted and needed absolute rest. But how could she refuse to go to Athens? We left July 28. We found the Greek capital tremendously hot, the air dry and the winds sweeping. It was a murderous climate for an opera singer. At the hotel we had booked an apartment on the top floor, because it would be less noisy, but the wind was unendurable up there. Then next to the hotel we found there was a dusty, noisy shipyard. Maria didn't feel well and she was exceedingly nervous. I had Dr. Kotzaridas examine her; he said that her throat was healthy, although one vocal cord seemed slightly inflamed.

At the dress rehearsal my wife complained that her voice was not responding. We notified the organizers of the Festival, because Maria assumed they could find a substitute. They would not even consider it. "It's you or no one," they said. Shortly before the concert, Maria was not well. "Don't worry about it," the directors of the Festival told her. "We'll inform the audience and they'll understand."

The Canceled Performances

Maria actually didn't feel that bad. She could have sung, even knowing that her voice would not have done everything she wanted it to do. The public would have been happy and she would have collected her big fee, but the general attitude of the sponsors rankled. "I will never allow myself to appear before the public in a weakened physical condition, no matter what the cost," she said. And she did not sing.

All hell broke loose. She was attacked and reviled by the Greek press. The organizers publicly grumbled about her fee. Her mother, sister, family, and benefactors who had helped her when she was young, were brought into it and they complained that they were betrayed and forgotten by that ungrateful woman. Maria wanted to pack her bags and leave. I fought to keep her there and convinced her to sing at the second concert. It took place on August 5 as scheduled and was a triumph. The directors came to apologize and they invited her to return. "Never again," she said.

Two days later, we were back in Milan. Maria's health was worse than when she had left. Dr. Semeraro reexamined her and said, "You must rest."

"But I must leave with La Scala for the Edinburgh Festival," Maria replied.

"That's absurd," he said. Semeraro wrote the following certificate: "Maria Meneghini Callas has symptoms of nervous exhaustion to a serious degree, caused by overwork and fatigue. I prescribe a period of at least thirty days of absolute rest."

I handed the certificate to Oldani, La Scala's administrator. "You must find a replacement for my wife," I told him.

"That's impossible. It would be better to cancel the visit rather than go without Maria. The guarantee of her name was the basis for our contract." He then added, "Maria is capable of working miracles, she will do it this time also."

Against my advice and that of her doctor, Maria decided to leave for Edinburgh.

"La Scala will be eternally grateful," Oldani told her.

Four performances of *La Sonnambula* were stipulated in her Edinburgh contract, which ran from August 17 to the thirtieth. La Scala asked her to sing a fifth, but she declined because she was obliged to go to Venice at the beginning of September for the party being given in her honor by Elsa Maxwell.

When she arrived in Edinburgh, Maria discovered that La Scala had promised them that she would sing all five performances of *Sonnambula*. The broadsheets and the newspaper advertisements naturally listed five appearances. Not even the directors of the festival knew that she would not be singing the last performance. Perhaps La Scala was trying to confront my wife with a *fait accompli*, hoping that she wouldn't have the nerve to withdraw at the last moment. But they should have known that Maria would never tolerate a trick of that sort, and their plan backfired.

Maria didn't comment on the extra *Sonnambula*. She sang exceptionally well. Everyone was enthusiastic. The BBC referred to her as "the diva of the festival." After she finished the four performances stipulated in her contract, she packed her bags. The news of her departure struck like a thunderbolt. The artistic director of the festival, Robert Ponsonby, came to the hotel. "What's going on?" he asked. Maria showed him her contract and he was astonished that La Scala hadn't said anything about it to him. He went to Oldani and indignantly demanded an explanation. Oldani rushed to Maria, begging her to "save La Scala." Ghiringhelli was in Milan. There were exchanges of phone calls and heated words. Maria did not give in. "I'm not saving anything," she said to Oldani. "You should have thought of that before."

Robert Ponsonby knew that my wife was right. It was necessary to inform the press and public. What could they say? If they told the truth, it would have reflected badly on La Scala.

They asked Maria for permission to explain the cast change by citing reasons of health. Vocally she had been in fine form, but it was a fact that she was weak and exhausted. She agreed to go along with it. A doctor filled out a report in which he stated that "Maria Callas left the festival because of her precarious health."

The ploy was not successful. The press refused to accept the official explanation. One paper wrote, "Maria Callas demonstrated once again that she is a prima donna of the storybooks: she simply walked out on the Edinburgh Festival."

We flew to Milan from London and from there we continued directly on to Venice, where Elsa Maxwell was awaiting us for her party. The news had scarcely circulated that Maria, instead of being sick in Milan, was in Venice enjoying herself, when everything erupted. The Edinburgh incident was blown out of proportion. Even Maria's fans were indignant and disapproved of her behavior. And they were right. The mistake this time was in Maria's agreeing not to tell the truth, in order to allow La Scala to save face.

In Venice, Elsa Maxwell had organized the festivities in grand style. Her party took place September 3 in the ballroom of the Hotel Danieli [during Venice's thirteenth annual film festival]. There were 170 guests, including Prince and Princess Ruspoli, Contessa Natalia Volpi di Misurata, Henry Fonda and his wife Afdera Franchetti, Arthur Rubinstein with his, the multimillionaire Arturo Lopez, Baronessa Lomanaco, and so on. We stayed on in Venice for four more days because Maria needed some relaxation. We continued to socialize with Maxwell and other guests. We ate at the beach and went dancing in the evening. Aristotle Onassis was among the people with whom we associated during those four days.

My wife's depression and irritability became more acute as soon as we returned to Milan. I was concerned, especially since we were to leave for San Francisco, where Maria was engaged from September 27 to November 10. I took her back to her doctor. This time she underwent clinical analysis which confirmed her state of exhaustion as well as an organic loss of strength. She was also examined by Dr. Carlo Trabattoni, a professor in a clinic for nervous and mental disorders. He corroborated that she was indeed very ill, and said that if she did not undergo a cure immediately, a period of rest in a clinic might be unavoidable.

I contacted the head of the San Francisco Opera, asking at least for a postponement of her debut there. Kurt Adler, the director of the company, had read about the Edinburgh cancellation and the subsequent party in Venice, and he replied testily that "he was skeptical about Maria Callas's indisposition," and that, in any event, he would not allow a postponement of her engagement. I mailed off the medical reports, but it was to no avail: they simply did not believe Maria. When she did not appear in San Francisco on the day stipulated in her contract, a formal complaint was filed with the American Guild of Musical Artists, a strict organization which, among other things, concerns itself with opera singers and their conduct.

AGMA is very powerful in the United States and it can be the undoing of even the most famous singer. It has the authority to protect the interests of the performing group and determine who may work. It is in a position to impose fines and periods of suspension from work. It can set in motion a boycott of an artist found guilty of breach of contract which encompasses all the theaters in the United States.

It was a most serious situation. If Maria was found guilty of breach of contract, she would not have been able to work in her own country. Learning of the formal complaint, Rudolf Bing wrote immediately, recommending that she resolve the matter in the best possible way; otherwise, she would be unable to appear at the Metropolitan.

On January 26, 1958, Maria appeared before the AGMA

panel, which had, in the meantime, made its own inquiries. Fortunately, everything went well. Although the members of the panel felt that her absence from San Francisco "was not fully justified," they accepted as valid her medical documents and did not censure her for breach of contract.

Chapter 22

Callas Leaves La Scala

Of all the regrettable incidents that happened to Maria during 1957, the one involving the Edinburgh Festival upset her most. It was also the one most harshly condemned by the press, especially since my wife, who ostensibly left for reasons of health, went on to Elsa Maxwell's party in Venice, instead of going to bed. It had never happened: an artist leaving an opera company high and dry to go dancing! My wife was severely criticized and censured by an indignant international press.

Maria, knowing she was in the right and that the blame for this mess [of committing her to an additional performance of *La Sonnambula* without her knowledge or consent] rested with Ghiringhelli, took a firm stand and demanded official exoneration by La Scala. "I will not continue to sing at that theater," she told me, "if Ghiringhelli does not step forward and tell the truth." Even while we were still in Edinburgh, Maria telephoned Ghiringhelli, asking him to clarify the situation. He promised to help, but did nothing. Upon returning from Venice, Maria began her siege. She bombarded him with phone calls, but Ghiringhelli was never to be found. Oldani, the administrator, did not know what to tell her. Maria also involved me in it. She insisted that I go to the opera house, find Ghiringhelli, and escort him to our house. We spent some very tense days. With every telephone call, letter, or newspaper article in which she was criticized because of Edinburgh, she practically had a nervous breakdown.

This was the situation during September and part of October. On October 15, I finally managed to speak with Ghiringhelli and I summarized what had been happening. He agreed to an appointment on the seventeenth. We went to his office, where Maria proceeded to read him the riot act. He had to agree with what she said.

"I want you to speak out publicly on my behalf," she told him.

"Your request is most reasonable," he replied submissively, "and I will defend you." It was agreed that by October 25 Ghiringhelli would distribute an official statement detailing the actual circumstances concerning Edinburgh, exonerating Maria of any wrongdoing. My wife seemed content and relaxed a bit, but Ghiringhelli did not keep his word.

October 25 passed, and then the thirtieth, without La Scala issuing a statement. Maria hit the roof. "Now they are giving me the runaround," she said, more exasperated than ever. I once again had to track down Ghiringhelli. He was afraid and was in hiding. I managed to speak with him around November 5, and he set a date for a new appointment.

He again admitted his mistake and promised to make amends. "You must do it immediately," Maria said. "Telephone Emilio Radius [editor of the most popular Italian magazine at that time] and ask him to send a reporter here as soon as possible." Ghiringhelli shilly-shallied, but Maria was adamant. The superintendent telephoned Radius to placate her, and requested a journalist, but for the following day. His explanation was that, as it was a delicate situation which compromised the reputation of La Scala, he had to study the wording of the statement carefully. But, again, it was just another delaying tactic.

Two weeks elapsed without the anticipated exoneration. Maria telephoned Emilio Radius herself; he confirmed that he had sent a reporter at Ghiringhelli's request, but the superintendent changed his mind at the last minute. Also, after keeping *Oggi's* correspondent waiting for two hours, Ghiringhelli told him that he had no statement.

Maria was not prepared to let Ghiringhelli have his way, and she continued her battle. She involved influential people, including Milan's mayor. It was suggested in the end that Maria should write an article herself, telling the true story of the Edinburgh "walkout." Ghiringhelli, with the help of the mayor and others, succeeded in convincing her that this was the honorable solution for everyone. Maria, who shouted a lot but was basically naïve, accepted, not understanding that she had once again been duped, for Maria's defense would have been credible only if it came from Ghiringhelli.

The article did appear and at least on the surface there was temporary peace between her and Ghiringhelli. Maria also had to turn her attention to the forthcoming season, whose opening night was imminent. The choosing of the repertory had been very difficult. Three tenors had refused to sing with her. It was eventually decided to open the 1957–58 season with Verdi's *Un Ballo in Maschera*, to be conducted by Gavazzeni. Maria's other operas were to be Bellini's *Il Pirata* and a revival of *Anna Bolena*.

Opening night, December 7, went well and the stormy year ended quietly, but the truce was short-lived. On January 2, 1958, my wife became embroiled in another situation, the ugliest of her entire career, and one which is still remembered as the most publicized scandal in the history of opera in this century. On that day Maria was to open the season of the Rome Opera with a performance of *Norma* [it was also to be broadcast throughout Italy]. It was an especially gala affair because President Giovanni Gronchi of Italy was to be there with his wife, along with other dignitaries. There was great expectancy surrounding the event.

The days immediately preceding that evening were trying for us because Maria was not feeling well, but with the help of various medications the doctors managed to ameliorate her condition enough that she felt she could fulfill the assignment. The human voice, however, is not like a string or keyboard instrument, and it is always subject to unexpected changes. At the end of the first act, my wife said that she was not well enough to finish the performance. The situation was certainly regrettable, but it need not have been desperate. These unforeseen problems occur regularly in all the opera houses in the world. It would have sufficed if the Rome Opera's administration had moved quickly, announced that she was sick, and replaced her with another soprano. The performance would then have continued quietly. But it was not the case of just any singer, but Maria Callas. They had banked everything on her name and had not even considered arranging for a cover.

What to do? How could one inform the President of Italy and the rest of the audience that the performance was being terminated because the principal singer had lost her voice? Anyone could reasonably have answered, "Replace the singer." But the directors of the Rome Opera did not have another Norma at hand, and none of them had the enterprise to locate one. The intermission was stretching to embarrassing lengths. President Gronchi was becoming nervous and some members of the audience were whistling for the commencement of Act II. In the meantime, the theater's superintendent and other officials had gathered in Maria's dressing room, trying to convince her to continue. "You are a great actress," they told her. "You can go on even without a voice. It's fine if you just go out there and declaim your lines."

Maria understood the gravity of the situation, but there was nothing she could do. Her high notes had started to slip away, and she was even having difficulty producing notes in her middle register. She had almost cracked on a note during the "Casta diva" and someone in the audience had shouted: "Go back to Milan. You cost us a million lire!" If Maria went out and started reciting, instead of singing her lines, God only knows what would have happened. And especially with Gronchi present, it was unwise to take any chances. Maria was adamant; she could not go on.

After an interval of almost an hour, Gronchi was informed that the performance was being suspended. The President and his wife quickly left the theater. Immediately, the public was informed by loudspeaker that the performance had been terminated. It is impossible to convey how explosively the news was received in the auditorium. Outside the stage door, hundreds waited hours for my wife, threatening to lynch her. We left the theater after midnight through a passageway that leads from the opera house to a nearby hotel. Groups of fanatics stood under the windows of our hotel room throughout the night, shouting insults and obscenities.

The lynching of Maria continued the next day, in the press. They all described the incident with indignant headlines. The blame was ascribed exclusively to Maria. No one chose to believe that she was sick. The newspaper articles implied that she had broken off the performance because the applause accorded her after Act I was not sufficiently enthusiastic. Others postulated that Maria had lost her voice from having celebrated the New Year at parties in the homes of Roman patricians. The end result was a moral condemnation such as had probably never happened before. And Maria was not guilty of anything, except being ill.

The actual circumstances leading to the debacle require explanation. We arrived in Rome on December 27 and Maria began rehearsals immediately in the opera house, which was unheated. All the singers protested, but to no avail. Fedora Barbieri became ill and they had to replace her before the dress rehearsal. Then Maria caught a cold and was obliged to go to bed. The head of the Rome Opera came to the hotel. "Maria, you must get better, you absolutely must sing," he pleaded.

My wife did everything she could, taking medicine, and using hot compresses and vaporizers. She was attended by the house doctor and was also in touch by telephone with her personal physician in Milan. She managed to get back on her feet. Although she knew that she was not in her best form, she was confident she could manage to sing.

She was examined an hour before curtain time and her condition seemed to be satisfactory. However, as I have said, the human body is not a machine. By the end of Act I, she had lost her voice and could not continue. This is the story behind the imbroglio, but the newspapers did not want to accept it.

Maria was examined the following morning by two specialists sent by the Rome Opera. They verified that she had a fever and an inflamed throat. Within four days, Maria had recovered. She notified the theater that she was at their disposal for the remainder of the series, but they informed her that they no longer had need of her: she had been replaced by Anita Cerquetti. Maria protested. They told her that it was a precautionary measure taken on instruction from the prefect of Rome, who feared that the public would riot if Callas were to appear on stage. We had no choice but to return to Milan, but we filed suit against the Rome Opera for breach of contract. The litigation was interminable and was concluded only in 1971. The Supreme Court of Appeals not only found Maria innocent of responsibility for what had happened the night of January 2, 1958, but it ordered the Rome Opera to pay damages. By 1971, though, Maria was no longer a *monstre sacrée*; none of the papers mentioned the decision.

The consequences of that evening were exceedingly deleterious to Maria's career. It is accurate to say that the Rome debacle precipitated the end of her operatic activities in Italy. Callas, in fact, did not appear again on any Italian stage in the 1950's except at La Scala, where she sang in two other operas that season for which she had been engaged some time earlier.

There was definitely an intervention on the part of the Italian government, from which Ghiringhelli received specific instructions not to use her anymore. I learned of this from the director of Brussels's Théâtre de la Monnaie, where we were to have gone in the summer of 1958 with the Scala company [for the World's Fair season]. The director of the Monnaie telephoned Ghiringhelli in March to inquire about the finalizing of the agreement and Ghiringhelli told him, "We are unable to come, the Italian government has decided that Callas will not be permitted to tour with La Scala."

Ghiringhelli would no longer have anything to do with us. All the projected Callas productions, even for the following season, were canceled. Having to make commitments, especially since she was receiving offers from other countries, Maria wrote letters querying Ghiringhelli. His responses were always evasive. The mood at La Scala had become cold and tense. It was obvious that Ghiringhelli had been instructed to be evasive. On the afternoon of March 11 we ran into him in front of his office: he looked away and walked by without acknowledging us. We saw him again that same evening at Biffi Scala. Before everyone present, he snubbed Maria.

In the meantime, the date was nearing for Maria's return to La Scala in *Anna Bolena*. Opening night of the revival was set for April 9. This was the first time that Maria was to sing in Italy after the fiasco in Rome. Even though she tried to hide the fact, she was very emotional about this homecoming. She loved the Milanese public and feared that she had become estranged from them because of what had happened.

The night of the *prima*, the stage door was patrolled by police. Officers in civilian clothes were seated throughout the house. At first the audience was hostile, then Maria broke the ice, and eventually she won them over, transporting everyone, friends and enemies alike. The evening was a triumph, ending with delirious applause.

Maria was also scheduled for *Anna Bolena* on April 12. President Gronchi was coming to Milan that day for the official opening of the annual Trade Fair, and in the evening he was to attend a performance at La Scala. Maria was pleased about this coincidence because she would have an opportunity to make amends for what had happened, through no fault of her own, in Rome. She looked forward to that performance, but she was not allowed to sing. The program was changed without any explanation whatsoever. La Scala issued a statement in which they said that on the evening of April 12 *Anna Bolena* would be replaced by Pizzetti's opera *Murder in the Cathedral*.

Relations with Ghiringhelli deteriorated rapidly. He never once came to my wife's dressing room after any of the performances of *Bolena*. If they had to communicate, they wrote letters, in which he returned to using the formal "you," as when they had first met. Maria responded by directing her notes to "the Administration of the Theater," rather than Antonio Ghiringhelli. They were hard, disdainful, dry letters, not devoid of sarcasm.

Even though she had a triumph every evening in *Anna Bolena*, she was the continuous target for abuse from rabid detractors. At each performance, especially early in the opera, there was always someone who tried to create a disturbance, distracting the public with comments and vulgar expressions. Among the many bunches of flowers thrown on stage, there were radishes, tomatoes, and other vegetables; one night there was even an old shoe.*

The harassment continued outside the theater. Every night,

---

* The late Walter Legge, who for twelve years produced most of Callas's greatest recordings, recalled in a 1977 article a performance of *La Sonnambula* at La Scala which ended with a shower of flowers and other

swarms of hooligans gathered under the windows of our home, shouting obscenities and defacing the walls with graffiti. One evening, as we were getting into our car to go out to dinner, we found on Maria's seat the remains of a dead dog. Another night we were returning late after a performance of *Bolena*. As she touched the garden gate, Maria emitted a terrible scream. I ran to her. The gate had been smeared with excrement. I managed to open it and I found that the *canaille* had befouled the garden walkway, the front door, and the walls.

The telephone rang at all hours with anonymous obscene calls, and every day unsigned letters arrived with the most disgusting insults imaginable. We reported all this to Milan's chief of police, but we never received any satisfaction. We had purchased a villa at Sirmione at the end of 1957. Seeing that it was no longer possible to live in Milan, we moved to the villa.

In May 1958, Maria essayed Bellini's *Il Pirata*, which had not been given for decades. It was a dramatic bel canto opera, ideally suited to Maria's temperament. In the mad scene her acting reached sublime heights and I am convinced that no other artist ever managed to equal her. Maria knew that *Il Pirata* was her final opera at La Scala, at least for the foreseeable future. She had decided not to continue working in such a hostile ambiance, even though she was realizing the greatest artistic successes of her career.

During this same period she suffered from hemorrhoids, with attacks so violent as to justify her canceling performances, but this was something she could not consider doing. Before the third *Pirata*, the problem became so acute as to demand immediate surgery. The operation was May 24. No one knew about it. At that time, this particular operation was very painful.

---

items from the gallery: "Callas, trading on her well-known myopia, sniffed each bunch as she picked it up; vegetables she threw into the orchestra pit, while flowers were graciously handed to her colleagues. Not even Strehler could have staged that improvised scene better."

Her doctor ordered at least five days of rest, but Maria could not heed his advice. May 25, the day after the operation, she was on the stage of La Scala, where she sang *Il Pirata* with such splendor as to move the audience to frenzied ovations. She sang the Bellini opera again on Wednesday the twenty-eighth and, for the last time at La Scala, on Saturday the thirty-first. The day afterwards, she informed the press: "I will not be returning to La Scala, at least while Ghiringhelli is there."

Her most faithful admirers had surmised that this was her final appearance, and they arrived at the opera house on May 31 with great masses of flowers to pay homage to her. The police, however, refused to allow them to bring them into the theater. The evening began with the atmosphere of a bullfight. Maria was very tense. She wanted to bid farewell to her public but at the same time call attention to Ghiringhelli, his resentment and his spitefulness. That night the superintendent was sitting toward the back of his box. In the mad scene, which is the culmination of the opera, Imogene has just learned that her lover, Gualtiero, has been condemned to death for murder. She loses her reason and imagines she sees her lover ascending the steps to the scaffold, at which point she launches into the cabaletta "Oh, Sole! ti vela di tenebra fonda" ("Oh, Sun, veil yourself in darkest gloom"). Maria usually delivered these lines facing the audience, with a wild look in her eyes, and a vocal quality that gave one chills. That night she turned toward Ghiringhelli's box, and as she extended her arm in the direction of Ghiringhelli she sang the line, "La vedete il palco funesto" ("There, see the fatal scaffold [or theater box]"). She continued to sing, pointing menacingly at his box. The public understood the allusion and all heads turned toward the box with curiosity. Ghiringhelli got up and left.

At the end of the performance, Maria was accorded an incredible ovation which lasted almost thirty minutes. The public did not want her to leave. People were shouting, "Come back,

Maria, return to us." Many were weeping. Ghiringhelli, angered by this display of affection, had the fire curtain lowered while Maria was still on stage acknowledging the applause. This was Ghiringhelli's way of saying, "The performance is over now and everyone must go home." He then sent a fireman to tell Maria, "By order of the theater, the stage must be cleared."

She walked sadly to her dressing room. She changed quietly and we left the theater. A group of young people were waiting for her and they crowded around her. Some policemen tried to disperse them. "Let them be," Maria said. "They are my friends, they do not mean any harm." Surrounding her, they walked her to her car. When she got in, she had tears in her eyes.

Chapter 23

An Opera Singer's Fees;
Rudolf Bing and the Met

Maria's break with La Scala and Ghiringhelli caused a great stir. The Italian papers discussed it for several days. At the beginning of June 1958, we went to London, where Maria made a concert appearance, gave performances of *La Traviata* at Covent Garden, and appeared in a recital which was televised by the BBC.

We spent July and August on Lake Garda and in Venice, enjoying a genuine vacation. In September we were back in London, where my wife recorded some arias for EMI. The following month, we went to America. Maria was engaged for concerts in Atlanta, Montreal, and Toronto, followed by performances of *La Traviata* and *Medea* in Dallas. It was while we were in Dallas that another operatic news item made the front pages: Callas was fired from the Metropolitan Opera.

Maria had arrived at a turning point in her career. She was tired of working at that hellish pace, performing standard repertory which, besides being enervating, no longer brought her much artistic satisfaction. She longed to organize her future activities with engagements that were more infrequent, thereby affording her the opportunity to take better care of her health. The solution was fewer full-length operas and more concert work. She wished to limit her operatic endeavors to the rediscovering of forgotten masterpieces, where her special capabilities would help make them viable again.

This plan to modify her performing schedule had been suggested in part by the fact that sponsors in various cities in the United States were constantly asking to have her appear in concerts, and they were offering astronomical sums. It was, therefore, absurd for her to continue with her exhausting operatic work with its considerably less attractive financial rewards. The United States, even then, was an extraordinary marketplace for opera. Naturally, in order to be a box-office draw around the country, it was necessary to have been a success at the Metropolitan. Maria was aware of this and had agreed to appear there even though the Met paid very little in comparison with other theaters. In fact, when she sang for the first time at the Met, she was paid $1,000 a performance, while during the same period she was earning $2,500 a performance in Chicago.

Within the year, however, Maria had become the most famous opera singer in the United States, and the prestigious endorsement of the Metropolitan was no longer relevant. Why, then, should she continue to exhaust herself in that theater without adequate recompense? It was better to free herself from that company. It was I, in particular, who broached this subject with Maria, because, in truth, she never thought about the financial side of singing. From the very beginning of her career we agreed that I should devote myself to the economic aspects of her work so that she could dedicate herself totally to singing. We had an ideal and practical relationship. I informed her in minute detail of what I wished to do and she would make some suggestions, but then she let me do what I pleased. "I have confidence in you alone," she would say.

It never happened, not once, that I caused difficulty by entering into an arrangement with which my wife was not in total agreement. If left to her own devices, she might have sung even for starvation wages, as at her debut in Verona. It was I who established and exacted her fees, and I did it with cold, precise reckoning. Callas became the highest-paid singer in the history of opera. Not even Caruso, Gigli, Francesco Tamagno, or anyone else earned as much as she.*

It was not long after I had met Maria that I realized that she was an exceptional artistic property. I was a professional man, and in agreeing to be her manager, I decided to apply all the rules of the business world. As a singer, Maria was in my eyes a valuable product. Instead of selling bricks, as I had done successfully for years, I began to market a voice. The most important prerequisite was that the product be of first-rate quality, and since Maria's voice was not only first-rate but unique in the world, I did not hesitate to demand the highest fee possible. It was my conviction that Maria's *cachet* should escalate continuously. In this way her prestige would keep pace with her earning power and at the same time contribute to the aura of greatness and unattainability. If she had been financially within the reach of every single theater, she would never have become "La Divina." That, at least, was my theory, and the facts bore this out.

Naturally, with this attitude I invited the anger of the various directors of the opera houses. They detested me, and I was well aware of that. My wife also knew it, but it didn't matter to her in the least. My requests for augmented fees were actually justified. When Maria Callas appeared, theaters had the benefit of her box-office appeal and the glamour associated with her name: it was only fair that they pay for what they were getting. For

* The highest-paid singer in opera history in total income was probably Adelina Patti (1843–1919). Her career spanned fifty-six years, and by the 1880's she was commanding a minimum of $5,000 a performance, payable in gold, in advance. In America, when someone complained that she earned more than the President of the United States, she replied, "Let *him* sing."

example, when she sang for the first time at the Metropolitan, we learned that the box-office receipts totaled a record $75,000.

Maria, as I have explained, began her main career singing *La Gioconda* in Verona for 40,000 lire [about $60] a performance. After *Gioconda*, she was unable to find work for five months. In December 1947, her second engagement finally materialized, *Tristan and Isolde* in Venice; I increased her fee a little, to 50,000 lire. *La Forza del Destino* in Trieste in April was 60,000 lire; *Tristan* in Genoa the next month was 75,000 lire; *Turandot* in Rome in July was 90,000; and for *Aïda* in Turin in September 1948 her fee was raised to 100,000 lire. In nine months her *cachet* had more than doubled.

In Venice in January 1949 she earned 130,000 lire for each performance of *I Puritani*; by September of the same year her fee had reached 200,000 lire. At the end of 1950 it was 300,000 a performance; in 1951 it was 400,000; in 1952 and 1953 it was 500,000. In 1954 her fee was 700,000 lire in Italy and $2,000 in the United States, in Chicago; in 1955 her Italian fee had climbed to 900,000, and in 1956 it reached the million mark. In 1957 her fee jumped to 1.5 million lire in Italy and $5,000–$6,000 in the United States. This rapid escalating of her fee is particularly remarkable when compared with the sums received by other major artists of the same period. It should be mentioned that these fees were the net amounts earned. To the fees were always added traveling expenses for two, the costs of learning a new role, and other related incidental expenses.

In order to be able to pay Callas's fee, theater directors sometimes had to resort to legerdemain. On one occasion [in 1956] the Teatro San Carlo in Naples engaged me as assistant stage director and added me to their payroll, and in that way met my wife's fee [of one million lire per performance].

The technique I used when dealing with impresarios who asked for my wife's services was always the same. Whatever amount they offered, my answer was, "No, that's out of the question." Since they wanted Maria and no one else, the interested parties were psychologically prepared to go to any lengths to engage her. On one occasion, in the United States, when Maria was being paid $5,000 a performance, representatives of the Alliance Française came to see us. This institution is important and affluent. They wanted Maria to sing at one of their benefit concerts, and they would not take no for an answer. Maria was very busy at that time. "It's impossible, my wife is fully booked," I explained. "She has to rest during the few free days that are left. She wouldn't be able to come even for $10,000." I had made the last comment without thinking, citing that figure simply because it was so prohibitive. But the men replied: "That is no problem. We are prepared to pay $10,000 to have Maria Callas." I hemmed and hawed a bit, and then accepted. It was a fabulous sum, but it soon became her standard fee in the United States.

Another time, in Milan, a representative of a recording company wanted Maria for one of his firm's projects. "Impossible," I replied. He was so insistent that I came up with an amount I assumed they would never be willing to pay. He turned pale. "I cannot give you an answer now," he said. "I must consult with the directors. I will be back in five days." Ghiringhelli, when he learned of it, told me I was crazy asking for so much money. "I intentionally asked it to get him off my back," I replied. "Maria doesn't have time now to do that recording." Five days later, the man did return: "My company has agreed to meet your demands. We want Maria for this recording."

I was able to comport myself in this manner because I was Maria Callas's husband, that is to say, a person totally concerned with her career and reputation, rather than her money. I never took a commission of any sort, so it did not matter to me if a contract was rejected. Regular managers, on the contrary, rather than run the risk of losing an engagement, might accept a low fee and/or a contract without clauses, after which the singer finds himself at the mercy of the theater. Maria always had a flexible relationship with the various opera houses, one without any ties. If she chose not to sing in a particular theater, she could leave when she wished, because I had added clauses to the contracts which safeguarded her freedom. No theater ever succeeded in negotiating a "hangman's contract" with me.

In October 1958 Maria was in Dallas for *La Traviata* and *Medea*. She was very popular in that city. The musical director of the Dallas Opera, Nicola Rescigno, was a personal friend. The staging of the *Traviata* was by another friend, Franco Zeffirelli. The audiences were magnificent and unstinting in their approval. Maria was happy and relaxed there. Speaking with some promoters of concerts, I saw an opportunity to make a major tour of the United States, with fabulous financial returns and the involvement of television. Maria had just been through two exhausting years of controversies and scandals which had sapped her strength and taken their toll on her nervous system. This concert tour, as projected on paper, was leisurely and lucrative. In short, a golden opportunity which was not to be passed up. But we had one stumbling block in the form of an agreement with the Metropolitan for twelve performances that winter, to be followed by the company's spring tour.

We had, unfortunately, signed a binding letter of intent, and to renounce it would have constituted breach of contract. We would have been involved once again with the terrible American Guild of Musical Artists.

"We absolutely must free ourselves from that Metropolitan," I said to Maria.

"If you can manage that, you're good," she said and laughed, imagining what machinations I would have to devise to achieve my goal.

My adversary was Rudolf Bing. Germanic blood ran in his veins and he was known in New York as "the Prussian corporal" because of his intransigence.* He served the Metropolitan with devotion, and he would never have allowed a problem to go unheeded. The scandal in Rome involving *Norma*, for instance, could never have happened in his theater. For every opera in the repertory, the Metropolitan had, in addition to the scheduled interpreters, a cover for every singer, and sometimes two. One afternoon Maria was in her dressing room and she felt she was too ill to sing a performance of *Lucia di Lammermoor*. This indisposition would not have been a disaster, because he could have replaced her with another fine singer, who was, in fact, prepared to go on.†

Bing couldn't stand me. He said that I was greedy, grasping, that I only thought of money. He claimed that I accompanied my wife into the theater and kept her locked in her dressing room until he had paid me in cash. He also stated that I always insisted on counting the money before I would permit Maria to go on stage. He once said: "Someday I'm going to play a trick on that miser. I'll pay him his wife's fee in dollar bills. We'll see how he likes that." I had the word passed along that I would make certain to be comfortably seated, and I would count the money carefully twice to be sure we were not being cheated. I added that that time I would really forbid Maria to go on stage until I had finished.

This gives some indication of the rapport between Bing and me. You can imagine, therefore, how unwilling the "Prussian corporal" was to allow himself to be outwitted by me. I was not

---

* Sir Rudolf was, as Meneghini mentioned earlier, of Austrian descent. Though he was known as "the Prussian" around the Met, it was not a nickname used by New Yorkers generally.

† Bing recalled that matinee of *Lucia* in his first volume of memoirs: "I literally ran to her room, and found her genuinely ill, with Meneghini and a doctor in solicitous attendance; by the time I got there, I suppose, I looked sicker than she felt, and after a few encouraging words from me she agreed to go on, saving us from what would have been a riot" (5,000 *Nights at the Opera*, 1972).

the least bit worried, however, and I began to maneuver to get out of the written agreement with the Met. Bing was a head-strong man. It was necessary to exasperate him to a point where he would lose his temper and cancel the contract himself.

At the beginning of November 1958, Bing telephoned us in Dallas to say that he had sent Maria's contract, and he asked that we return it to him signed. "I have to study it first, and then Maria will sign it," I told him. This remark annoyed him immediately.

"There is nothing to study," he replied. "The contract reflects all of the terms of the previous agreements."

"We'll see about that," I said, and hung up.

The contract arrived two days later. The twelve performances scheduled for the winter season did not offer any pretext for disagreement. There were, however, some details for the spring tour which allowed leeway for discussion. The schedule pivoted around *La Traviata* and *Macbeth*, which were to be performed alternately, with only a couple of days between them. As they are dissimilar works, requiring totally different vocal qualities, it is almost impossible for a soprano to undertake Lady Macbeth one night and Violetta forty-eight hours later. Maria was the only singer in the world who was capable of tackling this kind of assignment, but she did not want to. She had managed similar feats at the beginning of her career, but it was absurd for her to attempt it in the summer, with the heat and in her current state of health.

Bing telephoned again two days later: "Did you receive the contract?"

"Yes," I answered.

"Send it back to me immediately, signed," he said.

"We have some reservations," I interjected. "Maria cannot manage the schedule which you have devised for the tour this summer. The time between the operas must be changed."

"Let's not even talk about that," Bing said. "Our negotiations concerned those two productions. You agreed to them in writing and those are the operas we are giving."

"Of course our agreement specified those two operas," I said calmly, "but there was nothing decided about the sequence in which they were to be sung. To prepare for *Macbeth*, Maria must have at least a week for the appropriate vocalizing. And then, after *Macbeth*, she needs another ten days to get her vocal cords ready for *La Traviata*. You are a professional and surely are aware of these things. How can Maria sing *Macbeth* and then *La Traviata* forty-eight hours later, the way you have it scheduled? No one can manage that."

"Maria has done that sort of thing before," he countered.

"That was years ago," I replied. "Now my wife's situation is different. Her voice is no longer the same instrument. You absolutely must change the program."

"Never," he snapped. "I am giving you two hours to send me a telegram in which you accept unconditionally all that is set down in that contract"—at which point he hung up the telephone. Maria, who had been listening to the call, began laughing uncontrollably.

"We've done it," I said. "If he's waiting for my telegram, he's in trouble." I knew we had succeeded. In being so inflexible, Bing had played into my hands. Instead of sending off a wire, I went out to dinner with my wife. When we returned to our hotel, we were told at the desk that Rudolf Bing had telephoned four times. "If Mr. Bing telephones again, please tell him that we have not returned to the hotel," I said.

The following morning we received a telegram from Bing in which he formally stated that if we did not wire back accepting his terms within two hours after having received his message, he would annul the contract and all other agreements with the Metropolitan. Naturally I did not respond.

That afternoon, Bing called a press conference to inform the news media that he had fired Maria Callas from the Metropolitan because "the singer had tried to push through some changes in the company's schedule." He also said that he was happy to have taken this action because "it had now become impossible to work with Callas." He explained: "Her assumed right to alter or abrogate contracts according to her volition or whims has led to this specific situation, which is simply a repetition of the experiences which almost every opera house has had in dealing with this singer." Bing then cited the incident with the Rome Opera, her break with La Scala, the trouble with the Vienna State Opera, and the other major imbroglios.

The newspapers made the most of it. "Impetuous diva defies boss of Met" was the front-page headline of one of New York's afternoon dailies. Others used picturesque titles for their articles: "Cyclone Callas," "Hurricane Callas," "The prima donna with the tempestuous temperament."

That very evening in Dallas, Maria enjoyed an extraordinary triumph with [her first United States] *Medea*. The Texas newspapers marshaled in her defense against those in New York. "With all due respect to Rudolf Bing," wrote the music critic for the *Dallas Morning News*, "Maria Callas has not been barred by all the opera companies of the Western World." With Texans rallying to her defense, they created something of the atmosphere of a Western movie. Several millionaires announced that they were prepared to finance on the spot a production of *Medea* for Callas in New York, just "to show New Yorkers how one really presents an opera." "Callas has only to give us the word," they repeated.

This supercharged emotional climate, exhilarating and not a little entertaining, lasted for several days. Maria was the recipient of an outpouring of affection on the part of her public. American opera-goers for the most part sided with her instead of with Bing. She had emerged victorious from that match. Bing later had to bring her back in *Tosca* (1965).

With the temporary termination of our association with the

Met, we had the opportunity to turn our attention to that relaxing and profitable concert tour which probably would have resulted in something quite wonderful. We were not able to progress very far with it, however. Six months after that turning point in Maria's career, Onassis arrived on the scene, and that was the total destruction of everything.

Chapter 24

How Onassis Robbed Me of Maria

The first time my wife met Onassis was in September 1957, during the famous ball in Venice organized by Elsa Maxwell. On that occasion the Greek shipowner was pleasant but not overly cordial. The second time we met him was in Paris, December 19, 1958, at the gala concert which Maria gave at the Opéra as a benefit for the Légion d'Honneur.

That concert is still spoken of as one of the most elegant and successful given after the war. Tito Gobbi, Albert Lance, and Jacques Mars sang with Callas, and Georges Sébastian conducted. All Europe was able to enjoy it, thanks to the medium of television, and it received praise from the international press. For me it constituted a personal vindication, but I didn't know that it was to be, alas, the final great testament of my total devotion to Maria before she betrayed me.

Many people are praised when they speak or write of that concert—the directors of the Paris Opéra, those of the Légion d'Honneur, the President of France, and Georges Cravenne, husband of actress Françoise Arnoul (at that time known as the "pocket Venus" of the French cinema), who was designated organizer general of the gala. But the person who actually conceived, promoted, and realized that evening was myself.

When serious negotiations were underway at the end of April

1958, the diatribes were swirling about Maria with the greatest ferocity. The scandal of the Rome *Norma*, which was canceled after the first act despite the presence of Giovanni Gronchi, at that time President of the Italian Republic, had aroused a wave of hostility. Her enemies took advantage of it by fostering a campaign of vilification. At La Scala, the atmosphere had become insupportable. Even though her stage appearances were a series of triumphs, the administration was against her. It was no longer possible for Maria to work in Italy, and we decided to leave.

The gala concert, presented in a country bordering on Italy, in the most chic capital of Europe, had to be a success *sans pareil* to make the Italians realize that they had treated Maria badly. With this goal I set to work. I told the French that my wife would agree to the recital only if it were done in a grandiose manner, so that it would be the event of the year, and they threw themselves into it marvelously.

The evening was divided into two parts: the actual concert at the Opéra and a gala dinner immediately afterwards. Since this was to be a benefit recital, it was necessary to take in the largest possible amount. Maria was engaged for five million francs, the highest fee ever paid in the history of opera. At the end of the concert, my wife generously turned over the entire amount to a member of the Légion d'Honneur, as her contribution to the benefit.

The 2,130 seats of the Paris Opéra were sold for 35,000 francs each, and they were gone in a few days. Boxes went for as much as 300,000 francs. Even the program cost 2,000 francs; it was a volume weighing over two pounds, with a biography of Callas, her newest recording, and a ticket for the fund-raising lottery. The recital was followed by a dinner, served in the foyer of the theater, for 450 guests. Each place was an additional 15,000 francs. The event was preceded by a long publicity campaign that generated considerable interest. Appropriating the title of a well-known film, French magazines called the concert "The greatest show on earth: edition 1958."*

We had our first contact with the French organizing committee at the end of June. I wanted to be kept informed of even the most minute details. It is accurate to say that there was not one aspect of that evening that had not been examined and discussed by my wife and me.

Maria sang divinely that night. The orchestra, led by Georges Sébastian, whom Maria had known in the United States in 1946 when both were out of work, supported her with absolute devotion. The papers the next day were effusive in their praise—"La Callas triumphs" were some of the headlines.

From the social point of view, one could not have asked for more. Political, military, and financial leaders, as well as the most celebrated names in the arts, were present to hear and pay homage to Maria. In the box of honor was René Coty, President of the French Republic, with the Italian ambassador, Leonardo Vitetti. In the auditorium was the president of the National Assembly, Chaban Delmas; the ambassadors of Great Britain, the United States, and the Soviet Union; the secretary general of NATO, Paul Henri Spaak; the Duke and Duchess of Windsor; the Ali Khan; the Rothschilds; Françoise Sagan and other writers. From the theater world there were Charlie Chaplin; Juliette Gréco; film stars Martine Carol and Brigitte Bardot; composer-singer Sacha Distel, and many more. It was not possible to have a greater success. Even though they tried not to publicize it in Italy, there were far-reaching repercussions which compensated, at least in part, for the smear campaign against Maria.

Among the millionaires present at the concert was Aristotle Onassis, with his entourage. I believe the Greek shipowner was

---

* The gala was also the Paris debut of Callas, and René Coty's last official public appearance as President of France.

very much impressed by what he saw. He, with all his money, would never have aroused so much interest or attracted so much attention to himself, even among important men of politics. I believe it was this consideration that put into his head and set in motion the idea for his diabolical project: "If I take that woman for myself, I will impress everyone." I don't know if, in the midst of all the confusion that evening, Onassis managed to get near Maria to greet her. A few days later on the telephone he was very sociable, displaying an amiability and a cordiality I hadn't noticed the previous year in Venice.

After Paris we went to the United States for a concert tour, and returned to Italy at the end of spring. We were invited to Venice for another ball in honor of my wife, this time organized by Countess Wally Toscanini Castelbarco. It was on this occasion that Onassis invited us for a cruise on the *Christina*, his luxurious yacht. He spoke at length about the *Christina* and about the personalities he had invited, insisting that we also accept. Maria answered that she still had many engagements and would think about it.

From Venice, Maria continued her tour of Madrid, Barcelona, Hamburg, Stockholm, Munich, Wiesbaden. At the end of May, while we were in Milan, Onassis telephoned from Monte Carlo. This time it was his wife Tina who extended the invitation. Then Onassis spoke, and he was very insistent. Maria explained that she was leaving for London, where she had an important engagement for Cherubini's *Medea* at Covent Garden, and that she was not in a state of mind to think about a cruise. "I will come to London for your answer," Onassis said.

The Greek turned up punctually in London for the first performance of *Medea*. To ingratiate himself with Maria, he tried to copy what I had organized in Paris. As an afterthought, he managed to purchase about thirty tickets, which he distributed among his friends. He had invitations printed announcing: "Mr. and Mrs. Onassis have the pleasure to invite you to a party in honor of Maria Callas, which will be held at the Dorchester at 23:15, Thursday, 17 June 1959."

Onassis arrived at the theater very early the night of the *prima*. He waited at the bar in the foyer for his guests, to whom he distributed the tickets for the performance and to whom he offered glasses of champagne. He succeeded in assembling important names, including the Churchills (with the exception of Sir Winston); the Duchess of Kent, with her daughter Princess Alexandra; the Queen's cousin Lord Harewood; and the actors Douglas Fairbanks Jr. and Gary Cooper.

The party following the opera made headlines. The papers proclaimed it the social event of the London season. Even though it was organized in her honor, Maria, at first, did not want to attend. It was I who insisted, promising her that we would stay only a little while. We had scarcely entered the Dorchester when Onassis rushed forward to embrace her. After a little while Maria told me she wanted to leave, and with the excuse that she was very tired, we returned to our hotel.

The series of *Medea* performances ran until the end of June, after which Maria had concerts in Amsterdam and Brussels. July 15, we returned to our villa at Sirmione. We had before us a month and a half without obligations. Maria wanted to rest. The doctor had prescribed sea air, so we thought we would go to Venice to relax, for about three weeks.

July 16, around eleven in the morning, the telephone rang while Maria and I were in the garden. Our housekeeper Emma informed us that Mr. Onassis wished to speak with Maria. "We are absolutely not here," replied my wife.

"Tell him we're in Milan," I added.

A half an hour later the telephone rang again and Emma returned: "It's Onassis again. He says they told him in Milan that you are here and he insists on speaking with Madame Callas."

"We're not here," Maria shouted.

Around one, Onassis called again. "This will continue all day long," Maria said, as I went to answer the telephone. Onassis was euphoric. He addressed me by Maria's nickname of Titta, and used the intimate form of "you." "I want you on the *Christina*. We'll have a good time," he told me. "Persuade your wife." Then he put Tina on the phone. Then the two of them wanted to speak with Maria. Together they insisted so much that Maria said, "Okay, we're coming."

My wife was not convinced she had made the right decision. She seemed to sense something disquieting in the air. I tried to reassure her: "This invitation comes at just the right time. The doctor recommended sea air. It would be an absurd expense to buy a boat for just the two of us. Where would we keep it? Who would run it? They say the Greek's yacht is very comfortable. Let's give it a try. If you don't like it, at the first port we can return home."

The departure from Monte Carlo was scheduled for a week later, the evening of the twenty-second. Two days before the trip, I accompanied Maria to Milan to prepare our luggage. At the door of our villa in Sirmione, I said to Emma, just as we were stepping into the car: "Keep everything ready. We may be gone a week, we may come back in a day. It depends on the people we find on board."

Maria went shopping in Milan and made some absurd purchases. I think she was afraid of looking out-of-place among the other guests. She spent millions of lire on bathing suits, ensembles, and lingerie. It all seemed rather excessive to me, but I didn't say anything. I had never seen her so intensely concerned.

On July 21 we left Milan and flew to Nice. From there we took a taxi to Monte Carlo and checked into our hotel. The next morning a letter was delivered to us from Elsa Maxwell, who was staying at Monte Carlo's Hôtel de Paris. That gossip already knew everything and was meddling with the slobbering advice of a bird of ill omen.

Among other things in that letter, unctuous and malicious, Maxwell said: "Dear Maria, I am only writing to wish you and Battista a splendid voyage on board that marvelous yacht, with that marvelous and intelligent 'master of the house' Ari, and the ex-man-of-state (now perhaps a little in decline) who saved the world in 1940. In fact, you are taking the place of Garbo, now too old, on board the *Christina*. Good luck. I never cared for Garbo, and I loved you. From this moment on enjoy every moment of your life. *Take* (and this is a delicate art) everything. *Give* (that's not a delicate art, but an important one) all that you can bring yourself to give: this is the way to true happiness which you must discover in the wilderness. I no longer even wish to see you. The world will say—in fact they are already saying—that you only wanted to use me. This I deny categorically. The little I have done, I did with my eyes wide open, and with my heart and soul. You are already one of the great, and you will become even greater . . . (P.S. Yesterday Ari and Tina invited me to dinner with you. I couldn't say no.)"

The following day, July 22, we had lunch with Onassis's sister, and in the evening we dined at the Hôtel de Paris with Onassis, his wife, and Elsa Maxwell. We then went on to a dance, and at 2 a.m. we returned to our hotel. Thus began the tragic adventure.

On board were important people—Winston Churchill with his wife, his daughter Diana, Lord Moran and the Montague Browns. Churchill had brought along his little dog Toby, from whom he was inseparable. There was Gianni Agnelli with his wife Marella, and many other Greek, American, and English personalities.

The first stop was Portofino, then Capri. From the Mediterranean we passed through the Aegean Sea to the Gulf of Corinth. For most of these people, life on board was light and carefree. Their manner of comporting themselves was very different from that to which Maria and I were accustomed. We had the impression of being among people a little crazy. Many of the couples split up and found other partners. The women, and also the men, often sunbathed completely nude and fooled around in broad daylight, in front of everyone. In simple and precise words, I had the impression of finding myself in the middle of a pigpen.

One of the things that made the strongest impression on me was seeing Onassis naked. He didn't seem to be a man, but a gorilla. He was very hairy. Maria looked at him and laughed. He was, however, a considerate and cheerful traveling companion. He would say he was "a slave and chambermaid" on this ship and that he "played the clown to forget his troubles." I assumed he was referring to his business ventures. In fact, I often saw him at the numerous radio telephones which kept him in contact with his companies scattered around the world and which he personally continued to run from his yacht.

Onassis enjoyed playing cards with Churchill. He had a genuine veneration for the old man. Churchill was very feeble. He could neither stand easily nor walk, and he was incontinent. In addition to his wife and daughter, Churchill was assisted by a secretary-nurse, but it was Onassis who remained closest of all to him, and he was always ready to help him with even the most humble needs.

In order to take his friend around the islands we visited, Onassis had a special vehicle constructed in which the infirm statesman could remain seated comfortably. It was transported on the yacht, and was lowered to the ground in the various ports, with Churchill inside, by means of a special winch.

Many distinguished people came aboard the *Christina* to pay their respects to Churchill. July 29, while we were in the deserted bay of the Bosphorus, Greek Premier Constantine Karamanlis and his wife came for lunch. We made side trips at every port of call, sometimes on foot, and other times on the backs of mules. It was extremely hot and those excursions were, for me, damned exhausting.

On August 4 we stopped at the Turkish province of Smyrna, which was Onassis's birthplace. That evening the Greek wanted me to go to dinner with him and meet his old boyhood friends. Near the port we went to various local dives, which Onassis knew intimately, and we made merry all night in the company of dealers, prostitutes, and assorted sinister characters. At five in the morning I managed to persuade him to return to the yacht. He was so drunk he couldn't stand up.

From Smyrna we sailed for Istanbul. Here Onassis invited the Turkish Prime Minister Adnan Menderes to the yacht. Since he knew he wouldn't be able to wake up early, he deputized me to receive the Prime Minister, and to keep him company until it was time for lunch. While we were moored in the port of Istanbul, I noticed that the water was black and fetid. "We're in shit," I commented to the *Christina*'s captain, who spoke fluent Italian. He replied, "The real shit, my dear sir, is that which lives on board."

We stopped at the foot of Mount Athos on August 6, and the following day we received the Patriarch Athenagoras. It was on that day that, unexpectedly, destiny changed my life. The patriarch knew of Onassis and Maria, for they were both famous Greeks. Speaking to them in Greek, I don't know why, he blessed them together. It almost seemed as if he were performing a marriage rite.

Maria remained profoundly troubled afterward. I could see it in her eyes, which were luminous and wild. When she returned to the ship that evening, I saw that she was totally changed. She didn't wish to go straight to bed, as usual. When I said I was tired and wanted to go to sleep, she replied, "Do whatever you want. I'm going to stay here." It was that evening that the affair began. I only learned about it, however, a few days later.

How Onassis Robbed Me of Maria

At first I didn't fully grasp what was happening. Later Maria reproached me, accusing me of not having done anything to save her. "When you saw that I was going to be swept off my feet, why didn't you do something?" she said. It had never occurred to me, even remotely, that she would find herself in that kind of difficulty.

Many inaccurate and unjust things have been written about my marriage to Maria. When we were married, I was fifty-four and she was twenty-six. I have always been accustomed to thinking things through carefully. I had calculated and knew very well that when I was seventy, Maria would be only forty-two. I had called her attention to this fact many times, but it did not matter to her; she wanted to marry me, no matter what.

Our ten years of matrimony were stupendous. I believe that few have known a love so constant and untroubled. We were so close that Maria, for example, never went to sleep if I was not there. If I had to go out at night on business, she waited up for me even until one in the morning because she did not want to go to bed alone. The proof of this most tender and strong love is preserved in the numerous and passionate letters which she wrote me during the first years, when she was obliged to travel because of professional engagements. By the end of 1950, at her own insistence, we always traveled together; otherwise, she said, she would no longer continue singing. Since we were now together, there was no need for her to write me letters, yet her heart was so full and overflowing with affection that she wrote me little love notes almost every day, putting them in bunches of flowers, on the bedside table, or on my desk. Her last notes were written just before we left on the cruise.

Even on Onassis's yacht, everyone was aware of how much we were in love. Our reserve and our romantic comportment made them smile. They said that, because of our presence, it was a love cruise. It was Maria's wish that we were always elegant, at every hour. Together we decided what suits and outfits to wear.

The words that best summed up our mutual feelings were constant nervous excitement. Comparing our life style with that of the millionaires, Maria said, "They have what they have, yes, but I have you, always, always." Maria was everything for me; she saw only me and still behaved like a young girl on a honeymoon.

My inner happiness during the first days of that cruise was perfect. If I happened to see a church or a bell tower in the distance, the thought would come to me spontaneously to thank God: "Let it be, oh Lord," I prayed, "that Maria is always well and that it will always remain the way it is now." In the evening we knelt together in our cabin and prayed before the little painting of the Madonna from which Maria was never separated.

This was our relationship until August 7. Before that date, I noticed absolutely nothing that could have foreshadowed the tragedy. That evening, everything changed. Maria seemed more vivacious than I had ever seen her. She danced continuously, and always with Onassis. I was almost happy about it. "Maria is still a young girl," I thought while observing them. "She's letting herself go. It'll do her good." I had encouraged the voyage in the first place because of her health, and her vitality now was a sign that the sea air suited her.

August 8 and 9, things continued in the same fashion, with Maria always vibrant and dancing. The following day was Sunday, and we had arrived at Athens. We went to a party in the evening from which we returned at four in the morning. Onassis and Maria wanted to continue the festivities on the yacht. "I'm going to bed," I said.

I was more dead than alive, and I fell asleep immediately. I awoke at 9:30 next morning and realized that Maria was not there. I was worried and I went around the yacht looking for her. I ran into Onassis, who was smiling and ebullient. He said that he had been to sleep and had already shaved. A horrible suspicion passed through my mind. If Onassis had been asleep, then where had Maria been? I felt faint. I went to my cabin and she was there, having just returned. "You gave me a big fright," I said. It seemed as if she didn't hear me. She was vague and preoccupied. She began to rhapsodize about the beauty of the night, and the magic of the dawn over the sea. Then, suddenly changing her tone and assuming a derisive, offensive attitude, she launched into an acrimonious tirade, telling me that I should stop being her shadow.

"You act like my jailer," she said. "You never leave me alone. You control me in everything. You're like some hateful guardian, and you've kept me hemmed in all these years. I'm suffocating!" Then she began to criticize my shape, my way of doing things. "You're not adventuresome, you don't know languages, your hair is always uncombed, you can't manage to dress smartly."

It was a terrible blow. I knew that something had happened to her. Onassis suddenly came to mind, the way they were together, dancing that night. I began to understand, but I couldn't bring myself to believe that something of that nature could have happened to Maria.

I remembered that a couple of days before, Maria and I had thought of asking Onassis's advice about a delicate question involving my wife's career. She had been asked to appear in a major film. I thought perhaps her long conversations with Onassis might have concerned that subject. "Onassis," I told myself, "is a man of great experience, astute in business matters, and he would be able to give her sound advice." I was thinking such things, perhaps only to keep at bay the awful reality that was forming before my eyes.

That same day I received the news that my mother had suffered another heart attack. I endured terrible hours that day. On other occasions Maria had always been attuned to my suffering, but that day she was not aware of anything.

By evening, I was destroyed. Around midnight I said to Maria that I would be going to bed. "Go then, I'm staying here," she said simply. I stretched out on the bed, but was unable to sleep. Around 2 a.m. I heard the door open. I thought it was Maria. In that darkness I saw the figure of a woman almost completely naked. She entered the cabin and threw herself on the bed. "Maria," I said, embracing her. Immediately I realized it was not my wife. The woman was sobbing. "What's going on?" I said, jumping up. It was Tina Onassis.

"Battista," she said, "we are both miserable. Your Maria is downstairs in the lounge in my husband's arms. Now there is nothing more that can be done. He has taken her away from you."

I had developed a friendship with Tina. She was a very beautiful woman, good and kind. We often spoke together. She had revealed to me that her marital life with her husband had never been happy, and that Onassis was a brutal drunk.

At first I couldn't imagine why Tina was confiding all this to me. Later I realized she was probably doing it so I would pass it along to Maria and in turn open her eyes. Now Tina was there, on my bed, weeping. "I'm especially sorry for you," she said. "I had already decided to leave him, and this will be my opportunity to initiate divorce proceedings. But you two were in love. When I met you, I envied the love and affection you two shared. Poor Battista, but also poor Maria. She'll learn soon enough what kind of man he is." *

Tina went back to her cabin, leaving me in a piteous state. I continued to toss about on the bed in anticipation of an overwhelming sorrow. Maria reentered at 6:10 in the morning. I asked her how she could be so late, but she didn't answer.

I didn't see her the entire next day. In the evening I went to bed early and passed the night without closing my eyes. Maria came in shortly after five the next morning.

* In her divorce suit, Tina Onassis chose not to name Callas as correspondent and cited a woman with whom Onassis had had an earlier liaison.

How Onassis Robbed Me of Maria

I pretended to wake up at that moment. She told me the sea was splendid, even though it was squally. Nothing else. I prayed to God that the accursed cruise would end soon. I was certain in my heart that, once we arrived back at our home, everything would return to normal.

I wanted to believe that everything that had transpired with Maria was only a flirtation, a passing infatuation, precipitated by the sea and the vacation. On August 13, at two in the afternoon, we arrived at Monte Carlo. Two hours later we were in Nice's airport. By five in the evening we were back in Milan. Between us, for the entire trip, there was a glacial silence.

Chapter 25

The Diary of a Betrayal

I was convinced that by the time we reached Milan, Maria would have put behind her what had happened on the *Christina*. Onassis would continue his peregrinations around the world and my wife would resume her career. Everything would be as it was before.

In the final days of that accursed cruise Maria had acted irresponsibly, perhaps she had even been unfaithful, and she had been impatient with me, but she had not made any final decisions. Now the moment had come to reflect calmly, and consider the situation realistically. Recalling Maria's demeanor, her conversations, her deliberate way of examining things during our twelve years together, I was certain she would never renounce those values which, until a couple of weeks before, she honored above all else. But I was mistaken. Maria was now a different person. She seemed to have become the succubus of some hellish demon.

Our destiny was fixed during that turbulent month following our return from the cruise. I passed those thirty days in a terrible state of anxiety, enduring humiliations and the most bitter disappointments. My mother was also gravely ill. I was traveling constantly between our residences in Milan and Sirmione, Zevio, where my mother lived, and Turin, where I went to the lawyers to work out the details of the separation. I almost never slept, I could hardly manage to eat, I was feverish, it did not matter to me if I died.

Much was written later about our separation, but no one really knew the sequence of events. The press was unaware of our estrangement as it was happening. When the story broke on September 7, 1959, everything had been concluded between us. I kept a diary during those fateful days, if only to express some of the pain and desperation which I was not able to reveal to anyone. I believe this diary is the most accurate record of what transpired:

Thursday, August 13. We arrived at 5:00 in Milan, at Malpensa airport, having come from Nice. Contrary to what we had agreed upon earlier, Maria said that she preferred not to go on to Sirmione, but wanted to spend the next couple of days in Milan. She apparently wishes to be alone. "It's better that you go to Sirmione, where you're closer to your mother, who needs you so much." I protested, saying that I have business to finish at home in Milan. "You can work during the night," she answered. It is the first time that she has allowed me to work throughout the night. She always said in the past that she could not fall asleep without me.

Friday, August 14. I went to bed at two this morning. Maria slept soundly and peacefully. I awoke at five and continued to work in my studio. I was ready to leave for Sirmione by nine and I returned to the bedroom to say good morning to Maria. She seemed affectionate, but I sensed that her thoughts were elsewhere. She then said without preamble: "What would you do if I no longer wanted to stay with you?" I felt the blood rush to my head. Everything around me started spinning. I managed a little laugh and said, "Oh, I'd retire to one of those rocky gorges where the monks live on Mount Athos." I wanted Maria to believe that I did not take her question seriously, but I knew my wife too well to have thought that she was making an idle comment. I've begun to realize the enormity of the tragedy engulfing me. It is now all over for me.

I was in Zevio by early afternoon. My mother asked about Maria. "She's fine and she sends her greetings," I told her. Maria telephoned an hour later from Milan. She was calm. She said that she would call me later after I returned to Sirmione, but it's now after midnight and she hasn't telephoned. I would like to call her, but I fear that's unwise.

Saturday, August 15. I telephoned Maria at eight. She was both surprised and annoyed because I didn't call her last evening. "I thought that you were going to call me," I told her. "Perhaps I misunderstood, and I apologize." She returned to the subject of wishing to be alone in Milan. "I rest better," she explained. "If there's news, we can keep in touch by phone."

Maria telephoned at 12:15 and asked me to come to see her immediately in Milan. "Right away, without losing a minute," she emphasized. "I have decided to discuss things with you and inform you of everything. I cannot put if off any longer. Come, your Maria is waiting for you."

Her choice of words left me perplexed. She had said, "Your Maria is waiting for you," and I couldn't figure out if "your Maria" meant what it always did or if she just said it out of habit. I packed. Since it was late, my housekeeper Emma insisted I at least gulp down a bowl of soup, which I did, standing so as not to lose a moment. I hurried to Milan with my heart in my throat.

I arrived at 3:00, half an hour later than I had promised, having been delayed because of holiday traffic.

Maria had prepared something for me to eat. When I told her I had already had a bowl of soup, she turned into a Fury. I forced myself to eat to placate her. She seemed to be in a better mood, but when I finished, she commented disagreeably, "You never change: you never lose either your sleep or your appetite."

After that unpleasant meal, Maria invited me to join her for a conversation. "Do you want to talk here, or should we go somewhere else?" she asked.

"Wherever you wish," I replied. I felt a terrible weight pressing on my chest which made it almost impossible for me to breathe. Maria closed the door so the servants couldn't hear us. She came right to the point. With an icy voice, she said: "It's all over between us. I have decided to stay with Onassis." She paused for a moment, perhaps to hear my response, but I didn't say anything. She then continued, and her voice was almost sweet: "Ari and I have been caught up in this twist of fate and we are unable to combat it. We have done nothing wrong. We have behaved according to the rules and we have not crossed the bounds of honesty, but he can no longer be apart from me, and I cannot be away from him. He is here in Milan. He likes you very much and has great respect for you. We are counting on you to help us extricate ourselves from this situation. He wants to see you and talk with you."

I listened, half-numb. I managed to say: "Certainly, let him come. I will meet with him willingly. I will be strong. I will be able to handle myself well."

Onassis arrived at ten. He was dressed in a strange outfit so that he would not be recognized. Neither of them seemed able to initiate the conversation, so I began: "First of all, it's necessary to think of Maria's health. Then we should try to keep the scandal to a minimum. Apparently there is no other solution or way out of this. I will help to expedite your plans, but be aware of exactly what you are doing, the sin you are committing, the lives you are ruining."

It seemed as if I were speaking to two twenty-year-olds in love. Onassis tried to comfort me by saying that he himself had gone through a similar experience. "These are things that happen in life," he told me. I wanted to kill him.

Sunday, August 16.   The conversation lasted until 3 a.m. I went to bed destroyed. Maria remained downstairs with Onassis for another hour. When she came to bed I pretended to be asleep. She slid into bed slowly, into her usual place, and then dozed off. I was trembling like a leaf. Perhaps I was feverish.

At six I got out of bed, and without disturbing anyone, I left my home. As I closed the door behind me, I was weeping.

I stopped on the way to see my mother, who once again asked: "How is Maria? Where is she? Why doesn't she come?" I reached Sirmione at four in the afternoon. (It took me three hours to drive thirty-five kilometers.) I feel disoriented. I cannot recall if I've had anything to eat all day. I'm unsteady, and badly shaken.

I dozed off in an armchair. My thoughts were with Maria, who was dining with Onassis in my house in Milan. Maria had asked if I would allow them to eat there so they wouldn't be noticed together by others. I had replied that it didn't matter to me.

Monday, August 17.   Maria telephoned me this morning. She said that she would be joining me at Sirmione, but she wasn't certain how she would be arriving. I told her to inform Onassis that I wanted to meet with him in some suitable place, perhaps Malpensa airport, on Wednesday or Thursday.

Maria telephoned again in the early afternoon. She asked if she could come with Onassis because he had to leave immediately afterwards on business and was not free either Wednesday or Thursday. "Do as you wish," I answered.

At eight an enormous car passed through the gates of my villa in Sirmione. Maria got out, followed by Onassis, Bruna (our maid in Milan), and the two poodles, Toy and Tea. The chauffeur remained at attention. Onassis was euphoric. He greeted everyone warmly, loudly. His breath smelled of alcohol. The driver told me later that between Milan and Sirmione Onassis had drunk almost a full bottle of whisky. "I bought it before we left," he said, showing me the bottle.

Maria must also have been drinking. She was acting peculiarly. I had never seen her this way. Onassis said that his plane was ready at Boscomantico, near Verona, so he would be able to receive a telephone call he was expecting and could depart immediately.

We ate at nine. Maria behaved like a silly, stupid child. She wanted a fire lit in the dining room fireplace. It is the seventeenth of August and hot as the tropics. The burning trunks of olive trees in the fireplace only intensified the heat in the room. I was sweating like a burro and was unable to eat.

We went into the garden after dinner. Maria wanted to show the house to Onassis. She even took him up into the little tower, so that he could admire the lake. Onassis was not enthusiastic. He told me, "You have a nerve confining a woman like Maria to the edge of a puddle like this lake of Ciprione." I don't know if he was doing it out of pettiness or ignorance, but he kept saying "Ciprione" instead of "Sirmione."

Around eleven we went into the living room and began to talk. Many things were said, the most inane, irritating, disgusting remarks. I was no longer passive and subdued, the way I was two days earlier. I taunted Onassis and fought him every inch of the way. At once he became angry because he said that I was going back on the promises I had made two days earlier. He accused me of being cruel and of hoping for their unhappiness.

Then I really lost my patience and lit into him. I insulted him and called him the epithets he deserved. Maria began to tremble and to sob convulsively. Then Onassis began to cry, saying: "Yes, I'm a disgrace, I'm a murderer, I'm a thief, I'm no good,

I'm the most revolting person on earth. But I am also a million-aire and powerful. I will never give up Maria, and I will take her away from whomever it's necessary, using whatever means, sending people, things, contracts, and conventions to hell." At this point we were shouting back and forth. He said: "How many million do you want for Maria? Five, ten?"

I replied: "You are a poor drunk and you turn my stomach. I would like to smash your face in but I won't touch you because you can't even manage to stand up."

Now Maria was screaming hysterically. She kept repeating, "I have ruined your life, I will never have peace." She begged for my forgiveness. Suddenly Onassis seemed overcome with re-morse and asked if we should continue alone. "It's not necessary," I answered. "As far as I'm concerned, this discussion is closed."

I went out to get some air. It was now three in the morning. The staff was still up. Onassis asked for more whisky. He said that he couldn't leave before dawn because planes could not take off from Boscomantico airport in the dark. I said that I was going to bed. "Then let's shake hands," Onassis said. "I don't shake hands with refuse like you," I replied. "You invited me on your damned yacht and then you stabbed me in the back. I am placing a curse on you that you never have peace for the rest of your days."

I went up to bed. Maria started to follow me, but then she asked if she might stay a little longer with Onassis. "Do what-ever you want," I told her.

I rested on the bed, fully dressed. At four, Maria tiptoed into the room. She took some piece of clothing. I assumed she would return shortly, but by five I hadn't seen her. I got up and went downstairs. There was no one there. There was only the poodle Tea, sleeping in her usual spot. Onassis's limousine was no longer in the driveway. I looked into Bruna's room, but her bed was unmussed.

The Diary of a Betrayal

Tuesday, August 18.   Maria telephoned at 7 a.m. and said that she was at the house in Milan. She asked me to send Ferruccio, our butler, with her passport and the Madonnina, the little painting I had given her the day we met, and which had been our companion for twelve years of struggles, disappointments, tears, and also happiness.

She said that she agreed with my suggestion of settling everything quickly, making a clean break and, as much as possible, sparing everyone a lot of shame and disgrace. I advised her to think it over again, and then do what had to be done.

At eight I tried to locate Emanuele, a close friend of many sad and joyous days. At nine I telephoned Zevio for news of my mother. An hour later, Maestro Nicola Rescigno telephoned. I didn't know what to tell him and I asked him to call back. At eleven, Walter Legge called from London. At noon an impresario telephoned from Copenhagen. Everyone connected with Maria's career continued to contact me about her engagements, not being aware of the tragedy that had overtaken us. Maria had asked if I would continue to look after her business affairs, at least until the end of the year, but I said no. I am for a clean severing of all ties.

Wednesday, August 19.   Maria telephoned shortly after noon. She confirmed her decision to have a separation and requested that it be effective immediately. She wanted all of her accounts. She wanted to be informed of everything. "I must have my complete freedom," she told me, and added that I was not to annoy her with letters and entreaties.

Thursday, August 20.   Maria telephoned at two in the morning to inquire how I was. She called again at ten in the morning. She was almost sweet with me. She seemed changed. We spoke at length about pointless things.

The attorney Caldi Scalcini arrived at 2:30 and we began to discuss the details of a legal separation.

Friday, August 21. Maria was to have telephoned in the morning to confirm her departure for Zevio, where she was to visit my mother, but she didn't call. I left for Zevio at three in the afternoon and returned to Sirmione at eleven. Emma told me that Maria had telephoned, asking about me. I called Milan, but Ferruccio informed me that Maria was out with friends.

Saturday, August 22. I arose at 5 a.m. and went to Turin, where I spent the morning examining documents. On the return trip I had trouble with my Mercedes and had to stop in Milan. I arrived at Via Buonarroti at seven. Maria wasn't home. She had left with friends the night before. She had written down her address: Hôtel Hermitage, Monte Carlo." I ate and went to rest. Maria telephoned at ten. She said that she was well and happy.

Stampa Sera mentioned that Maria Callas had been seen driving through Cuneo [in northwestern Italy] with Aristotle Onassis.

Sunday, August 23. I worked all day organizing our correspondence files and papers. My young financial assistant arrived around noon. I apprised him of what had happened and he was shocked. The phone had not rung all day. I lifted the receiver and the line was dead. I recalled there had been thunderstorms the day before. I contacted the telephone company only to learn from a representative that they had received a request that the service be cut off. Who could have played a joke like that on me?

I took a train from Milan to Sirmione and arrived at eight. I'm in my studio, where I try to continue working. I'm terribly unhappy without Maria.

Monday, August 24. There were no calls or messages. I went to visit my mother in the afternoon, and returned to Sirmione at 10:30. Emma told me that my wife had telephoned twice. She was back in Milan, she was fine although a little tired, and she was going to bed. Would I call her the next morning at eleven?

Tuesday, August 25. I spoke with Maria at eleven. She said she wanted me to have peace and security in my later years. "I," she said, "have that security in the future. It is important that you also be in the same position." She made it clear that she wanted the house in Milan. She said, "You will also give me my jewels."

"Those are matters to be discussed," I replied.

She advised me to stay at Sirmione. She said that it was the ideal place for me.

"When this business is concluded," I told her, "I want to spend some time in Venice or Cortina."

"No, no," she said, "you must remain at Sirmione." She was afraid of scandal. She begged me not to speak of the dissolution of our marriage with anyone. "The name of the other person absolutely must not be mentioned," she said. "Ari and I are the ones who are disgraced, the unfortunate parties. Everyone will blame us for this."

Wednesday, August 26. Maria telephoned at eleven. She asked that Emma bring her clothes, lingerie, and evening dresses. She was most insistent that I send all of Elsa Maxwell's letters to her. She begged me to do this immediately, so that this episode could be terminated definitively. She invoked all her patron saints to come to her aid, "because [her words] I need to have peace."

"I also have need of peace," I told her, "and you have ruined my life."

"You can consider yourself fortunate to have reached your age in such good health," she replied. "You have had a full life. You must be prepared to step aside. I, on the other hand, have my entire life before me and I want to enjoy it. I was with you for twelve years. That is enough now. I have a right to seek a change."

I pointed out that when we married we did not do it conditionally or with an expiration date. At that time we had a very different understanding. I also reminded her that in recent years it was she who had insisted constantly that we buy a tomb in the cemetery at Sirmione where we could be together in death. ("After having bought me this villa which you gave to me for my old age," she would say, "I want you to have a place in readiness for us, so that we may be together even when we are no longer on this earth.")

"Now go talk to all your patron saints and ask them for advice, ask them if you are in the right," I told her, "but also pay a visit to your Madonna in the Cathedral in Milan, the Madonna you saw so very many times, before whom you genuflected and prayed. Maria, what have you made of our promises, our pledges, our prayers, our work together? You have committed an unspeakable sin."

Thursday, August 27.   There were no telephone calls. I went to Zevio in the afternoon. My mother had intuitively sensed everything. She was now very feeble, about to pass into the next world, and once again caught up in another family tragedy. Poor Mamma.

Friday, August 28.   I went to see my lawyer in Turin. I suggested denouncing my wife and Onassis. He pointed out that Maria is an American citizen and therefore could not be incriminated.

Maria telephoned while I was at the lawyer's. She was not in Milan, but in Nice. That evening I went to the house in Milan to work for a couple of hours. I noticed that Maria had left without taking her little painting of the Madonnina from which she had never been separated. I asked Bruna how this could have happened, and she replied, "That painting no longer matters to Maria."

Saturday, August 29. I sorted out the files concerning Maria's taxes. I had to get three years in order. I met with our lawyer Trabucchi and explained the situation. I spent the afternoon in Zevio. My mother also suffered because of what I was going through but, as usual, she had enormous fortitude in the face of misfortune.

Sunday, August 30. The first hints of dissension between Maria and me appeared in the newspapers. Nothing specific, however. Maria is in Monte Carlo.

Liduino telephoned in the afternoon. He said that he was in Milan waiting to discuss with me many possible engagements for Maria. He asked, "When do you two end your vacation at Sirmione?" He then put conductor Nello Santi on the phone. Santi spoke of a production of *I Puritani* in Catania. "Okay," I told him, "if you haven't heard anything yet, you will soon learn of some news concerning Maria and me, and then everything will be taken care of, including your production of *Puritani*."

When Maria had some little temperamental flare-up in the theater, the press jumped on her back. Now that she has been running around with Onassis for almost a month after having left her husband, not one reporter is on top of the situation.

I went to dinner with some friends. One of the women present told me that just the night before the Contessa di Belgioioso had confided having heard, at Consuelo Crespi's, talk of a disagreement between Callas and Meneghini. Someone had even hinted at a separation, but the story had seemed so improbable that nobody took it seriously.

I left Sirmione at nine and arrived in Milan at midnight. Maria was not there.

Monday, August 31. I worked throughout the night, surrounded by letters, papers, contracts, and accounts.

At nine in the morning I telephoned Maria's cardiologist, inquiring about her. He had often spoken to me of his concern for my wife's health. Now he informed me that on her last visit, only four days before, her heart was fine. "It has returned to normal," he said. "Her blood pressure, which has always been dangerously low, has climbed to 110. We should thank the Lord for the benefits your wife has received from that cruise," he said in conclusion, leaving me without a response.

I left for Sirmione at eleven. Bruna came with me to pick up some of Maria's things. My wife left Milan last Thursday. Today is Monday. Where is she?

Tuesday, September 1. A quiet day. Liduino telephoned at four to tell me that the impresario Sandor Gorlinski would be having dinner with my wife that evening in Milan. I decided to go to Milan also, but I learned that Liduino's information was jumbled: Maria was still in Nice. Bruna told me that Maria had telephoned saying that she would be returning to Milan the next day.

I worked late into the night and then went to sleep on the makeshift bed in my studio.

Wednesday, September 2. I got up early and decided to leave before Maria arrived, but I did have a great desire to see her. I headed for Malpensa airport. The only regularly scheduled flight was in the afternoon. My wife had told Bruna that she would be landing at Malpensa around noon, so I assumed she would be arriving in Onassis's little two-engine plane.

By 10:20 I was at the airport. It was still early. I parked alongside the exit ramp. The sun was beating down strongly and my Mercedes was becoming stifling. I got out and walked around a bit to get some air, but I never took my eyes off the runway. Each time I spotted a tiny aircraft, my heart started pounding.

Unexpectedly, I ran into my friend Emanuele, with whom I hadn't spoken on the telephone in quite a while. "What are you doing here?" he asked. I was embarrassed, and stammered, "I'm here to pick up Maria." He told me he had seen her leave by another exit. And she hadn't said anything to me. I got back into my car and drove off.

Thursday, September 3. Bruna telephoned at eight to say that my wife was not feeling very well. Thinking that I might come to Milan this evening, as I had mentioned on the telephone yesterday, Maria had Bruna ask me to postpone the trip for a few days so she could rest quietly at home. "Certainly," I answered. "Her peace won't be disturbed."

Friday, September 4. I left for Turin at 5 a.m. Passing by Milan, I telephoned Bruna and inquired after my wife's health. "She's better," Bruna told me. This was the day she was to go to La Scala to begin recording *La Gioconda* for EMI.

I had a fight with my attorney in Turin and I relieved him of the assignment. I returned home in the early evening. At the toll booth on the highway I saw, on the front page of one of the afternoon papers, an article describing a rendezvous between Callas and Onassis. Furious, I telephoned Bruna and exploded. "My room and office," I told her, "must always be ready and in order, because I intend to come to my own house whenever I please."

Saturday, September 5. I spent the day in Verona with my new attorney. That afternoon I went to lunch with a couple of old friends and told them about my marital situation.

Sunday, September 6. The news broke first in Verona. The local press had pieced together bits of gossip that had been making the rounds in the city. Reporters arrived. I tried to convince them they were mistaken in thinking there was a story, but they didn't believe a word of what I told them.

Monday, September 7. La Notte fired the first shot and then the other newspapers followed. The affair was now common knowledge. The telephone rang continuously. In front of my house there was a constant coming and going of reporters, photographers, and curiosity-seekers. Friends, lawyers, and members of my family telephoned, but I had no desire to speak with anyone.

The days which followed were chaotic. My diary indicates an endless series of meetings with attorneys, financial assistants, and intermediaries, for Maria did not wish to speak with me. She then vanished with Onassis, so the journalists had no choice but to pursue me. At one point I was exhausted from the ordeal and I gave an interview in which I spoke my mind. The newspapers made the most of it. Maria, who was in London, learned of it and telephoned me in a rage. She began to insult me; I lost my temper and answered her in turn. She then said, "Be careful, Battista: one day or another I'm going to arrive at Sirmione with a revolver and I'm going to kill you." "Fine," I shouted at her, "and I'll be waiting to machine-gun you down." That was the final break: violent and irreparable. It seemed impossible to believe that we were so in love only a few weeks before.

Chapter 26

The Last Years

That terrible phone call in which Maria and I, blinded by rage, threatened each other, was our last. From that moment she canceled me from her life. Thereafter we had no other personal contact whatsoever. It was typical of her character to behave this way, and I, unyielding, stubborn man that I am, withdrew into myself, contributing with my silence to the irremediable widening of the gap between us.

Little by little, Maria began returning to the people with whom she had quarreled: Ghiringhelli, Bing, and various other theater directors. She agreed to these reconciliations to show that it was I who had been behind the battles and difficulties in which she had found herself in the past. During this period she spoke unkindly of me and wrote very cruel things. I did not respond, because nothing mattered to me. I was sad only for Maria, because I knew for a fact that as soon as she was in difficulty, all these people would vanish, leaving her in absolute solitude.

I followed Maria's life and her activities through the newspapers. Now and then she needed to be in touch with me for something, usually concerning the legal details of the separation. All negotiations were handled by our lawyers, but unimportant matters could easily have been settled informally between us. Maria, however, chose to communicate through mutual friends. She never spoke to me again. We passed each other several times in court, but she never even glanced at me.

At one point Maria wanted, more than anything in the world, for me to sign a document in which I would agree to concede her a divorce. Onassis had led her to believe that he would marry her if she could obtain that paper. Using an acquaintance as an intermediary, Maria tried everything to persuade me to sign, but I refused. It was not so much that I wished to block her marriage to Onassis as that I was certain the Greek's request was only an attempt at demonstrating to Maria his good intentions. He would never marry her. Maria did not understand this, however, and she despised me even more.

Perhaps this was the reason behind her unkind criticism of me. She said and wrote things in total contradiction of what she had always professed during the twelve years of our union. Her remarks stung me to the quick, and I would have liked to speak out in my defense, but I did not. The press took up her remarks and proceeded to depict me in the most unflattering terms. Journalists wrote that Maria, finally out of my grasp, was beginning to live, and they foresaw a rich and glorious artistic life. But history did not bear out their predictions. Maria did not have a happy life with Onassis, and in the end she was abandoned. Artistically she did little, especially in comparison with her great career of the past.

My life was also very difficult after our separation. I was not young like Maria, nor was I surrounded by the chic members of the jet set who could help me to forget. I was totally alone. I had alienated myself from family and friends because of Maria. Now, in losing her, I was also no longer part of the musical world in which I had lived for so many years.

For a few months my life seemed meaningless and I suffered from enormous depression. Then I decided to pull myself together. I tried to rediscover a normal, carefree existence. I was also goaded by spite, for I wanted to prove to my detractors and

Maria that I was capable of putting my bitter experiences behind me. I started seeing other women. At one point I even considered remarrying, but when it actually seemed that I might, the memory of Maria won out. No one would have been able to take her place. I was always in love with her.

In my heart remained the hope that she would return. I realized that it was an absurd hope, but I never stopped thinking about it. Every now and then I sent her some kind of message, even though it was indirect, trying to find out if she still thought about me. If I read something unfair that had been written about her, I wrote a letter to the editor, speaking out on her behalf. Then I would send a copy of what I had written to Maria, but she never acknowledged any of them.

When Onassis married Jacqueline Kennedy, I was aware, knowing Maria's character and sensibilities, of how great her sorrow and humiliation must have been, and I was worried that she might do something rash. But Maria showed her mettle. She soon involved herself in new interests [such as her film with Pier Paolo Pasolini and her master classes at the Juilliard School in New York]. She then recommenced her career with a series of concerts with Giuseppe Di Stefano, but this proved to be little more than an interlude that ended in a taste of defeat, which she did not deserve.

As I had guessed, all of the fair-weather friends who had surrounded her in her moments of glory quickly vanished. In Paris, Maria spent her last years alone and unhappy. If she had made and then surveyed a list of the people with whom she had shared her life over the years, she would have had to admit that the only person who always championed and loved her was me.

Perhaps she did reflect upon this and desire a reconciliation. When a German reporter asked her when she would write her memoirs, she replied: "There is only one person who could write them, because he knows everything about me: my husband."

She confided to a mutual friend a few days before her death: "I have so much nostalgia for Sirmione." She then added: "I have done much that was good in my life, but I also made many mistakes, and now I am paying for them." When telling me these things, my friends urged me to make the first move. "You know that Maria is a proud woman," they said. "Don't expect her to be the one to break the ice. Get on the telephone, go see her, you will see that you two will be back together again." But I, a stubborn old man, replied, "It was she who walked out of this house and it is she who must take the initiative."

On May 1, 1977, in the garden of my home in Sirmione, I suffered a serious heart attack. I survived, thanks to the timely intervention of the people nearby and the skill of Dr. Lo Manto, who lavished so much care on me. I spent a month in the hospital, followed by four months of closely supervised convalescence.

On September 16, 1977, the day Maria died, I was still unwell. I had just started going out into the garden once a day for a little walk of a few minutes. That afternoon, when I awoke, I asked my housekeeper Emma to accompany me on my walk. I noticed that she was silent and distressed. I thought she might have received a negative report about my progress. Only later did I learn that she had received word of Maria's death a few hours earlier, and didn't know how to break the news to me, for she feared for my health. She had sent her husband and son to find a doctor so that he could be present. When the doctor arrived, it was he who informed me of Maria's death. It came as a terrible shock. I wanted to hear the radio and television reports and see the newspapers for myself. They then filled me with tranquilizers and helped me to bed.

The next day I wanted to go to Paris, but my doctors were opposed, saying that I would not even make it as far as Linate. I then asked Emma to represent me at the funeral. Emma had known Maria well, had been very fond of her, and had remained loyal to her. "I will go, but only with the understanding that they will at least let me see her," Emma said. In fact, we had heard strange reports on television. Upon learning of Callas's death, many people went to her home to pay their last respects, but no one was allowed to view the body. Not even her oldest and closest friends, such as Giuseppe Di Stefano. All this seemed bizarre and incomprehensible to me.

Emma telephoned Bruna, Maria's maid in Paris, who was a good friend. "Don't come," Bruna said. "It is not possible to see the body. Try to remember her as she was in life."

I followed all the news concerning Maria with the greatest attention. In light of the unexpectedness of her death, I assumed there would be an autopsy. However, nothing. No relative requested it and there was not even an inquest. Her funeral was Tuesday, September 19. The body was taken to the Greek Orthodox church in Paris and from there to the cemetery. The funeral was so hastily arranged and shrouded in mystery that everyone was amazed. Princess Grace of Monaco was unable to conceal her anger.

At the cemetery the body was taken to the crematorium instead of being buried. "Why? Upon whose instructions?" I asked myself in anguish. I was trembling because I had been powerless to do anything about it. This was certainly not in compliance with Maria's wishes.

I anxiously waited to learn what Maria had written in her will. I wanted to know if she had perhaps left a letter for me, a conciliatory word, but no matter what avenues I pursued, even with the help of friends and acquaintances, I never succeeded in learning if there was, indeed, a will.

It all struck me as very strange. Maria was exceedingly meticulous and she was in the habit of organizing her life even to the most minute detail. When she lived with me she often spoke of our later years, of what we would do, where we would like to die and be buried. She asked me constantly to go to Sirmione's town hall and purchase two plots for our tombs, so that we could be beside each other even in death. We almost had an argument once because I had not found the time to comply with her request.

As for the terms of her will, she had very specific ideas. "Since we don't have any children," she said to me on various occasions, "it would be nice to leave our estate to the Institute for Cancer Research. This horrible disease will be conquered someday by doctors and scientists, and I would like to have helped in that fight." In 1974, during the period of her joint recitals with Di Stefano, they gave a private concert in Milan for the patients in the Institute for the Cure of Cancer: an indication that her old project was still very much on her mind. I felt certain that she had made a will with this disposition, but it was never found.

One night Maria came to me in a dream and said, "Battista, remember the will." She repeated that phrase three times, as if wanting to imprint it on my mind. I woke up and began to think about the dream. "What was she trying to tell me?" I asked myself, and I made a thousand suppositions. Finally I remembered something that had occurred many years before. Maria and I had gone to the office of our lawyer, who at that time was Trabucchi, to sign some papers before we flew to the United States. Trabucchi said: "The two of you travel constantly. Haven't you ever thought of making a will in which each of you makes the other beneficiary? I assure you that nothing is going to befall you, but if some accident did happen, at least the survivor would not have any financial worries."

"You're right," Maria said. "It never occurred to us, but it's a good idea and we should take care of it now." I wrote, on a plain sheet of paper, as dictated by Trabucchi: "In the event of my death, I leave everything to my wife Maria Callas," and I signed it. Maria did the same and we left the two sheets of paper with Trabucchi.

Recalling that incident, I realized that Maria may have been alluding to that testament, which would still have been valid if there were no others. But how to find it? That was over twenty years ago. I always had a mania for annotating everything. I said to Emma's husband Ferruccio, "Look in the attic for a letter file with 'Trabucchi' written on it." Ferruccio went to the attic, but it was impossible for him to find the file because the mice had gnawed the boxes and he was unable to make out the writing. I refused to give up. I went to the attic myself and looked at the pile of cartons. Suddenly, almost by inspiration, I said to Ferruccio, "Give me that folder over there." I opened it and found my papers from Trabucchi's office. As I had suspected, among the various documents was a note recording the fact that on May 23, 1954, Maria and I had made out our wills and had left them with our lawyer.

Trabucchi, however, was dead. He was also notorious for his lack of organization. His files consisted of a mountain of papers, and only he could put his hands on a specific document. After his death, all his papers had been divided among his associates. Who among them would know where Maria's will might be filed?

The next morning I telephoned a lawyer who had worked in Trabucchi's office in 1954. "I'm sure it's impossible to find that piece of paper, but I'll look for it." He had the same bizarre luck that I had had. He arbitrarily picked up an old folder and in it was Maria's will.

Now that I had located the document, it was necessary to take it to Paris. This time I wanted to go myself. I managed to convince my doctors I was strong enough to make the trip. A month had passed since Maria's death. I was not interested in her estate. I was touched by the fact that apparently she had never changed her original testament. It suggested that she had continued to think of me, that she did not harbor resentment, and that perhaps she had never really stopped loving me.

On October 18 I left for Paris with two friends, one of whom was a lawyer. A third person awaited us in the French capital to put us in touch with the appropriate people responsible for examining the will and having it probated.

My trip also had another purpose: it gave me the opportunity to pursue the unanswered questions concerning Maria's death and to learn exactly who had ordered the cremation. But before anything else, I wanted to go to her tomb. A custodian of the cemetery accompanied me into a vault whose walls were covered with tiny marble plaques, each with numbers on them. "Here is the person you are looking for," the custodian said, indicating the plaque with the number 16.258. I touched the tiny marble tile and began to cry. My friends rushed over to help me. I felt dizzy.

After a while they led me out of the vault. We went to the office of the cemetery. "I want to know why my wife was cremated," I asked the director. He was very kind. He showed me the register with the record of the request. To the person who had accompanied Maria's coffin, the official had asked the usual question: "What is the disposition?" "The body is to be cremated," was the reply. "And to whom are we speaking?" "I am Jean Rouen."

But who was this Jean Rouen? I never knew of anyone in Maria's family by that name. I also learned from the director that the cremation was not done the day after the arrival of the body, as is customary, but immediately. Thirty minutes after the bier arrived at the cemetery, the body was cremated. Why such haste? With infinite sorrow and pain I stood before the crematory and stared at the chimney from which had issued the smoke produced by Maria's beloved body. I thought I would lose my mind.

In the following months I returned often to visit Maria's final resting place. At Christmas of that year I remained for twelve days, but someone had played a cruel joke on me. I had given instructions to the authorities to begin the formalities to have

Maria's ashes transferred to Sirmione, and to place her mortal remains where she had wished. Word of this had reached the ears of those who, I do not know why, wished to separate me even then from my wife. To obstruct my request, they had arranged to have her ashes placed in a bank vault. For an entire week I had given vent to my emotions and placed flowers before the plaque, behind which there was nothing.

And then fate arranged the final chapter of the mystery: the scattering of Maria's ashes over the Aegean Sea—an indefensible act. Now nothing more remains of Maria.

But I did not give up. I wanted to learn the truth. With all the means at my disposal, legal and illicit, I tried to gather information concerning my wife's demise. Maria's servants had given this version of her death: Maria had died suddenly, after she had taken a bath and was trying to reach her bedroom. That morning she had had breakfast, then she had asked for orange juice because she had a great thirst. Bruna had brought it to her in the bathroom, and Maria gulped it down. As Bruna was returning to the kitchen, she heard a thud. She ran back and found Maria unconscious on the floor. She called the other servant, Ferruccio, and together they carried Maria to her bedroom. When they placed her on the bed, she was no longer breathing.

Is that what really happened? When I divided Maria's possessions with her mother, I asked that I be allowed to have her papers. The court was unable to comply with my wishes, because almost everything had vanished from her studio. Among the few things that were left was a prayer book which Maria always kept on the night table by her bed. In the pages of the book I found a note that raised disturbing questions about her death.

It was a piece of blue note paper with the letterhead of the Hotel Savoy in London, on which Maria had written five lines, in pencil. In the upper right-hand corner she had written, in Italian, "Summer '77," which indicated that the lines had been written just a few days or weeks before her death. Under the date were the words, "*A T.,*" which was certainly "To Titta." In fact, that "T." was typical of Maria when she was writing my name. And then, the five lines: "*In questi fieri momenti, tu sol mi resti. E il cor mi tenti. L'ultima voce del mio destino, ultima croce del mio cammin*" ("In these terrible moments, you alone remain to me. You alone tempt my heart. It is the last call of my destiny, the last cross on life's road"). These are the opening words of Gioconda's great aria on suicide in Ponchielli's opera, *La Gioconda.*

It is obvious that Maria did not write those lines to refresh her memory, but rather to leave a message. The most important events in our lives were linked with that opera. *La Gioconda* was the first opera Maria sang after she arrived in Italy in the summer of 1947, exactly thirty years earlier, and it was during the rehearsals for that opera at the Verona Arena that our love was born. Maria had also recorded *La Gioconda* at the beginning of September 1959, in the days in which she had decided to leave me to go off with Aristotle Onassis. But I was certain the key to the message was the significance it had in the context of the opera. Gioconda sings it at the beginning of Act IV, in the dramatic scene in which she decides to kill herself. The aria begins with the one word which Maria did not write: "*Suicidio!*" (suicide).

Who knows, perhaps Maria did take her own life. And if she did not, she certainly thought about it. But why was she reduced to that mental state? I did know that in her last years she was desperately alone. After the death of Onassis, she no longer went out. Almost every afternoon, if it was not raining, she had Ferruccio drive her to the park, where she walked her two poodles, which were now old and blind. She had a fear of being alone. Her servants had Sundays off, but she would do everything she could to persuade Ferruccio to keep her company. Saturday nights she would play cards with him, and in the middle of the game she would stop, saying, "Let's continue tomorrow evening."

"But I have plans," he would say. She would answer, "You can't leave the game unfinished." The next day she would badger him to stay in and finish the card game and he, out of consideration for her, almost always forfeited his free evening.

That is what had become of Maria Callas. It was this overwhelming solitude which killed her. The blame for that loneliness rested not with me but with those who had done their best to separate us. I was, to be sure, old-fashioned, not very elegant, not young, and certainly not worldly or a man-about-town; but I was the man who always adored her and lived only for her. During our twelve years together, Maria had repeatedly told everyone how happy she was. And I had wanted only to assure her happiness, even to the very end.

Index

Opera houses and arenas in which Maria Callas appeared are listed by city

[323]

Index

Benassi, Memo (actor), 115–6
Bergman, Ingrid, 185
Bernhardt, Sarah, 207
Bernstein, Leonard, 173, 182
Berrettoni, Umberto (conductor),
57, 117
Bing, Rudolf, 41n, 96n, 131, 205,
226–9, 249, 276–80, 311
Bison, Massimo (tenor), 66
Boehm, Karl (conductor), 250–1
Bohème, La, 36
Bologna, Teatro Duse, 145
Bonardi, Liduino (theatrical
agent), 41, 41n, 43–4, 126,
131, 226, 307–8
Borriello, Mario (baritone), 74
Broselli, Beppe (music reviewer),
56
Bruna (Callas's maid in Paris),
308–9, 315, 319
Bruscantini, Sesto (bass), 146
Brussels, Théâtre de la Monnaie,
266
Brutti, Emma, xi, 184, 208, 286,
314–5
Brutti, Ferruccio (in the employ
of Meneghini), 303, 317
Buenos Aires, Teatro Colón, 85–6,
89, 93n, 94
Bussetto, 136, 140

Calabrese, Franco (bass), 146, 200
Callas, Evangelia, x, 120–2,
124–30, 132–3, 229
Callas, George, 121–5, 127, 133
Callas, Jackie, 121
Cammarano, Salvatore (librettist),
138
Canali, Anna Maria (mezzo-
soprano), 55, 146
Caniglia, Maria (soprano), xi,
119, 159n

Capuano, Franco (conductor), 118
Caraza-Campos, Antonio (opera
impresario), 128
Cardi, Augusto (stage director), 13
Carmassi, Bruno (bass), 55, 74
Carmen, 143, 204
Carol, Martine (actress), 284
Carosio, Margherita (soprano), xi,
69–70
Caselotti, Louise. *See* Bagarozy
Castellani, Leandro (film director),
189
Catania [Teatro Massimo Bellini],
117, 169, 307
Catozzo, Nino (theater
administrator), 42, 44–5, 48,
68–70
Cavalleria Rusticana, 52n, 129
Cazzarolli, Giovanni (Meneghini's
brother-in-law), 67, 79, 219–9,
225
Cecilia (Refice), 109
Celli, Teodoro (music reviewer),
170, 172
Cerquetti, Anita (soprano), 265
Chaplin, Charlie, 30, 284
Chicago, 21n, 241, 250–1; Lyric
Opera Company, 227–8, 237–9
Chigi Saracini, Guido, Count, 188
Christoff, Boris (bass), 53, 71,
96n, 149, 175n
Churchill, Sir Winston, 288–9
Cipriani, Nicola, 146
Cleva, Fausto (conductor), 229,
251
Cocteau, Jean, 30
Coen, Gino (Rome businessman),
217–9, 225
Colasanti, Irma (mezzo-soprano),
56
Confalonieri, Giulio (music
reviewer), 171

Index

Index

Index

Index

Index

Index